Establishing Competitive Advantages in the Service Sector in EU Member States

Marzenna Anna Weresa (ed.)

Establishing Competitive Advantages in the Service Sector in EU Member States

PETER LANG

Frankfurt am Main · Berlin · Bern · Bruxelles · New York · Oxford · Wien

Bibliographic Information published by the Deutsche Nationalbibliothek
The Deutsche Nationalbibliothek lists this publication in the Deutsche
Nationalbibliografie; detailed bibliographic data is available in the internet at
http://dnb.d-nb.de.

Cover Design:
Olaf Glöckler, Atelier Platen, Friedberg

ISBN 978-3-631-60650-6
© Peter Lang GmbH
Internationaler Verlag der Wissenschaften
Frankfurt am Main 2010
All rights reserved.

All parts of this publication are protected by copyright. Any
utilisation outside the strict limits of the copyright law, without
the permission of the publisher, is forbidden and liable to
prosecution. This applies in particular to reproductions,
translations, microfilming, and storage and processing in
electronic retrieval systems.

www.peterlang.de

Table of Contents

Preface 7

Chapter 1

The Role of ICT as a Strategic Driver of Service Sector Competitiveness and Productivity: Focus on Process Industries 9

Elias G. Carayannis

Chapter 2

An Analysis of the Possible Causes of Product Market Malfunctioning in the EU: First Results for Manufacturing and Service Sectors 31

Fabienne Ilzkovitz, Adriaan Dierx, Nuno Sousa

Chapter 3

Liberalizing Trade in Services

A New Agenda for Growth and Jobs in Europe? 87

Suparna Karmakar

Chapter 4

Changes in the Competitiveness of Service Sectors in New EU Member States: The Role of Business Process Outsourcing 111

Magdolna Sass

Chapter 5

Investment Attractiveness of the Service Sector in Poland 133

Marzenna Anna Weresa

Chapter 6

The Development of the Service Sector in European Regions 153

Małgorzata Dziembała

Chapter 7

Towards a Policy for Supporting Innovation in the Service Sector: The Rationale for Policy Action and Further Steps 177

Beata Lubos

Preface

The service sector plays a crucial role in developed economies, accounting for a predominant portion of their GDP and employment. International trade in services has been growing continuously and a rising wave of global service offshoring has been observed. Moreover, in a knowledge-based economy, services are critical for the competitiveness of enterprises in all industries. As the service sector is increasingly important in European economies, productivity growth and further improvements in the competitive position of EU member states are highly dependent on the successful development of service industries. Therefore, it is necessary to boost innovation in the service sector in order to improve its performance and enhance the competitiveness of European countries.

Furthermore, technological advancements in areas such as communication technology have led to a fragmentation of services. This has triggered a process of relocation of certain service activities to locations where they can be carried out at a lower cost and/or where better quality can be ensured. Due to this process, coupled with the liberalization of trade in services, especially within regional economic blocs such as the EU, countries are increasingly starting to compete for investments in the service sector. As a consequence, the establishment of competitive advantages in the service sector has become an important component of sustaining a country's competitiveness and productivity growth.

This book focuses on general developments in the service sector and their consequences for the competitiveness of EU countries. It aims to identify factors that influence the competitive advantage of the service sector. The book examines the development of service sectors in several EU countries and assesses their competitiveness. The material is divided into seven chapters.

The first chapter underlines the strategic meaning of the ICT industry as a driver of service sector competitiveness. By profiling in detail the role of e-commerce as a strategy-enabling technology and identifying best practices, it provides readers with useful approaches to improving quality and productivity in services.

The second chapter focuses on the four dimensions of service market malfunctioning in the EU (regulation, integration, competition and innovation) and thus helps identify opportunities and threats as well as the business potential of European service markets.

The third chapter evaluates the benefits of increasing globalization in service sectors, the role of policy initiatives and multilateral trade negotiations in the process of opening markets. This section of the book also assesses the prospects for countries to further their growth and employment objectives by pursuing a liberal cross-border service trade regime; it could therefore serve as a strong reference for policymakers.

The fourth chapter provides a detailed analysis of the extent, characteristics and impact of the relocation of certain service activities to third countries and thus identifies business opportunities for both individual companies and countries.

In chapter five, selected aspects of the development of Poland's service sector are analyzed. In particular, the attractiveness of the Polish service sector for foreign direct investment is assessed and compared with the appeal of service sectors in other EU countries in Central and Eastern Europe. Poland, the largest new EU member and by far the most popular service FDI destination in Central and Eastern Europe, is presented as a best practice example.

Chapter six assesses the development of service sectors in various European regions on the basis of an analysis of the structure of employment. It provides academics, business professionals and policymakers with valuable insights into the competition structure of European regions as well as their competitiveness.

The seventh chapter incorporates the policymaking perspective. It addresses the crucial question of how to support innovation among entrepreneurs operating in the service sector. It attempts to determine if service investments in technology are more likely to obtain public support than projects based on the implementation of non-technological innovation and if they are consequently of special interest to entrepreneurs.

The book is an outcome of a research project carried out at the World Economy Research Institute, Warsaw School of Economics. The research results presented in this book allow concluding that Europe needs to support services and innovation in the service sector in order to enhance growth and competitiveness across the EU.

Marzenna Anna Weresa

Chapter 1

The Role of ICT as a Strategic Driver of Service Sector Competitiveness and Productivity: Focus on Process Industries

Elias G. Carayannis[1]

Abstract

Information technology, and especially the Internet, are exerting an increasingly large and broad influence on industrial structures and measurement and evaluation of such fundamental concepts as risk, the value and benefits of intangibles such as intellectual capital, brand-related goodwill, and service sector productivity. Identifying the key value adding factors underpinning productivity in the service sector has always been a significant challenge but with the advent of the WWW and the broad diffusion of Internet-enabled technologies and transacting modalities such as electronic commerce, this challenge has become even harder.

We use a number of empirical case studies from industry where the use of electronic commerce has served as a strategic differentiator in pushing the service productivity envelop and in maximizing customer value added. Specifically, we examine the impact of electronic commerce on the process and petroleum industries. We profile in detail the role of electronic commerce as a strategy-enabling, infrastructural, path-breaking and general-purpose technology that if properly leveraged, can lead to radical improvements in both quality and productivity in services, thus helping re-define and re-shape the core structure and relationships in the industries it impacts.

We end by identifying best practices in deploying electronic commerce as a strategic agent of change within and across firms and industries in the pursuit of increasingly higher levels of service sector productivity and quality.

---

[1] Professor of Science, Technology, Innovation and Entrepreneurship, Director of Research, Science, Technology, Innovation and Entrepreneurship, European Union Research Centre (EURC), Co-founder and Co-Director, Global and Entrepreneurial Finance Research Institute (GEFRI), School of Business, George Washington University, email: caraye@gwu.edu.

Introduction: From Declining Superpower to the New Economy

The geo-economic status of the United States seems to have shifted dramatically since the late 1980s. The U.S. is now seen as a model that other nations should emulate to achieve economic success. The difficulty is in identifying what accounts for that success. One popular explanation is that the U.S. economy operates in an emerging paradigm, the so-called "New Economy," while other nations have not yet adjusted to this new reality. Proponents of the "New Economy" argument generally point to three key factors contributing to U.S. economic prosperity (see Chandler and Pearlstein, 1997):

1. Growth of global markets
2. Strategic and organizational flexibility
3. Deregulation of infrastructure industries

The inter-relationships among these factors point to a competitive outlook among U.S. firms which is qualitatively different from the situation ten years ago. New markets for U.S. products overseas provides more opportunities for profits, and also new outlets for U.S. goods. Consequently, U.S. firms can produce at higher rates without flooding the market or building up unused inventories. At the same time, in response to global competition, successful U.S. firms have built up competences in rapid strategic decision-making and implementation. This shift to time-based competition leverages inherent strengths in the U.S. labour market, which is more resilient in the face of rapid downsizing and restructuring than labour in other nations. Finally, it is cheaper for manufacturing and other firms to operate in the U.S. than in many other nations. The reason is that key infrastructure industries, notably transportation, financial services, and telecommunications, have been deregulated over the past twenty years. The costs for these critical services is now much lower in the U.S. than in the past.

All of these trends are occurring in the context of a more service-oriented economy. For the past ten years or more, manufacturing has accounted for a consistent 20 percent of U.S. gross domestic product. But manufacturing employment has dropped steadily over that same period. In contrast, the service sector now accounts for 80 percent of all employment in the U.S., and 70 percent of the value-added in the GDP (Fingleton, 1999). The new nature of competition, particularly in the service sector, highlights the importance of "intellectual capital" rather than physical capital in the New Economy (Stewart, 1997). Strategic advantage is now based more on the knowledge embodied in companies, not their facilities. The time-based competition forced by globalization means that companies must adopt an offensive strategy based on rapid innovation, rather than a defensive one based on protecting past advantages. The knowledge retained by a company's workforce is its key resource for overcoming the competition and maintaining leadership.

One potential influence on the shift to a "New Economy" is the increased use of information technology throughout the U.S. economy. In particular, technology executives point to the increasing pervasive influence of the Internet on business practices and productivity, under the label of "e-commerce" or "e-business." To support this argument, it is necessary to show how investments in information technology and especially Internet technologies have resulted in productivity growth across a wide portion of the U.S. economy. Productivity growth has been very healthy in the manufacturing sector. However, there is little evidence of any change in productivity in the U.S. service sector for many years.

This analysis will seek to show that an improvement in productivity is but one of many strategic advantages gained by the service sector through the introduction of electronic commerce. We illustrate these advantages using case studies drawn from the petrochemical industry. The framework for analyzing the benefits of EC can then be applied to the service sector. In our view, the more important impact of EC will be the fundamental restructuring of business relationships in the service sector, and between firms in service and manufacturing industries.

Information Technology and the Productivity Paradox: A Review

Proponents of increased spending on information technology argue that the spread of computing power throughout the business, combined with the ability of individuals and computing devices to communicate through networks, will lead to very different forms of business transactions and relationships (see, for example, Schwartz and Leyden, 1997). According to this theory, the diffusion of information technology will have four significant effects which change the rules under which economies operate:

- **Internal efficiency.** The spread of high-powered computing throughout corporations means that the average worker can now process more information in the same amount of time. Information technology investments comprised 19.1 percent of business capital stock in 1996, compared to 12.7 percent in 1990 (Roach, 1998). The major impact of this investment has been on 'white-collar' work, especially streamlining tasks performed by administrative and clerical staff. The reengineering of paperwork reduces the overhead expenses of each company, enabling them to downsize while increasing sales.

- **Transaction costs.** Just as the internal operations of a firm generates administrative costs, transactions between firms have overhead. Coordinating a sale can be quite expensive, considering the effort involved in negotiating contracts and auditing transactions (Williamson, 1985). Automating the electronic exchange of trade information between organizations can eliminate much of the paperwork and delay in commerce, thus reducing the overall costs of doing business in the marketplace.

- **Industrial restructuring.** Transactions costs are cited as a main justification for bureaucracy: it is cheaper to coordinate workers when regulated by a higher authority, instead of trying to obtain cooperation from autonomous workers (Williamson, 1985). But electronic networking reduces transactions costs, so that it is now feasible for many small firms to collaborate as "virtual corporations" instead of combining within a single large corporation (Davidow, 1993). This combination of networking and flexibility has led U.S. firms to downsize, outsource and restructure over the past five years.

- **Knowledge management.** As noted earlier, the current economic environment rewards firms based on what they know, not what they own. More importantly, with the flood of information available over networks, know-how (knowledge of a process for doing something, such as building a car) is more valuable than raw facts. Networks enable companies to disseminate critical knowledge faster within organizations and with key partners, thus contributing directly to knowledge-based competitive advantage.

According to this analysis, investment in information technology will create abnormally high returns compared to other capital investment, due to the greater efficiencies achieved through networking and computerization. The implication of these trends is that as U.S. corporations continue to purchase and install new information systems and technologies, U.S. economic growth will accelerate well above the rates of other, less computerized industrial countries. Nearly fifteen years of research on the economic benefits of computerization have yet to support this hypothesis unequivocally.

As early as 1986, some economic analysts had noticed the rapid rise in information technology spending by U.S. corporations, particularly in the service sector. In particular, IT penetrated white-collar offices for the first time as business began to adopt personal computers more widely. These analysts also noted what would become known as the "productivity paradox:" despite large and growing investments in IT, U.S. economic productivity did not rise significantly.

As stated succinctly by Robert Solow, a Nobel Prize-winning economist at MIT, "You can see the computer age everywhere but in the productivity statistics." Related research at the microeconomic level also questions the benefits of computerization. An analysis by Paul Strassman, formerly CIO at Xerox Corporation and Director of Defence Information at the U.S. Department of Defence, found no correlation between the amount of investment in information technology by U.S. firms and their overall profitability (Strassman, 1997). There are several reasonable arguments as to why the productivity paradox may appear to be true, but is in fact misleading.

First, statistics about U.S. GDP and productivity growth may understate the actual growth rate. Economic research at the investment bank Morgan Stanley, over 85 percent of existing investment in information technology is in the service sector (Roach, 1996) where productivity is very difficult to measure. In many of these sectors, productivity is estimated as a function of input, meaning that gains in efficiency are not included in U.S. government statistics.

Second, many of the benefits of information technology are felt in ways which are not directly reflected in productivity statistics. For example, the adoption of automated teller machine (ATM) by banks did not greatly increase the output of each employee, but it did have significant benefits to bank customers in terms of convenience and efficiency. Also, IT often results in cost savings which companies pass on to consumers in the form of lower costs, not increased profits or productivity. Lawrence Chimerine, chief economist at the Economic Strategy Institute in Washington, DC, believes that heightened competition forces firms to use cost savings to deflate prices rather than increase profits. Therefore, the results of IT may be seen more in consumer benefits, which are not measured by government, rather than productivity growth (Hitt and Brynjolfsson, 1994).

Third, the benefits of IT to business are not realized through increasing the scale of investment in IT, but by improving the management of IT within firms. IT in particular appears to have a long learning curve, because the spread of computer processing power through a company tends to force organizational changes which may meet initial resistance from management (Nolan, 1973). While mainframe-based computer systems of the 1960s reinforced hierarchical control and bureaucracy, PCs and networking are most effective after organizational structures have been aligned with new technologies. Paul David makes the analogy between the diffusion of computers in business and the development of electric power in U.S. industry (David, 1990). His research reveals that manufacturing firms were initially unsuccessful in using electric power, because they attempted to apply it in ways suitable for mechanical power. Significant gains in productivity were seen only after firms had developed engines and other machines specifically designed to run on electricity, and after organizational structures had changed to match the capabilities of those devices. These changes did not occur until 40 years after the introduction of electrical power; coincidentally, computers were first introduced in business approximately 40 years ago.

Information Technology in the Service Sector: The Shift to E-business

Another problem with linking information technology and economic productivity is that IT will tend to have disproportionate effects on efficiency and output across industries. While all industries are becoming more information-intensive, there are clearly some industries which depend more on information for output than other industries. In manufacturing, IT is applied to both production (factory-level) activities and to administrative or overhead activities—in common English, blue-collar versus white-collar functions. At the factory level, the main functions of information technology are automation (removing workers from the production process) and flexibility (increasing the variety of outputs produced by a manufacturing process). As might be expected, increased IT usage in manufacturing is correlated strongly with reductions in employment, reflecting the use of IT for automation.

In contrast, a 1991 study of IT usage in the service sector by Stephen Roach of Morgan Stanley and others found that increased IT spending was correlated with increased white-collar employment (National Academy of Science, 1991).

Mr. Roach concluded that in the service sector, firms did not face enough competition to force improvements in efficiency. Instead, firms were using information technology to increase the control of information through expanded bureaucracies. It is very likely that today, service firms are facing more competition due to globalization, deregulation, and reduced barriers to entry. Since the early 1990s, service firms have begun to reduce their employment levels. This indicates that service firms are using IT now to increase productivity and efficiency, but that achieving those goals required more radical reorganization than was necessary in the manufacturing industry.

There are several general factors, however, which lead to increased IT spending by industries. First, the increased deregulation of industries, particularly in the service sector, intensifies competition, and makes the strategic use of information technology even more important. In the United States, large surges in IT spending were recorded in the airline industry in the 1970s, in the banking industry in the early 1980s, and in the telecommunications industry in the late 1980s. These increases correspond to waves of deregulation in those industries. For example, the end of government limits on bank interest rates in the late 1970s allowed banks to develop new packages of services and savings plans. These required banks to use information technology to coordinate these new products. Also, fierce competition for new customers led banks to install networks of automatic teller machines, which improved their customer satisfaction by providing 24-hour service and increasing the geographic coverage of bank services. More recently, financial services reforms which enable cross-investment between banking and insurance is creating new financial "supermarkets" such as CitiGroup, which depend on information systems to coordinate the activities of their vast global operations.

Second, as service industries reach a growing customer base, through innovation and deregulation, they require information technology which supports their new businesses. The banking industry first began automating operations through information technology in the late 1950s, when check processing volumes increased quickly. That automation was also a response to the development of a new service, consumer loans. Consumer loans decreased the average size of the loans offered by banks while increasing the volume of loans; this resulted in a rapid rise in paperwork involved in loan operations. In the telecommunications industry, the diffusion of digital communication technology in the late 1980s increased the range of service that carriers could offer to customers. In turn, this required large investments in new billing systems, network management operations, and other business systems supporting those services.

Third, just as new entrants to a market can force an increase in IT spending, a sudden wave of mergers and acquisition which reduces the number of competitors in an industry can lead surviving companies to expand their information systems. The creation of large conglomerates is possible only if they can transfer information effectively for coordination and control of geographically-dispersed operations. Parallel increases in average firm size and information technology investment have been seen in the retail industry (following the rise of Wal-Mart, Kmart, and other large discounters), airlines, as well as financial services.

Fourth, as competitive pressures mount, firms often need to cooperate with each other to develop new products and services and to respond more quickly to customer needs. Cooperation is aided by electronic networking to speed the transfer of critical information and to coordinate actions. Most commonly, firms use information technology for vertical networking with their suppliers and major corporate customers. A number of industries, notably retail, automotive manufacturing, and chemical processing, use Electronic Data Interchange (EDI) technology to exchange common business documents (invoices, purchase orders, etc.) with suppliers. Large banks give dedicated terminals to their key customers, the finance departments of large businesses, to facilitate electronic account management and transactions.

Finally, cooperation among competing companies in information technologies may be needed to enable the development of new capabilities or services which benefit all firms. One example is the linking of individual bank ATM networks, so that customers can withdraw cash even in areas where their banks do not operate. Similarly, telecommunications carriers need to link their traffic management systems to calculate and transfer "settlement" payments for calls transmitted across multiple carriers. Even vertical networking between firms and suppliers often includes horizontal cooperation to standardize such communications, so that suppliers can deal easily with multiple customers.

In the United States, retailers cooperated with wholesalers and manufacturers to develop the Uniform Product Code (UPC) system for bar-coding goods so that they can be tracked and transferred more easily. Drilling down to the level of the firm, information technology can have any of the following benefits, only some of which are related to increasing productivity:

Firms experience increased ability to expand their market shares through economies of scope. Since information technology is very flexible and can be reconfigured rapidly, it allows firms to increase the variety of products and services that they offer to customers. In manufacturing, this application of IT is called "flexible production" or "mass customization"—the production of many products highly customized to individual customers. In service industries, IT introduces "economies of scope." With the same IT platform, a company can offer a large range of services or bundles of services, each designed to meet the very specific needs of each customer.

IT investments increase the ability of firms to manage risk and avoid potentially damaging business losses. Telecommunications firms and credit card companies are using sophisticated artificial intelligence programs to identify usage patterns which may reflect user fraud. In the airline industry, information technology is vital to ensuring the safety of passenger jets, which could cause catastrophic losses if unattended. The insurance industry uses IT heavily for data analysis to ensure that they are not taking on unnecessary risk in providing policies. These types of investment have no measurable effect on worker productivity, and the net benefit may not be directly traceable to spending on IT, but failure to make these investments reduce revenues or even threaten the continuing operation of the business.

Firms may invest in information technology simply to create an infrastructure which can later be used to create new products or services. As an example, banks originally invested in ATM networks to provide their customers with more convenient access to cash. Now, they are looking to use ATMs for managing investments and stock transactions and other capabilities. Information infrastructures also enable companies to react more quickly to changes in their competitive environment. As stated by Apple Computer co-founder Steve Jobs, "If you knew what was going to happen in advance every day, you could do amazing things…Well, it turns out that most people don't even know what happened yesterday in their own business. So, a lot of businesses are discovering they can take tremendous competitive advantage simply by finding out what happened yesterday as soon as possible" (Huey, 1994).

Another form of IT investment creates a new internal management environment which helps to forecast future activities and reduce the effects of business cycles. A prime example is the investment by Boeing Aircraft Company over the past two years in information technologies which enable the company to better control the flow of its production lines in response to wide swings in orders. While Boeing typically would need to fire and hire workers in large numbers according to the cyclical swings of the aircraft industry, it now is able to maintain a more stable workforce due to better manufacturing planning.

Information technology also plays an important role in helping firms to cope with the shift to time-based competition, where firm performance depends on the ability to identify and respond to shifting market conditions and customer needs. Firms can improve their reaction times by transmitting information from customer sites to the company's own databases. For example, Wal-Mart's suppliers use the EDI system supplied by the retailer to receive information about the sales of their product in Wal-Mart stores. The suppliers can detect immediately when a store's inventory for a specific product is getting low, and can then ship replacement products before that inventory runs out. IT also enables closer relationships with customers. Federal Express developed the COSMOS package tracking system, and then offered customers their own terminals to connect to COSMOS to look up the status of their own packages. This transforms firms into so-called "sense and respond" organizations, which are better positioned to compete in the electronic age.

IT and Productivity: The Special Case of Electronic Commerce

Business investment in and usage of electronic commerce is clearly an extension of efforts to capture the full value of information technology advances. Many of the technologies cited above are in fact precursors to today's Internet commerce technologies (for example, automatic teller machine networks, electronic data interchange, and bar coding for retail distribution). Like these technologies, Internet-based electronic commerce enables a firm to improve coordination and control over transactions between internal organizational units, and between the firm and its trading partners (customers, suppliers, and even competitors). Based on these observations, we can distinguish four types of benefits which firms attempt to realize through the introduction of electronic commerce.

- **Effectiveness:** Electronic commerce enables firms to gain greater skills in their areas of core competence, which gives them additional advantage over competitors.
- **Efficiency:** Electronic commerce enables firms to achieve the same or greater levels of output with few resources (which does impact productivity directly).

- **Reach:** Electronic commerce enables firms to expand their range of business activities by leveraging economies of scope.
- **Integration:** Electronic commerce enables firms to form closer links to key business partners, including competitors, customers, suppliers, and complementors, which facilitate their efforts to meet specific strategic goals (see Brandenberger and Nalebuff, 1996).

These four dimensions of gains from EC are shown in Figure 1.

To simplify the use of the term, we will define electronic commerce as "The electronic exchange of value between two parties". *Value* can be defined as

- Financial or business transactions
- Operational information
- Transfer of digitized data, such as fax, text, drawings, sound or visual images.

Figure 1: Dimensions of Business Value from Electronic Commerce

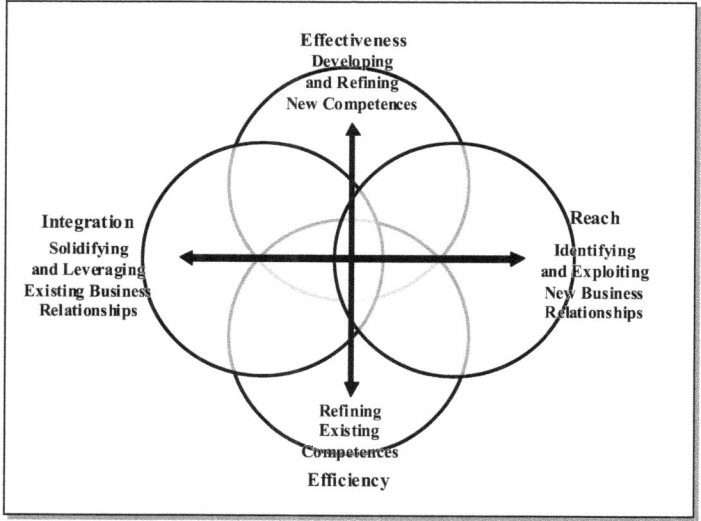

Many organizations are looking at electronic commerce for various reasons, including the ability it provides to reduce the costs of intra or inter-company transactions, increase revenues by establishing an e-channel for selling Internet commerce goods and services, and improve business process efficiencies through Customer Relationship Management (CRM), Enterprise Resource Planning (ERP) (such as SAP), Supply Chain Management (SCM). Using case studies drawn from the process industries, we show how firms are using EC to gain advantages along the four strategic dimensions noted above. We then draw parallels to the service sector, and discuss how similar EC activities in that sector will impact productivity and competitive advantage at the firm, industry and national levels.

Case Study on Supplier-Oriented EC: B2B EC for Procurement

Electronic commerce based on common or shared business processes between two trading partners has brought fundamental change to businesses such as BOC Gases. Its British parent, the BOC Group, has been pushing for on-line supplier and customer transactions supported by common business process for a long time. These common business processes implemented throughout its multinational operations, which include a wide variety of warehousing, distribution and cargo-handling services, have been in operational for over three years. And the benefits transcend for both BOC and its trading partners include not only from back-office efficiency but also into the execution into key business process such as "Order Fulfillment" and "Order-To-Cash".

Alex Cahill, a BOC purchasing manager in Murray Hill, cites the example of tungsten hexafluoride. The company sells the gas in six-foot steel cylinders that are worth $10,000 each when filled, making for an unwieldy, expensive inventory. "In previous years, our stock has been bloated to accommodate for miscommunication, upturn in demand, returns or problems with quality," Mr. Cahill said. "So it was typical to have three months of inventory in the system - which could be between 50 and 60 cylinders, with a bunch en route."

The primary reason for such "blind stocking" as Mr. Cahill puts it, was the inefficiency of the order fulfillment process. "We have quite a lot of people interested in each purchase order," he said. "All that communication was handled through faxes, E-mails or the phone, one on one – which is great until someone goes on vacation or sick leave, or they leave the office for a few hours, or transcribe something incorrectly."

Under the system, which the San Diego site put in place in March 1998, BOC negotiates a bulk purchase with suppliers for a year's worth of gas, and posts the information on a restricted-access Web site. This site, or "extranet,' is accessible only to select BOC suppliers and customers, and to BOC employees who place orders by choosing from an on-line catalogue of gases that has been screened for price and selection, based on the bulk purchase agreement. As the order progresses through delivery, both the supplier and BOC will update the Internet order page, noting the shipping dates, quantity, and shipping method. This gives key personnel instant access to the order's status, which cuts down the need for correspondence, slashes the amount of time spent processing purchase orders and greatly reduces the opportunities for human error. Perhaps more significantly, Mr. Cahill said the system's precision had enabled the company to reduce substantially the number of filled cylinders it keeps in stock, saving his division "several hundred thousand" dollars in annual inventory costs.

A long-time customer, the Massachusetts Institute of Technology, which has been buying gases from the company since 1989 for use in science experiments and other purposes pulled BOC into e-commerce. Four years ago, seeing the Internet's potential for more efficient business practices, MIT persuaded BOC and another of the university's major vendors, Office Depot, to offer their products for sale in virtual catalogue. Like BOC, Office Depot gave it a try, liked what it saw and has since become an e-commerce evangelist. BOC hired IBM in early 1996 to custom-design its extranet. But the system also includes a large amount of software written by BOC's own engineers, which helped keep the initial outlay below $1 million, according to Wilcox, who said annual maintenance now ran around $150,000.

Beyond money, though, companies embarking on E-commerce must also become accustomed to doling out ample portions of trust. BOC, for example, gives its suppliers unprecedented access to its own inventory data; in order to keep its stockpiles replenished. BOC customers like MIT give BOC access to their cost accounting systems, to avoid having to re-enter data as an order works its way through the process. Such trust is a departure from traditional business practices, Wilcox conceded. "But somebody's got to be willing to do something a little differently for this to work."

"The business-to-business process is just a lot more complex," Davis said. "And organizations don't always behave like consumers." With layers of bureaucracy to navigate, and with procurement and sales methods ingrained in the corporate culture, he said, those who champion Electronic Commerce within corporations must be prepared to move slowly. "The sun and the moon and the stars have to line up to make this work," said Wilcox, of BOC. "We're so intertwined with a customer and their processes, we can't just do things suddenly without re-engineering the whole process. That's why business-to-business E-commerce will have a more organic growth than the flash growth on the retail side."

Case Study on Customer-Oriented EC: B2B EC Marketmakers in the Chemicals Industry

Several start-up ventures are now seeking to facilitate the earliest steps in B2B EC, namely the mutual identification of buyers and sellers for a prospective transaction. A primary source of transaction costs in B2B EC is the time and effort needed to locate a supplier who can provide the appropriate goods at the best price. In addition, firms often incur a substantial opportunity cost by trading with a known supplier, although another supplier might exist which could provide an even better product for a lower price. Web-based intermediary sites can help subscribers to lower transaction costs by easing the discovery of the best trading partners. These intermediaries are often very specialized, often focusing on a segment within the B2B activity of a particular industry. This specialization helps the site to cater to the specific needs of its members, and to maintain a high level of sophistication in content and services.

Table 1: On-line Marketmakers in the Petroleum Sector

Marketmaker	Description
Anderson Unicom Group	Electronic catalogue of 700,000 life science, MRO, and office supply products
CambridgeSoft	Leveraging a large installed base of chemistry software users
CheMatch.com	Large-quantity standardized bulk commodity chemicals
ChemConnect	Electronic marketplace for bulk industrial chemicals
Chemdex	Online distributor focused on laboratory chemicals
E-Chemicals	Small-quantity industrial chemicals
Fobchemicals.com	Demand-aggregation model for commercial chemicals purchasing
Industry to Industry (I2I)	Chemicals Exchange focuses on chemicals and plastics
SciQuest	Online distributor focused on laboratory chemicals

Source: Adapted from S.G. Cowen, 1999.

The chemical production industry has a number of B2B segments with very different characteristics. Customers of chemical producers (who are often chemical firms themselves) use bulk chemicals in certain products, which are essentially commodities as products from different vendors are difficult to distinguish. Others use highly specialized chemicals which are essentially custom-produced by suppliers. Some chemicals are bought in extremely small quantities for laboratory use, while others are traded in tons by the day. These varied characteristics make it difficult to standardize all business processes involved in B2B EC for the chemical industry.

For this reason, marketmakers in the chemical B2B space are becoming highly specialized by product type and application. While buyers would typically prefer a one-stop shop set-up for all of their chemical supply needs, these vertical portals add value by collecting producers of like chemicals for like applications in a single on-line database. Once a customer knows the type of chemical needed, finding the appropriate Web-based marketplace for the purchase is easy. The table below shows the range of marketmakers operating in the chemical industry. Many are backed by particular firms; for example, ChemConnect received capital from Dow, while CheMatch is funded by DuPont and Millenium Chemicals.

Case Study on Horizontal EC: Inter-Industry Coordination

Envera (based on the Latin term for 'in truth') was founded by Ethyl Corporation, a mid-sized player in the chemicals industry, in August 1999. The original site was developed based on Ethyl's own experiences in building a B2B extranet for its customers. Ethyl then developed the idea to open the extranet to a larger number of chemical producers, while maintaining the focus of the system on selling to core chemical purchasers. The key technical development was the creation of a clearinghouse for all transactions, which Envera refers to as the "single point of contact," using XML to enable standardized exchange of industry data. Now an independent entity, Envera refers to its system as "B4B" (business for business) site, since it is building the basic infrastructure to enable B2B EC.

In March 2000, Ethyl announced that Envera had recruited a number of "strategic participants" for the site. The core partners are Ethyl, Eastman Chemical, and Sunoco, which are providing the human resources to develop the system. Other participants, who have made financial investments in Envera, are shown in Table 2.

Table 2: Other Participants in Envera

• Albemarle	• Occidental Chemical
• Aristech	• PPG
• BF Goodrich Performance Materials	• Rohm & Haas
• Castrol International	• Solutia Inc.
	• Ultramar Diamond Shamrock

While none of these participants is one of the major leading producers, such as Dow Chemical or Dupont, these partners have combined revenues of $100 billion per year. Envera aims to have 50 investors by the end of the year 2000, and hopes to raise at least $75 million in start-up capital. The site should be operational in the third quarter of 2000.

Envera is not a typical B2B trading hub, as it focuses more on the technological infrastructure for B2B trading than on matching specific buyers and sellers. For that reason, Envera is not positioned to compete directly with the many trading hubs addressing the petro-chemicals industry, such as Chemdex and ChemConnect (in fact, two Envera investors, Rohm & Haas and Eastman, are investors in ChemConnect). Instead, what Envera proposes is an integrated system for facilitating B2B transactions. For that reason, Envera may end up interconnecting to the other B2B hubs, so that business partners who initiate a transaction on another site can transfer to Envera to carry out the transaction.

The core technology behind Envera is contained in two components: the Business Clearinghouse and the Translator Server. The Business Clearinghouse is actually a suite of services which cover the various steps needed to conduct an on-line transaction. These include, among others:

- Product catalogue
- Order processing
- Shipment tracking
- Industry info
- Banking and electronic bill payment
- Logistics

Each of these components will be executed with a specific, pre-defined XML document standardized across the Envera system. Certain components are provided by outside partners. For example, electronic payment will be supported by First Union Bank. The Translation Server is a system which, when configured by Envera, will convert documents and data between each participant's proprietary, legacy format and the Envera XML standard. This will enable seamless integration of the participant's existing supply chain systems with the Envera system.

EC in the Service Sector: Some Observations

The cases described above illustrate the four key dimensions of strategic change enabled and induced by electronic commerce.

Efficiency. By automating formerly labor- and paper-intensive processes, such as procurement and inter-company trading, firms can reduce their transaction costs and directly increase their profits. The case of BOC Gases shows how simple electronic procurement processes reduce operating costs and increase profitability. On-line marketmakers also increase efficiency by facilitating price discovery in the competitive petrochemicals market.

Effectiveness. BOC Gases also found that its inherent capabilities in software and information systems development enabled the firm to create an extranet, extending its ability to serve key customers and coordinate its supply chain. Similarly, Envera promises to improve the ability of its members to serve their customers rapidly and effectively. This shows how EC can extend and even create core competences in user firms.

Reach. Electronic commerce is clearly increasing the reach of petrochemical firms. BOC Gases is now able to trade at relatively low cost with a global supplier base. By investing in on-line marketmakers, large chemical firms such as Dow and Dupont can identify new customers and better serve their immediate needs.

Integration. Most importantly, the three cases above show how electronic commerce is used to facilitate the direct exchange of value between firms in the form of transactional data and intelligence. With Envera, companies will be able to view the processing and fulfillment of orders as it occurs inside of their trading partners. BOC Gases is using electronic commerce to transmit its future capacity requirements and demand estimates to its suppliers, and its suppliers' supplier, helping to ensure a stable flow of primary goods.

Extending our observations about electronic commerce strategic changes from the petrochemicals industry to the service sector, we can infer that service firms will face equal opportunities to gain competitive advantages through electronic commerce. Subject to the limitations of measurement methodologies, the service sector should see gains in productivity and other dimensions as a result of the use of EC. Recent strategic moves in electronic commerce by large service companies indicate at least the expectation of such gains:

Electronic procurement. As with BOC Gases, many service companies have moved their procurement activities on-line, in cooperation with software vendors in this area (such as Ariba Technologies, Oracle Corporation, and i2 Technologies). This trend is particularly strong in commercial banking, where electronic procurement sites have been established by most large banks. More importantly, financial institutions are opening up their electronic procurement services to their customers. For example, corporate customers of the brokerage firm Merrill Lynch can buy their own supplies through the Merrill Lynch site. This is especially attractive to smaller firms, who can receive the volume discounts that vendors give to Merrill Lynch due to the sheer size of its procurement activity. For Merrill Lynch, providing this service could increase customer loyalty and retention. Other large financial institutions have followed the lead of Merrill Lynch, including Citigroup, Bank of America, Chase Manhattan Bank, and Wells Fargo. Several airlines have formed a joint electronic procurement system.

B2B electronic marketplaces. While B2B marketplaces are most commonly found in manufacturing industries (automotive, aerospace, electronics, etc.), some marketplaces are forming to increase the efficiency of service transactions.

One example is the National Transportation Exchange. On this site, trucking firms can post the routes that their trucks will travel and the available capacity on each truck for each route segment. Firms which have shipments to be transported can then log on and place spot bids for pick-ups and deliveries along available routes. This marketplace provides significant benefits to the thousands of small, independent trucking firms in the U.S. In the past, these firms would make a one-way shipment, and then run empty trucks on the return route before getting another delivery job. With the NTE, truck drivers can book their trailer space in real time, maximizing the revenue from each mile travelled. B2B exchanges are also common in banking (marketplaces for commercial loans), telecommunications (real-time trading of available bandwidth on public networks), and even professional services (on-line contracting for consulting and legal services).

Integrated B2B transaction systems. Some service industries have operated electronic systems to facilitate B2B transactions for years, but not on the Web. One example is SWIFT, the worldwide network for transferring funds between financial institutions. With the cooperation of global financial companies, SWIFT transactions can be transmitted over the Internet using the FIX (financial Internet exchange) protocol. Healtheon/WebMD is a firm which is attempting to set up a similar system for the health care industry, so that medical providers and insurance firms can exchange information seamlessly.

One potential outcome of this move to electronic commerce is the increased integration of multiple, nested value nets (see Figure 2). Electronic systems for supply chain management and customer relationship management are being merged in a new concept called Enterprise Relationship Management (ERM), where a firm can communicate with all of its trading partners from suppliers to customers to competitors and complementors. As each firm builds these "value webs," they will be able to access directly information residing in firms which are beyond their immediate network. As a hypothetical example, a company which manufactures the control knobs for car radios will in the future have direct access to the production schedules of the U.S. auto manufacturers, so that the company can plan its manufacturing volumes to provide exactly the number of radio knobs needed by the final assemblers (Thornton, 2000). Firms can form integrated supply chains and customer chains, so that they will in effect communicate directly with the suppliers of their suppliers, the customers of their customers, and so on.

Figure 2: Nested Integrated Value Nets

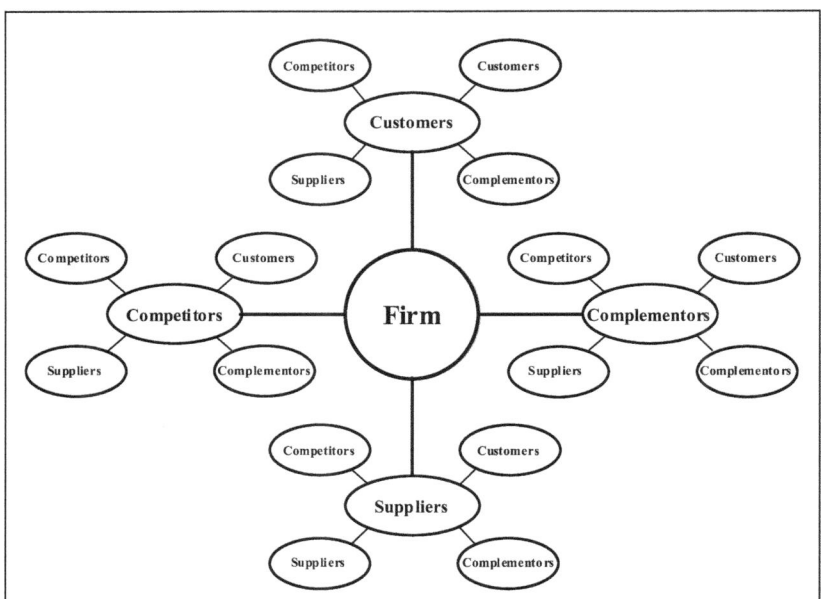

The analysis of service sector productivity often overlooks an interesting implication of the shift to electronic commerce: the effect of increased service sector productivity on manufacturing productivity. Service firms play an important role in facilitating various aspects of business-to-business and business-to-consumer purchases of manufactured products. Therefore, close integration between the service and manufacturing sectors through electronic commerce is critical. For example, the Envera consortium includes participation from First Union Bank to enable electronic payments. Service and manufacturing firms need to interface electronically to realize the full productivity benefits of electronic commerce.

This type of cross-sectoral integration is typical of the industry-level influence of electronic commerce on business strategies. In some cases, this increased integration is leading to complete mergers which attempt to capture the expected synergies from increased e-business.

In the service industry, vertical integration has accelerated rapidly. For instance, the Disney Company purchased Capital Cities/ABC to gain access to a new distribution channel for Disney's content. The merged company also combined the efforts of its two components to exploit a new distribution, the World Wide Web, through Disney's redesigned Go network. A similar merger is underway between America Online and Time Warner, with America Online hoping to use

Time Warner's cable systems to distribute its on-line services and content via broadband transmissions to consumer households.

Horizontal integration is also increasing as EC changes the definition of markets. The pending merger of MCI Worldcom and Sprint, two of the top three telecommunications carriers in the U.S. market, is being defended on the grounds that the Internet and other factors have made telecommunications into a global marketplace. In global terms, the merged company would be but one of several large carriers fighting for leadership. The auto industry also faces antitrust review as a result of its new integrated electronic procurement system, Covisint, which will combine the buying power of Ford, General Motors, Daimler-Chrysler, Renault, Nissan, and Toyota. These companies could argue that the efficiencies gained from consolidated on-line buying outweigh the anti-competitive effects of the combined system.

The final category of integration developing as a result of electronic commerce is *diagonal integration*—mergers which cross traditional market and sector boundaries. The deregulation of financial services has enabled banks to offer insurance (as in the merger of Citicorp and Travelers Group), and many banks are using the Web as a low-cost means of test-marketing their insurance products. Also, some manufacturing firms are using the Web to enter new industries—for example, new Web banks are planned by both General Motors (through the General Motors Assurance Corporation subsidiary) and General Electric (through GE Capital).

Summary and Conclusions

Business models provide general rules for organizations to adhere to when implementing new initiatives. The rules are derived from specific instances of success within the working environment. Traditional business models are dramatically changing as electronic commerce grows, and as a result, very few established business models exist for electronic commerce. Establishing the new business models necessary for organizations to evaluate and determine successful methods to execute electronic commerce is a significant challenge for organizations.

The overall success of electronic business will depend to a great extent on the organization's ability to form strong partnerships. The basic candidates are the ones you would expect; supplier, provider, customers, consumers and employees, but to be highly successful you need to go further. This includes trade associations, technology vendors, on-line gateways, financial service suppliers, fulfilment companies, government agency and the legal profession. Strong partnerships allow an organization to spread its exposure to risk, where the traditional organization increases its risk by standing still, maintaining an inflexible structure, or limiting its potentially by being position in a single supply chain. Partners who set common goals to focus on value, not volume, will form successful electronic operations. Several "Critical Success Factors" have been identified by successful organizations:

- Business or government executives need to provide support and have buy-in
- Establish electronic commerce definitions and measurements
- Determine revenue targets for each brand, customer group and/or initiative
- Create electronic commerce "imperatives" (reasons/incentive to use the web)
- Determine channel readiness of products, services or consumables
- Develop an electronic commerce infrastructure – high function /scaleable catalogue, configurations, registration, etc.
- Develop sound business cases focused on ROI and value propositions

Many organizations are implementing electronic commerce in numerous ways and receiving tangible benefits. But as electronic commerce matures and develops, these ways are likely to change based of the accelerating adoption rate. Based on our review, three specific implementation models are starting to appear in the marketplace. They include:

Transaction-Based. A single company establishes a common transactional method for conducting business with its major customers or key suppliers. This offering is common across all business unites within the company and includes common tools, techniques and infrastructure.

Process-Based. Two companies establish a common business process required for conducting business efficiently and effectively between the two firms. The two firms establish and share this common practice jointly, both within their firm and outside their organization with this predetermined trading partner.

Strategic Relationship Based. Two or more companies establishing a strategic relationship partnership based on all major interactions between the organizations. This includes transactions, process and any other collaboration between the two organizations. From a technology perspective this includes linking the CRM, ERP and SCM Systems between the two organizations. This way each organization can actually monitor sales activity, production schedules, inventory management, and technical service exchanges.

Among these three modes, strategic electronic commerce partnerships represent the best means to obtain added competitive advantage in the marketplace, but under very specific circumstances. In many situations, the risks incurred from undertaking strategic linkages with trading partners are not justified by the likely benefits. Some examples of EC relationships which are *not* strategic include:

As the world moves toward e-business, the traditional order/invoice process is being subsumed by a new, more-diverse order/deal management process that requires a portfolio approach to trading-partner relationship. Electronic marketplace, electronic catalogues, electronic bidding systems and Internet search agents are creating an open-sourcing environment for certain product classes.

Trends accelerating the adoption rate of collaborative activities include the following:

- a switch from enterprise-centric business models to customer-centric business models is mandating an external process view
- increase global competition and the emergence of the global logistics network is forcing some enterprises to band together to compete more effectively (e.g. the US apparel industry
- increased demand from customers for service that is "faster, cheaper and better" is creating a need to increase the velocity of goods and information up and down the entire supply chain

Overall, firms need to realize that only some modes of EC transactions will be suitable for particular needs. Some transactions may also require a hybrid approach bridging these categories. The key is to first identify the critical nature of the transaction, and then define the relationship needed with trading partners, which is then implemented in EC.

There are many *challenges* for business and governments to take advantage and utilize electronic commerce as a complementor for existing channels and to improve cost and revenue positions. And, the *opportunity* is sizable, almost $200 billion by 2001 of business-to-business electronic commerce, but is also the target of our traditional and emerging Internet competitors. We have defined a version of electronic commerce. Now business and government need to set targets to measure e-commerce in relation to revenue, reduced cost and industry spend share, and drive their electronic commerce initiatives to enable the achievement of these goals. But some key lessons have been identified and need to be part of the solution:

Electronic Commerce is highly collaborative and cross-functional. It impacts business, marketing, communication, legal, tax, and information technology and customers service.

Electronic Commerce requires mastery of many disciplines. Such as customer or consumer need, strategy development, managing partnerships & alliances and project and change management. It requires understanding of current technology standards such as XML, SSL. It also requires understanding the latest regulatory and legal issues and the latest social – economic thinking. It needs to be attempted at the lowest level and the grown into a more scalable solution.

References

Barnevik, P., (1994). *Global Strategies*. Harvard Business School Press. Boston.

Benesko, G., (1996). *Inter-Corporate Business Engineering: Streamlining the Business Cycle From End to End*. Research Triangle Consultants, Inc. Raleigh, NC.

Chandler, C. and Pearlstein S., (1977). "Debating the Myth or Miracle Behind the 'New Economy.'" *The Washington Post*. October 11, 1997, p. D1.

Drucker, P., (1989). *The New Realities*. Harper & Collins. New York.

Electronic Commerce in Europe. July 1998.

Fingleton, E., (1999). *In Praise of Hard Industries*. Butterworth Press. New York.

Hegel, J. and Armstrong, A., (1996). *Net Gain: Expanding Markets Through Virtual Communities*. Harvard Business School Press. Boston.

IBM (1997), *Think Leadership*. Vol. 2, No 1.

Kalakota, R. and Whinston, A.B., (1996). *Frontiers of Electronic Commerce*. Addison-Wesley. Reading.

Martin, J., (1996). *Cybercorp*. AMACOM. New York.

McRae, H., (1994). *The World in 2020*. Harvard Business School Press. Boston.

Ohmae, K., (1990). *The Borderless World: Power and Strategy in the Interlinked Economy*. Harper & Row. New York.

Ohmae, K., (1995). *The Evolving Global Economy: Making Sense of the New World Order*. Harvard Business School Press. Boston.

Samli, A. C., Still R. and Hill J.S., (1993). *International Marketing: Planning and Practice*. MacMillan Publishing Company. NewYork.

SG Cohen. (1999). *Business to Business E-commerce: Here come the on-line intermediaries*. Report released December 1999.

Tapscott, D., (1996). *The Digital Economy: Promise and Peril in the Age of Networked Intelligence*. McGraw Hill. New York.

Yip, G., (1992). *Total Global Strategy: Managing for Worldwide Competitive Advantage*. Prentice Hall. Englewood Cliffs.

Chapter 2

An Analysis of the Possible Causes of Product Market Malfunctioning in the EU: First Results for Manufacturing and Service Sectors

Fabienne Ilzkovitz, Adriaan Dierx, Nuno Sousa[1]

Acknowledgements: This report was undertaken at the Directorate General for Economic and Financial Affairs under the direction of Klaus Regling, Marco Buti, Jan Host Schmidt and Gert-Jan Koopman. The authors gratefully acknowledge the contributions of C. Buelens, Andrea Conte, Yann Ducatteeuw, Olivia Galgau, Viktoria Kovacs, Barbara Moench, Francesco Montaruli and Dominique Simonis.

Abstract

Within the context of the follow-up to the Single Market Review, the European Commission has screened EU manufacturing and service sectors for problems of market malfunctioning. This paper investigates the nature of these problems in the 23 selected sectors and focuses on the following four dimensions of market functioning: regulation, integration, competition and innovation. In spite of the data limitations, regulation appears to be a cross cutting factor affecting market functioning in many sectors. The service sectors, in particular, show signs of an unexploited potential in terms of market integration and competition pressures. In all selected sectors there are indications of an unsatisfactory innovation performance. Overall, the analysis appears to confirm the results of the initial sector screening.

Introduction

One of the initiatives put forward by the European Commission in the Single Market Review Communication of 20 November was the proposal to adopt a new approach to market monitoring. The objective of this proposal is to promote

---

[1] This article was written by Fabienne Ilzkovitz, Adriaan Dierx and Nuno Sousa, DIRECTORATE GENERAL FOR ECONOMIC AND FINACIAL AFFAIRS © European Communities, 2008. The views expressed in this Article are those of the authors and do not reflect the official position of the European Commission.

an approach towards policymaking which is less legalistic and more based on sound economic evidence.

In order to put in practice this proposal the Commission has recently conducted a screening exercise to identify the key sectors to which priority should be given for future in-depth market monitoring initiatives. This note aims at complementing this exercise with an investigation of the possible causes of the problems affecting market functioning in these priority sectors.

The objectives of this investigation are multiple: first, it checks the robustness of the screening results by analysing if all the sectors that have been selected as a result of the screening are indeed facing challenges from a policymaking point of view; second, it provides a starting point and guidance for the subsequent in-depth market monitoring analyses; finally, it aims at developing a consistent and comprehensive policy strategy most suited to address the particular needs of any given sector. It should nevertheless be kept in mind that the investigation is limited to supply-side issues and should be complemented with an analysis of demand-side issues.

The analysis starts with an overview of the regulatory framework that conditions the functioning of markets in the EU and then continues by exploring three distinct (albeit intrinsically intertwined) policy areas: first, integration in order to determine the extent to which EU markets are well integrated internally as well as externally within the global market place; second, competition to check whether EU markets are contestable; and finally, innovation to examine how dynamic EU sectors are in terms of benefiting from new technologies and introducing new products in the market.

The rest of this note is structured as follows: section 2 provides more information related to the background and context of this initiative; section 3 starts by describing the adopted methodological approach followed by a presentation of the analysis made of the four dimensions scrutinised, namely regulation, integration, competition, and innovation. Section 4 draws the main conclusions from the analysis and finally section 5 points out avenues for further work.

Background and context

The implementation of a more systematic and integrated approach to the monitoring of the functioning of key goods and services markets as envisaged in the 20 November Communication rests on the methodology that was developed by the inter-service group on product market and sector monitoring during the fist half of 2007[2].

---

[2] See European Commission (2007a) for a full description.

This methodology encompasses two steps. The first step consists of a horizontal screening exercise aimed at selecting the sectors which should be given priority in terms of market monitoring. This is done by identifying the most important sectors for growth, jobs, consumers and adjustment in the EU and that present signs of problems of market malfunctioning (both in terms of economic efficiency and consumer welfare). So far the consumer perspective could not be adequately taken into account due to the lack of data. However the development of the Consumer Markets Scoreboard will allow closing this analytical gap. The second step involves a market-based in-depth investigation of the sectors that have been identified in the screening in order to better understand the reasons for malfunctioning and to draw concrete policy recommendations. The economic examination should in particular investigate in depth the three elements that constitute the backbone of the organisation of sectors and markets: their industrial structure, the conduct of the firms and the performance in terms of efficiency and consumer welfare.

The first stage of the methodology (the screening) was already implemented by the Commission services leading to the identification of 23 sectors, see table 1[3]. These results were published in a staff working paper that accompanied the Communication of 20 November (See European Commission (2007b). The sectors that have been selected are evenly distributed between manufacturing and services. The former cover mainly investment (equipment) and intermediary goods sectors (both from more capital intensive industries and from the more high technology/skilled labour intensive industries). The latter include a variety of activities related to distribution (retail, wholesale, hotels and restaurants), financial services as well as network industries like "Electricity, gas and water supply", "Inland transportation" and "Post and telecommunications". In addition, professional services such as engineering consultancy, legal and architectural services and the like (sector 74 "other business services") have also been selected. In total these 23 sectors represented 44% of total EU value added and 46% of total EU employment in 2004.

---

[3] For a more comprehensive description of the main characteristics of the selected sectors see Annex 1.

Table 1: Sectors selected in the screening

SELECTED SECTORS
22 - Printing, publishing and reproduction
25 - Rubber and plastics
27 - Basic metals
28 - Fabricated metal
29 – Machinery
30 - Office, accounting and computing machinery
31 - Electrical machinery and apparatus
32 - Radio, TV and communication equipment
34 - Motor vehicles, trailers and semi- trailers
35 - Other transport equipment
36 - Furniture, other manufactured goods n.e.c.
37 – Recycling
E - Electricity, gas and water supply
50 - Sale, maintenance and repair of motor vehicles
51 - Wholesale trade
52 - Retail trade
H - Hotels and restaurants
60 - Inland transport
63 - Supporting and auxiliary transport activities
64 - Post and telecommunications
65 - Financial intermediation
66 - Insurance and pension funding
74 - Other business activities

Analysis of the causes of market malfunctioning

I. Approach

The objective of this analysis at the sectoral level is to provide a first assessment of the nature of the causes of poor performance (from a supply side point of view) in the sectors previously selected, notably to determine the extent to which the observed underperformance is related to market malfunctioning. The idea is to eventually explore alternative policy responses aimed at tackling the identified problems. While ultimately the problems affecting market functioning in these sectors should be examined in light of the overall welfare costs for consumers and producers, given the complexity of such task we have opted to structure this analysis along four "policy areas", namely regulation, integration, competition, and innovation.

A fifth policy area is also considered crucial to achieve a comprehensive analysis of the causes of market malfunctioning in a given sector: the consumer welfare[4]. However the necessary data at the sectoral level to make this analysis operational are not yet fully developed[5]. The current development of a Consumer Scoreboard by the Commission services in close cooperation with national authorities, statistical offices and stakeholders will in the short run provide the necessary indicators (covering issues such as complaints, prices, consumer satisfaction, switching and safety) for such an analysis.

For the sake of simplicity (and to keep the exercise as objective and manageable as possible), the analysis developed in this note deals with each of the four areas considered separately. However, clearly these four dimensions of market functioning are closely intertwined and therefore from a policymaking point of view an integrated approach is required (see Figure 1).

Figure 1: Analytical framework

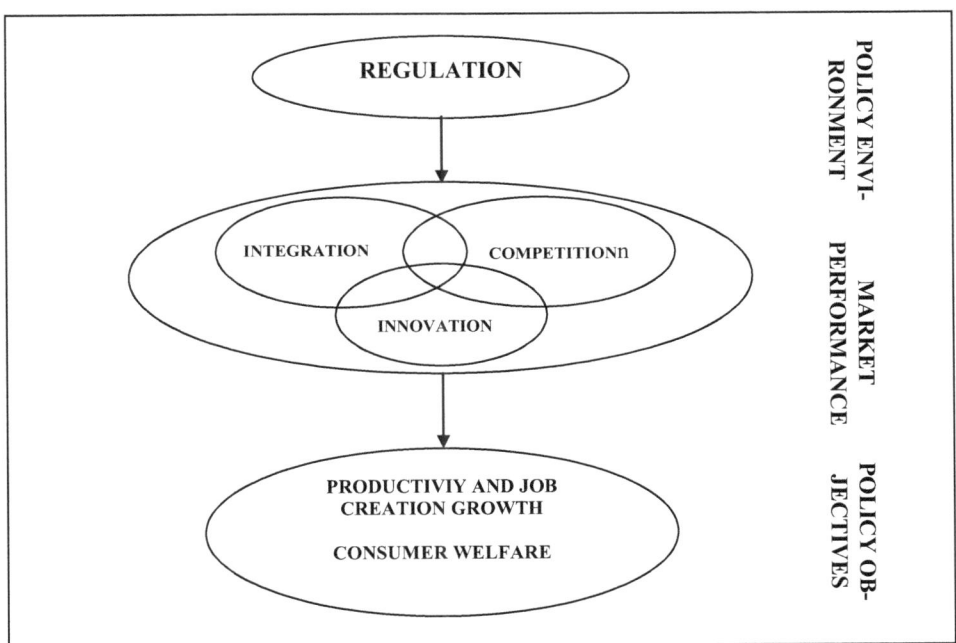

---

[4] In the screening methodology the level of consumer satisfaction was used as criterion to assess whether markets in a sector are functioning well. The rationale behind this approach is that markets can only be considered as well functioning if they guarantee an efficient use of resources but they must also respond well to the needs of users (consumers and businesses), by allowing an informed identification and selection of the suppliers that offer the best goods and services at an affordable price.

[5] Until now data on consumer satisfaction, particularly for sectors other than services of general economic interest are very limited both from a quantitative and qualitative point of view.

Regulation is as an exogenous policy driven dimension that frames the environment in which markets function. It directly results from the use of most policy instruments that can be called for to influence the behaviour of market players, crucially affecting the competition, integration and innovation dimensions in the markets. First, the regulatory environment directly affects the level of competition pressure that firms face. The intensification of competition pressure leads in turn to allocative efficiency gains while giving also firms the necessary incentives to increase their productive efficiency[6]. Moreover, competition pressure is increasingly associated with international market integration as markets often span beyond national borders. The lifting of trade and investment restrictions and the resulting competition pressure from foreign firms contribute to further discipline the monopolistic or oligopolistic behaviour of domestic firms, forcing them to behave in a more competitive way. Finally, integration and competition are also closely related to innovation as the increased competition pressures encourage firms to seek new ways of doing business to remain competitive, which in turn spurs entrepreneurial drive and innovation efforts[7]. Provided that other necessary framework conditions are there (namely in terms of skills availability) and if this competition pressure is sustained, in the long run the result will be a gain in terms of dynamic efficiency. Achieving a good performance overall in terms of competition, integration and innovation is a necessary condition for the better functioning markets that allow higher growth rates of productivity and employment as well as greater consumer satisfaction. As far as consumer welfare is concerned, this condition is not sufficient as both strategic behaviour of providers and behavioural biases of the consumers affect the markets' outcomes.

The conditions under which EU product markets operate have changed considerably since the 1990s[8]. The Single Market Programme and the introduction of the euro have led to increased market openness and price transparency, which have boosted the pressures of competition triggered by globalisation

---

[6] For a exhaustive investigation of this it would be necessary to look into other aspects of market performance such as entrepreneurship, financing, firms' entry and exit rates as well as firm-level adjustment. These issues are crucial for more in-depth market monitoring exercises, which would greatly benefit from the use of firm-level data.

[7] The relationship between market structure and innovation has been explored since Schumpeter (1942). Lately the literature has shifted from the view of market structure as an (exogenous) determinant of R&D activity to the recognition of a dynamic interaction between firm size, market structure and innovation (Scherer, 1992). Recently the existence of an inverted U-shape relationship between innovation and competition is acknowledged. While, at first, the intensification of competition gives firms added incentives to innovate to stay in the market and better resist pressures from competitors, further entry in the market entry when it is too strong may reduce mark ups to such an extent that the incentives to innovate are reduced because the costs cannot be recovered.

[8] For a more in-depth description of main developments, see Ilzkovitz et al. (2007) and EU Economy Review 2008.

and the diffusion of information and communication technologies. Several other product market reforms aimed at strengthening integration and competition have also been implemented in individual Member States within the context of the Lisbon Strategy for Growth and Jobs (see Box 1).

> **Box 1: Reforms carried out to improve the functioning of product markets since the 1990s**
>
> Within the context of the Lisbon Strategy for Growth and Jobs, several reforms have been implemented to improve the integration, competition and innovation in the European Single Market. These reforms are closely monitored by the European authorities, via the Member States' Annual Implementation Reports and the Commission's Annual Progress Report [9].
>
> Measures taken to improve the integration of product markets have included the implementation of Single Market directives and reforms aiming at modernising public procurement. The reform measures taken in the area of competition have aimed at improving the powers and means of competition authorities, at reducing unnecessary state aid measures and at improving the regulatory environment in specific sectors.
>
> Most measures included in reform programmes at both EU and Member State level are aimed at promoting investment in research and new technologies and at supporting business start ups, investment in risk capital and education and training. These include: *i*) Financial incentives for R&D have been created or expanded in all euro-area countries; *ii*) The tightening of the links between research and business via the promotion of public-private partnerships and the creation and development of innovation poles and networks or facilitation of university spin-offs; *iii*) Measures to upgrade general education; *iv*) Measures to promote ICT use in education and training, online government services and e-commerce and the investment in broadband internet infrastructure; *v*) Programmes to facilitate access to risk capital to young and small enterprises and the setting-up new firms.
>
> Finally a number of reforms have been aimed at reducing market distortions caused by public interventions, including: *i*) Corporate tax reforms aimed at removing or easing distortions; *ii*) Cuts in state aid; *iii*) The implementation of "better regulation" programmes, *iv*) Measures to improve the efficiency of public administration, namely via the setting up of on-line government services; *v*) The opening up of public procurement markets.

---

[9] Comprehensive information on European measures in favour of entrepreneurship and competitiveness until 2002 is also available at: http://ec.europa.eu/enterprise/enterprise_policy/charter_directory/index.htm.

Despite these positive developments problems persist in terms of regulation, integration, competition, and innovation which are experienced to a different degree by the various sectors. In this note, the different sectors will be analysed along each of these four dimensions on the basis of a set of pre-defined indicators. The regulation dimension is somewhat different in nature than the other three dimensions that are taken into account. The former captures the institutional framework in which firms operate but it does not directly reflect market outcomes. In contrast, information on competition, innovation and integration performance can be used more directly to make qualitative assessments about market functioning, which is in turn conditioned by the regulatory framework in place.

The assessment whether there are indications of problems in a given sector is made using a pre-defined benchmark. If possible, the performance of the same sector in the US is used as the benchmark because it allows tackling the issue of the sectoral heterogeneity. *A priori,* the US is an appropriate benchmark for this exercise given that it is a well integrated market of a size comparable to the EU. Given the other structural similarities, namely in terms of factor endowments, the US is a direct competitor to the EU for many products in the world market. Moreover the US is also a suitable benchmark for analysis of innovation issues given that it is generally regarded as a technological leader. Whenever a direct comparison with the US is not possible due to unavailability of data the performance of a given sector is benchmarked against the performance of other sectors at the EU level. In this case, when justified by the intrinsic characteristics of the sectors, we make the distinction between manufacturing and services sectors adopting the manufacturing average and the services average as two different benchmarks[10].

II. Regulation

The starting point for this analysis is an examination of the extent to which the observed problems in market functioning can be related to the policy environment. In this respect, the quality of economic regulation is a crucial issue to be considered. The regulatory framework governing product markets (both rules and institutions) affects market characteristics and performances[11]. Notice that in this note we focus exclusively on product market regulations and do not take

---

[10] The EU averages are constructed taking into account all sectors of the economy and not just the sectors that have been selected in the screening stage.

[11] The OECD (1997) defines regulation as "the diverse set of instruments by which governments set requirements on enterprises and citizens." Regulations include laws, formal and informal orders and subordinate rules issues by all levels of government as well as rules issued by non-governmental or self-regulatory bodies to which governments have delegated regulatory powers.

into account other types of regulation like for example labour and environmental regulations, which can also have considerable effects on the functioning of markets. However, these effects should nonetheless be considered in the more in-depth analyses of particular sectors or markets.

Generally, product market regulations are introduced to improve the functioning of markets by addressing public interest concerns about market failures including imperfect competition, externalities and asymmetric information. However, often these regulations do not meet the purposes they have been designed for or their implementation leads to unintended negative (collateral) effects[12]. For example, regulations can introduce or augment barriers to entry curbing the competition pressure in the market. They may also alter firms' incentives to invest, to adopt leading technologies available in the market and to innovate in-house. Moreover regulations can introduce further distortions in the market as their cumulative impact is likely to be especially important for small and medium-sized enterprises, which generally lack the resources to deal with the administration burden resulting from laws and regulations.

However, an in-depth investigation of the impact of the regulatory framework on market functioning would also require detailed qualitative data to fully take into account the different features and objectives of the regulation imposed on firms. By ignoring the qualitative features of regulations one risks conducting a partial analysis that overlooks many of the potential benefits of regulation, which often go beyond purely economic considerations. While we acknowledge these intrinsic limitations of quantitative indicators of regulation, for the sake of consistency with the rest of the analysis in this paper the focus will be put on the available quantitative information on regulation. Therefore, we use the OECD regulation indicator as the main source of information to draw an overall picture of the level of regulation in European markets[13]. The methodology developed by

---

[12] In Arnold et al. (2007) a number of economic and policy factors are listed to explain why the regulatory framework may be flawed. First, some regulations may drift away from their original public interest aims, resulting in the protection of special interest groups. Second, regulations (and their implementation) sometimes involve costs that exceed their expected benefits, leading to so-called "government failure". Third, technical progress, the evolution of demand and progress in regulatory techniques can make the design of regulation obsolete.

[13] The information contained in the OECD database is based on the answers provided by OECD Members to a questionnaire containing 805 questions in the following domains: general policies (antitrust, control, market access, etc.), regulatory and administrative policies, administrative requirements for business start-ups, regulation of professional services, regulation in transportation industries, and regulation in the retail distribution industry (see Nicoletti et al., 2000). The data allow building indicators of product market regulation at various levels of aggregation, using weighting techniques such as principal component analysis.

the OECD focuses only on those regulations that affect competition where competition is an appropriate policy objective[14]. In this way it implicitly acknowledges that many regulations are welfare enhancing by addressing market failures or by pursuing non-economic objectives. The OECD indicator aims at quantifying the degree to which regulatory settings are anti-competitive while making no attempt to measure the stance of regulation with respect to public policy goals or to evaluate the efficiency of the regulations in meeting such goals.

Figure 2: OECD indicators of product market regulation in 1998 and 2003

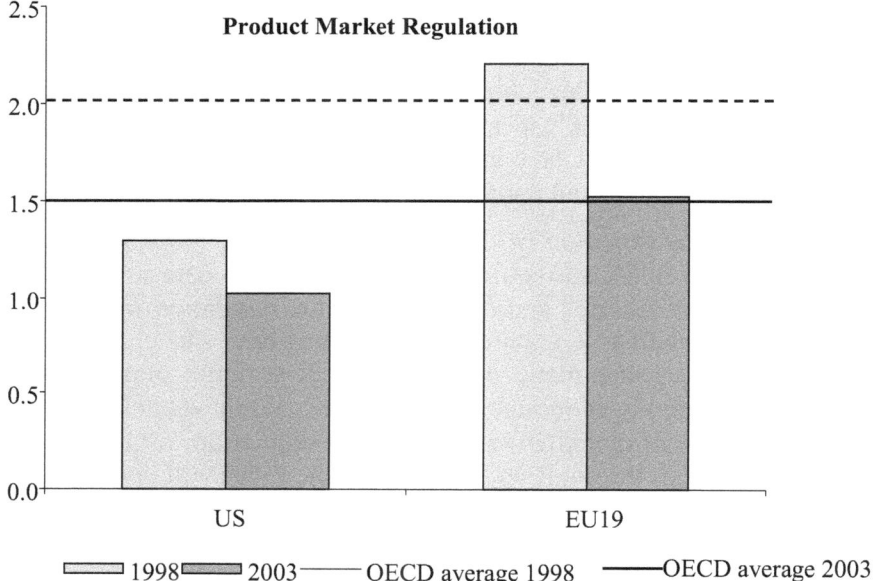

Source: Conway, P. et al. (2005).

Overall markets in the EU remained relatively heavily regulated in 2003, despite the several programmes of reforms put in place over the past decade and a half. Visible progress was achieved between 1998 and 2003 in reducing barriers to competition across the EU. Moreover it should be pointed out that since 2003 further deregulation has taken place in a number of sectors (e.g. telecoms, transport etc). Furthermore, there has been a process of convergence among Member States towards lower levels of regulation as on average the countries

---

[14] All these indicators are constructed from the perspective of regulations that create barriers to entrepreneurship and restrict competition in domestic markets where technology and demand conditions make competition viable.

that had the highest level of product market regulation are those that have carried out the most substantial reforms (see Conway et al., 2005).

In general, these liberalisation efforts entailed a decline in state control (via the elimination of price controls and direct controls of businesses) and the elimination of barriers to trade and investment (via lower tariffs and lower restrictions to foreign investment). Barriers to entrepreneurship (including in particular administrative burdens and legal barriers to entry in sheltered markets) have declined less dramatically, notwithstanding the increased use of one-stop shops. Nonetheless, it is clear that product markets are more regulated on average in the EU than in the US.[15] This makes the issue of regulation particularly important when analysing the functioning of markets in the EU.

While there is not much direct evidence of how regulation affects the functioning of markets *per se*, these quantitative indices of regulatory burden allowed the development of an increasing body of empirical research that shows that product market deregulation has a positive effect on market entry, productivity and growth. For example, Nicoletti and Scarpetta (2003) found that reducing barriers to entry in service in certain European countries, most notably Germany, France, Italy and Greece, would boost annual multi-factor productivity growth in the overall business sector by about 0.1 to 0.2 percentage points. Indirect effects would boost manufacturing-wide annual productivity growth by 0.1 to 0.2 percentage points, (see also Griffith and Harrison (2004) and Griffith et al. (2006)). The assumption is that measures aimed at reducing regulation that inhibit competition lead to a reduction of slack in the use of resources and improves the functioning of markets (namely by easing start up conditions, simplifying existing regulations and enhancing entrepreneurial activities) which trigger greater investment and increase innovation efforts ultimately spurring economic growth. The impact of regulation on the entry and exit of firms is particularly important a mechanism through which the functioning of markets is directly affected (and eventually economic performance). For example Scarpetta et al. (2002) found the contribution of entry and exit of firms to aggregate productivity growth ranges from 20% to 40% in several OECD countries[16]. Cincera and Galgau (2005) also find a clear link between deregulation and higher rates of entry and exit which in turn affect positively macroeconomic outcomes as measured by labour productivity growth.

---

[15] EU is a simple average of data referring to 19 Member States, namely: AT, BE, CZ, DE, DK, EL, ES, FI, FR, HU, IE, IT, LU, NL, PL, PT, SE, SK, UK.

[16] The results show that exit of low productivity firms has a positive contribution to aggregate growth across all countries and that in high technology sectors, the entry of new firms has a larger than average contribution to total growth, whereas in mature industries the exit of firms has larger contributions to growth.

> **Box 2: Measures of level of product market regulation**
>
> Three main sources of data can be used to assess the level of regulation in the EU and other economies (see Dierx et al (2007) for a more exhaustive overview). First, the Fraser Institute indicator of general economic freedom, combines data summarising the degree of regulation of credit markets, labour markets and business with information on the strength of property rights, the state involvement in the economy, financial stability and freedom of trade. The indicator has been calculated every five years since 1970 and annually since 2000. Second, the World Bank database "Doing Business" provides indicators on the cost of doing business by identifying specific regulations that enhance or constrain business investment, productivity and growth. Data are available for 2003, 2004, 2005 and 2006. Finally, the product market regulation database constructed by the OECD contains indicators of barriers to entrepreneurship, state control and barriers to trade and investment. Data have been collected for two years only: 1998 and 2003. While these three organisations use different data sources, simple Spearman and Pearson tests show a significant negative correlation between the 2003 OECD indicators of product market regulation and the Fraser indicators of economic freedom (except in the case of state involvement/control).

For the current exercise it is important to go beyond the comparative analysis of the aggregate levels of regulation imposed in the EU and the US and to investigate to what extent these regulations affect the functioning of markets in different specific sectors. Regulations are very often specific to particular sectors and/or markets and the exposure of firms to regulation (either sector-specific or economy wide) can vary importantly (depending for example on their position relative to the technological frontier).[17]

While the sector level may still be too aggregate to uncover the mechanisms by which regulations can affect the functioning of markets, even such an analysis remains difficult to implement due to the scarcity of information. To the best of our knowledge the only information collected on regulation at the sectoral level are published by the OECD. However, these indicators are characterised by two shortcomings. The first is the most recent OECD data are for 2003. This is particularly problematic for sectoral analysis as it overlooks all measures taken since 2003 which have targeted regulation in specific sectors. Currently the

---

[17] De-regulation (and the ensuing increase in competition pressure) may lead to stronger innovation efforts particularly in the firms that are closer to the technological frontier as they attempt to stay ahead of their competitors (the so-called escape-competition effect on innovation). The impact on firms that are further from the technology frontier is less clear-cut as these firms will feel discouraged from investing further on innovation as the effort necessary to take the lead may be considered untenable for them (a discouragement effect of entry), see Aghion (2005) and Aghion and Griffith (2006).

OECD is working on the updating these data which should be available by the end of 2008. The second shortcoming is that the sectoral coverage of the OECD database is very limited as it focuses on non-manufacturing sectors only[18].

However arguably these are the sectors where most regulations aimed at restricting competition (and market entry in particular) in developed economies are concentrated. Furthermore, the impact of regulations on the quality, the variety and the price of products is exacerbated in these sectors given that the consumers' and businesses' ability to get around them is curtailed by the limited degree of import penetration.

> **Box 3: The OECD Regulation Impact Indicators**
>
> The OECD Regulation Impact (REGREF) indicators aim at providing a measure of the overall impact of the regulation imposed in non-manufacturing sectors on all the sectors of the economy. This overall impact includes the indirect effects of regulation on the sectors which buy intermediate inputs from the regulated non-manufacturing sectors. However this measure is still incomplete as it does not include any regulations that are directly imposed on manufacturing sectors. The indicator therefore does not inform whether there is a specific regulatory problem in an individual manufacturing sector itself. For more detailed information on the methodology used in the construction of these indicators see Conway and Nicoletti (2006).
>
> The value of this indicator in a given sector is thus determined by: i) the level of anti-competitive regulation in the non-manufacturing sectors as measured by the OECD product market regulation indices (see annex 2) and ii) on how much the sector purchases of non-manufacturing inputs (measured using total input coefficients derived from harmonised input-output tables). The higher the value of the indicator in given sector the greater the impact of regulation of that sector.
>
> The REGREF indicators are calculated for 39 (ISIC rev3) sectors in 21 OECD countries over the period 1975 to 2003.

Bearing in mind all these caveats, on the basis of these indicators it is clear that in 2003 the level of regulation imposed on businesses in almost all of the sectors covered remained higher in the EU than in the US despite the important reforms introduced namely to liberalise network industries in the EU (see annex 2).

The exceptions are the liberalisation and deregulation processes in the electricity and postal industries which seem particularly well advanced compared to the

---

[18] Two groups of sectors are covered: i) energy, transport and communication and ii) retail distribution and some business services (namely accounting, architects, engineering and legal services).

US[19]. It should be pointed out, however, that compared to other sectors in the EU these remain relatively heavily regulated.

However to fully grasp the economic impact of the regulations imposed in the non-manufacturing it is important to bear in mind that their effects spill over to other sectors as they affect the cost structures of firms elsewhere in economy (particularly those that purchase inputs from the non-manufacturing sectors). The OECD Regulation Impact (REGREF) indicators use the available data on the regulation burden imposed on the non-manufacturing sectors (and on financial services sectors) to provide an overall measure of its impact across the economy including both the direct and indirect effects (on the sectors to which they sell intermediate inputs).

Table 3 shows the OECD regulation impact indicators for the sectors that have been selected in the screening phase in the EU and the US (the latter to be used again for benchmarking purposes). Overall, in almost every sector the impact of regulation is higher in the EU than in the US, which is unsurprising as it reflects the higher regulatory burden in the EU's non-manufacturing sectors. The only exceptions are the "printing, publishing and reproduction" sector (22) as well as "financial intermediation" (65) and "insurance and pension funding" (66), where regulatory impediments to competition seem somewhat higher for the US than for the EU OECD countries on average. Nonetheless the financial sectors remain among the sectors that are most affected by regulation in the EU. In contrast, "electricity, gas and water supply" (E), "other business activities" (74), and the transport sectors namely "inland transport" (60) and "support and auxiliary transport activities" (63) stand out as the sectors where the EU disadvantage *vis-à-vis* the US in terms of higher levels of anti-competitive regulation is largest.

On the basis of this table we identify the sectors where there are indications that the regulatory environment may present important challenges for market functioning: i) when the sector is heavily regulated and ii) where the degree of regulation is higher than in the US. We marked with ** and * when both or just one of these conditions is fulfilled respectively.

Despite the data limitations, there are indications that regulation is a cross cutting issue affecting market functioning in many sectors. Only two out of the 23 sectors that were identified in the screening do not show any indications of relatively heavy regulation. The regulatory framework is particularly stringent when it comes to creating barriers to entrepreneurship, therefore contributing to limit the entry of new firms in sheltered sectors. Therefore problems created by the regulatory framework are closely intertwined with competition and integration problems. For example, in "business services" (74) problems are particularly

---

[19] In contrast, in sectors like air transport and gas supply the gap *vis-à-vis* the US in terms of regulatory burden remained among the highest in 2003.

related to the conditions for entry into the professions and excessively restrictive codes of practice imposed on members of the professions (e.g. restrictions on advertising).

Table 3: OECD Regulation Impact (REGREF) Indicators in 2003

SECTORS	EU[20]	US	Signs of regulation problems
22 - Printing, publishing, and reproduction[21]	0.104	0.058	*
25 - Rubber and plastics	0.102	0.067	*
27 - Basic metals[22]	0.109	0.077	*
28 - Fabricated metal	0.109	0.077	*
29 - Machinery	0.103	0.094	-
30 - Office and computing machines	0.103	0.104	-
31 - Electrical machinery	0.102	0.067	*
32 - Radio, TV and other communication equipment	0.103	0.074	*
34 - Motor vehicles	0.109	0.101	-
35 - Other transport equipment	0.102	0.057	*
36 - Furniture, other manufactures	0.100	0.069	*
37 - Recycling	0.100	0.069	*
E - Electricity, gas and water[23]	0.341	0.195	**
50 - Sale, maintenance and repair of motor vehicles[24]	0.389	0.318	**
51 - Wholesale trade	0.389	0.318	**
52 - Retail trade	0.389	0.318	**
H - Hotels and restaurants	0.077	0.064	*
60 - Inland transport[25]	0.362	0.195	**
63 - Sup. and auxiliary transport activities	0.362	0.195	**
64 - Post and telecommunications	0.269	0.266	*
65 - Financial intermediation[26]	0.303	0.344	*
66 - Insurance and pension funding.	0.303	0.344	*
74 - Other business activities	0.313	0.220	**

Finally, it is important to notice that the regulation impact indicators used in this analysis are primarily based on the information related to the regulatory framework in services (see box 3).

---

[20] The EU average includes all Member States belonging to the OECD.
[21] Refers to "Pulp, paper, paper products, printing and publishing" (21t22).
[22] Refers to "Basic metals and fabricated metal products" (27t28).
[23] Refers to "Electricity, gas and water supply" (40t41).
[24] Refers to "Wholesale and retail trade; repairs" (50t52).
[25] Refers to "Transport and storage" (60t63).
[26] Refers to "Financial intermediation" (65t67).

For a more thorough investigation of regulation in manufacturing sectors it would be important to have data on sector-specific regulation directly imposed on these sectors. These data are not available at the moment. However, this is an issue which clearly needs to be investigated further in the more in-depth market monitoring exercises.

III. Integration

1. Motivation for the analysis

The level of integration, or in other words the extent to which the international trade and foreign investment flows have been liberalised and the prices of goods and services have converged across borders, is a crucial element to take into account in analysing the functioning of markets[27]. The effect of the removal of (tariffs and non-tariff) barriers to cross border transactions is equivalent to an increase in the size of the market, giving firms an opportunity to capture the benefits of increasing returns to scale both in production as well as in distribution and marketing activities (see for example Ades and Glaeser (1999), and Alesina et al. (2000)).

However, firms will take advantage of this opportunity only if they can overcome the increase in competition pressure that should be expected in the integrated market. Integration is a powerful device to discipline the monopolistic or oligopolistic behaviour of firms, forcing them to behave in a more competitive way and to seek new ways of doing business and innovate while driving the least efficient players out of business[28]. Eventually, provided that the competition pressure is sustained this process of industrial restructuring will also result in dynamic efficiency gains. Bernard et al. (2003) find evidence based on US plant data that the reallocation of resources in favour of more productive firms triggered by a 5% reduction in trade barriers due to globalisation can be quite large; the equivalent to 40% of total factor productivity growth in the manufacturing sector.

In the EU, the Internal Market Programme and more recently the creation of the EMU, the accession of the Central and Eastern European countries and the strengthening of the globalisation phenomenon have contributed to reinforce the integration of product markets via increased trade and FDI flows. However, the pace of market integration within the EU (and particularly among the EU15) seems to have slowed down over the recent period. The intra-EU trade to GDP

---

[27] For this exercise integration refers exclusively to the free movement of goods and services.

[28] The reduction of rent seeking activities inspired by trade and investment restrictions could spur entrepreneurial activities (see Harrison, 1994; Tybout, 2003; Pavnick, 2002; Bernard et al., 2003).

ratio increased strongly during the second half of the 1990s but stabilised since 2000. The convergence of price levels in the EU25 has also progressed substantially but within the EU15 price dispersion has remained more or less stable in recent years. While such a slowdown in the pace of integration is expected, given that the remaining barriers are increasingly difficult to remove, the potential for further progress does not appear to be completely exhausted as the US remains a more integrated trade area than the EU (see Ilzkovitz et al., 2007). Moreover, the remaining barriers to integration are often market specific and therefore their impact on market functioning will vary importantly across sectors.

2. Methodology used for the analysis

The adopted approach for this analysis aims to capture the different features of the process of market integration. Firstly, we look at the trade component of integration (or market access effect) which is triggered by the removal of tariff and non-tariff barriers to allow firms to enter new markets and/or introduce new ranges/varieties of goods. For this, we consider two complementary indicators; the first was developed by Knetter and Slaughter (1999) and captures the degree of thickness of intra-EU trade relations; the second is the degree of import penetration (both intra-EU and total), which is used to examine the relative importance of foreign suppliers in domestic consumption[29].

Alternatively foreign markets might be served via the setting up of production capacity abroad. This is particularly important in some services sectors where production often remains largely non-tradable. In this case trade based indicators are not suitable to fully assess the degree of integration. Therefore the share of intra-EU cross border mergers and acquisitions (M&A) in total M&A deals was used as an additional indicator to capture the entry of firms in foreign markets via the acquisition of foreign firms[30]. The importance of this aspect of market integration is measured by the number of intra-EU cross-border deals (the bidder and target companies are located in two different EU countries) over the total intra-EU deals in a given sector. However the impact of integration on M&A activity in the tradable sectors is ambiguous given the potential substitutability

---

[29] The market thickness indicator provides information on the number of trade flows taking place and therefore on the extensiveness of trade relations regarding the partners/sectors composition of exports. However it does not give information on the values of these trade flows and therefore of their intensity. This is why we have also used the import penetration indicator.

[30] Ideally, this indicator should have been constructed using data on total FDI flows to cover not only M&A but also greenfield investment which is another important channel for firms to set up operations in foreign markets. However, internationally comparable FDI data are only available for two years. Furthermore, these data were available at a more aggregated NACE level than the one used in this exercise and many of the EU countries were missing from the data set.

between arm's length trade and the setting up of subsidiaries to gain market access (in other words the low number of M&A activity can be an indication of easy market access through trade). At the level of the whole economy, there is no evidence of this substitutability between trade and M&A flows: the increase in intra-EU trade, which took place after the launch of the Single Market Programme was accompanied by a surge in intra-EU M&A activity. Nevertheless, in the case of tradable sectors the M&A indicator should be interpreted together with the indicators based on trade data in order to provide an overall picture of the international integration of the sector[31].

Finally, we also adopt an indicator of intra-EU price dispersion. The removal of barriers to trade and capital flows leads firms to reassess their strategy in the face of an integrated market where the opportunities for arbitrage and price discrimination are quickly exhausted eventually leading to a process of cross border price convergence. To capture the extent to which this process is underway the best is to examine price developments notably regarding the degree of cross-border price dispersion: the higher the level of integration, the lower the firms' ability to price discriminate and therefore the lower the level of price dispersion across the different national markets. However, it is important to be aware that price differences do not only reflect market fragmentation but also to some extent, differences in demand patterns (due to differences in income levels, preferences,...). Moreover, price dispersion may also reflect firms' pricing strategies to recover investments in R&D and innovation by selling different product varieties in different markets and/or charging higher prices for the same product in higher income markets compared to the prices charged for lower income markets. These are not necessarily signs of integration problems[32].

> **Box 4 - Indicators and data used**
>
> **1. Market thickness**
>
> • **Definition:** the share of total possible bilateral trade flows (in terms of exports) for which trade actually happens within a given sector. The indicator, as developed by Knetter and Slaughter (1999) captures how "thick" product markets are in terms of breadth of trade flows. It is defined as a count of the number of goods in which trade is observed between two countries divided by the total number of possible goods which could be traded between these two countries.

---

[31] Nonetheless in sectors where trade flows are still hampered by non-tariff barriers, this ambiguity is reduced and a high level of cross border M&A deals can be interpreted as a sign of greater integration.

[32] To take into account such sector specific ability to price discriminate associated with investments in product differentiation it would be necessary to use as benchmark the price dispersion level in the same sector in an integrated market with characteristics similar to the EU. Unfortunately this is not possible due to lack of data.

- **Interpretation:** The indicator is equal to 1 if every country pair has two way industry trade in industry i at time t and 0 if there is no bilateral trade between country pairs. The higher the degree of market integration (the fewer barriers to transactions between Member States remain), the higher the number of firms entering new export markets and the higher the market thickness indicator. To decide whether a given sector shows signs of problems in terms of market integration we compare the market thickness indicator in the sector with the EU average for manufacturing when dealing with manufacturing sectors and the EU average for services when dealing with services sectors[33].

- **Source of data:** The indicator was calculated both for 1995 and 2004 using COMTRADE bilateral intra-EU trade flows only (excluding the trade with the rest of the world). The indicator is only constructed for the NACE sectors for which trade data are available, which excludes most of the services sectors.

2. Import penetration

- **Definition:** ratio between the value of imports divided by the value of apparent consumption[34]. Two different import penetration indicators are considered, one taking into account only intra-EU exports and imports and the other using total (intra and extra EU) exports and imports.

- **Interpretation:** The two indicators were taken into account because a sector can have different levels of integration at the EU and at the world levels and this difference is relevant for policymaking. For example, a sector may have a low import penetration indicator at the EU level, while importing a considerable amount of goods from the rest of the world. In this case it is evident that the sector has no integration problems. The low level of intra-EU imports may simply reflect the fact that the EU has a comparative disadvantage in the sector and is a net importer from the rest of the world. On the other hand, in a given sector there may be considerable imports from EU countries but not from non-EU countries. Whether or not this reflects trade barriers vis-à-vis producers outside the EU is an issue to investigate.

As a general rule, we consider that a given sector has problems in market integration if both the intra-EU and total import penetration indicators are below the benchmark, but not if only one of them is below the benchmark. In the latter case some further investigation should be carried out in order to understand the difference between the two indicators. Two different benchmarks are adopted for manufacturing and services, namely the EU manufacturing average and the EU services average respectively.

---

[33] The need to adopt two different benchmarks for manufacturing and services is justified by the intrinsic differences in terms of the tradability of these two types of sectors.

[34] Apparent consumption is defined as domestic production minus exports plus imports.

- **Source of data:** The import penetration indicators were calculated for 1995 and 2004. COMTRADE data were used for trade flows while the gross output series were extracted from the EUKLEMS database. The data problems encountered for these indicators were similar to the ones of the market thickness indicator and therefore for most of the services sectors it was not possible to compute the indicators.

3. Share of cross border M&A deals over total deals

- **Definition:** The number of intra-EU cross-border M&A deals divided by the total (domestic and cross-border) number of M&A deals. The indicator was calculated for the periods 1997-2001 and 2002-2006.

- **Interpretation:** The interpretation of this indicator is similar to that for import penetration. The indicator is bound between 0 and 100 and generally the higher its value the greater the level of integration in the sector. In other words, *a priori* a higher ratio of cross-border M&A deals is taken as an indication that both the entry of firms into new markets and the industrial restructuring is taking place which is associated to increased market integration. While this interpretation is unambiguous in non-tradable services, for tradable sectors some caveats are needed. For example if an increase in M&A deals coincides with a reduction of import penetration in that sector the net effect in terms of integration is ambiguous. The adopted benchmarks were the EU averages for manufacturing and services respectively.

- **Source of data:** The data are taken from the Thomson Financial Services database on mergers and acquisitions activity and cover only intra-EU M&A activity[35].

4. Price dispersion

- **Definition:** The coefficient of variation of prices for a given sector, i.e. the ratio between the standard deviation and the average of prices across EU countries calculated for the 1996-2006 period.

---

[35] There are some drawbacks associated with this database which are important to consider: first, the M&A data used refer to a count of the number of deals and do not provide information on the value of these deals. Using value data is not advisable given that only around 40% of the values of the total M&A deals covered in the database are reported. Second, the number of deals may be inflated by the methodology used in the construction of the database: if a firm acquires the entire target company at once, this is counted as one deal, whereas if a firm acquires a target company in successive steps over several years, the buyout of this company will be counted in the database as several deals.

- **Interpretation:** A low level of the price dispersion indicator is interpreted as an indication of high level of integration. Two separate benchmarks were used, namely the median for manufacturing industries and the median for services[36].

- **Source of data:** Consumer price data according to the COICOP classification developed by Eurostat[37]. Ideally producer price data should be used but such data are unavailable. The fact that these price data refer to final goods sold to consumers (therefore including the mark-up added by the retail outlets as well as taxes such as VAT) is one important drawback of this dataset. Another is that since the data refer to retail consumer prices they are not appropriate to assess price dispersion of intermediate goods. In fact, some of the NACE sectors do not have a correspondence in the COICOP price category (for example "basic metals" (27) or "recycling" (37)).

3. Main findings

Market thickness

Table 4 shows that in 2004 only one of the selected manufacturing sectors had a below average market thickness indicator: "other transport" (35). The "building and repairing of ships and boats" and "aircraft and spacecraft" sub-sectors were responsible for this result. Below average market thickness in these sub-sectors could be attributed to a low degree of competition in public procurement which acted as a barrier hampering foreign firms' activities. Nevertheless, since 1995 the degree of market thickness has improved in these sub-industries.[38]

The market thickness indicator is substantially lower in the services sectors (for which trade data are available) than in manufacturing. The degree of market thickness in the "electricity, gas and water supply" (E) sector is particularly low. Several factors can explain the still limited cross border supply and distribution of electricity and gas: the lack of investment in interconnection infrastructures

---

[36] The mapping of the COICOP price categories into NACE could not be done for all the sectors that were not selected in the screening phase. This made it impossible to use the EU average as a benchmark.

[37] Given that the market screening phase of the exercise relied on the NACE classification of sectors, it was necessary to establish a correspondence between the COICOP price categories and the NACE classification. The availability of price data according to the COICOP classification does not allow us to obtain prices at the disaggregated product level. As a consequence, several COICOP categories correspond to one NACE sector. This is why the average of the COICOP price categories for a given NACE sector was taken as representing the price for that sector.

[38] In contrast, the indicator is above average for the "railroad and transport equipment" sub-sector.

which hamper the integration of the different national energy markets; and the fact that trade in electricity and gas occurs between neighbouring countries, thereby limiting the number of bilateral trade flows that can be established.

Market thickness was also below average in the "other business activities" sector (74). This is also not surprising given that: (i) in many of these sectors face to face contact between suppliers and consumers is required; (ii) important legal and other entry barriers for cross-border transactions remained in place until recently; (iii) demand is likely biased towards domestic suppliers due to cultural and linguistic affinities, thereby limiting the scope for further integration. Contrary to the evolution in most other sectors, the market thickness indicator has decreased since 1995. A more in-depth analysis of this sector seems necessary in order to offer a clearer picture of the reasons behind this evolution.

Import penetration

Since 1995 the level of import penetration has increased in most manufacturing sectors. Table 4 shows that in 2004 only six manufacturing sectors (out of the 23 selected in the screening) remained below the EU average for both the intra-EU and the total import penetration indicators: "printing, publishing and reproduction" (22), "rubber and plastics" (25), "basic metals" (27), "fabricated metal" (28), "machinery" (29) and "furniture and other manufacturing" (36). In these six sectors foreign supply via imports (both from within the EU and with the rest of the world) remains relatively limited suggesting the existence of problems in terms of market integration. Among these sectors, import penetration was the lowest in "printing, publishing and reproduction". This is not unexpected given that in this industry cultural and language barriers limit the scope for further integration. Similarly, in "fabricated metal", "basic metals" and "furniture" trade integration is also hampered by intrinsic characteristics of the sectors: in this case high transport costs. In contrast, the low level of import penetration in the other sectors can potentially be attributed to remaining economic barriers to market integration. For example, there is some evidence that a significant amount of technical barriers to trade persist in the "rubber and plastics" sector, particularly in the "plastics" sub-sector.

Among the manufacturing sectors "motor vehicles" (34) and "other transport equipment" (35) are interesting cases. For "motor vehicles" (34) while the level of total import penetration is below the benchmark, there are no indications of problems in terms of intra-EU import penetration. Hence, *a priori*, this sector can not be considered as presenting problems in terms of import penetration since it is well integrated into the EU. The relatively low level of imports from outside the EU may in fact reflect the comparative advantage of the EU relative to the rest of the world in the sector. In the "other transport equipment" (35) sector, intra-EU import penetration is below the benchmark, while total import penetration is close to the benchmark. Market segmentation is this sector may be associated with the low degree of competition in public procurement.

With respect to the services sectors, data were available for only two sectors among the list of sectors selected in the screening, namely "electricity, gas and water supply" (E) and "other business activities" (74). The degree of integration was slightly higher in the former. Moreover the level of import penetration in the sector has increased over the 1995-2004 period.

Cross-border mergers and acquisitions

Table 4 shows that on average this indicator is lower for the services sector than for manufacturing, which validates the general assertion that the former remain less integrated.

Among the manufacturing sectors a general increase in this indicator can be observed over the recent years. On average the share of cross-border deals in the 2002-2006 period increased in comparison to the 1997-2001 average in all of the manufacturing sectors with the exception of "furniture and other manufacturing goods" (36) where the average decreased slightly. Nevertheless, cross border M&A activity is below the adopted benchmark in 7 of the manufacturing sectors selected in the screening stage: "printing, publishing and reproduction" (22), "fabricated metal" (28), "office, accounting and computing machinery" (30), "electrical machinery and apparatus" (31), "radio, TV and communication equipment" (32), "motor vehicles and other transport equipment" (34+35) and "furniture" (36).

Regarding services, this indicator remains below the adopted benchmark in 6 sectors, such as: "electricity, gas and water" (E), "retail trade" (52), "hotels and restaurants" (H), "financial intermediation" (65), "insurance and pension funding" (66), and "other business activities" (74).

Nonetheless, in most of the services sectors, the degree of M&A activity increased over the 2002-2006 period compared with the 1997-2001 period. There are however three exceptions, namely "electricity, gas and water supply" (E), "retail trade" (52) and "hotels and restaurants" (H). The latter two sectors also show the lowest importance of cross-border deals. Given that these are sectors where the scope for cross border trade is limited or inexistent (the cases of "hotels and restaurants" (H) and "retail trade" (52)) this M&A based evidence can be interpreted as suggesting that significant barriers to integration remain.

Price dispersion

Since 1996 the degree of price dispersion has decreased substantially in all the sectors under consideration, which suggests a general increase in the level of economic integration.

However, as expected there are considerable differences between manufacturing and services. In 2006, the degree of price dispersion across the EU remains substantially higher in services than in manufacturing, reflecting the still fragmented nature of many services industries. Among the manufacturing sectors, price dispersion was above the median (the adopted benchmark) in "printing, publishing and reproduction" (22), "office, accounting and computing machinery" (30), "radio, TV and communication equipment" (32), "motor vehicles" (34) and "other transport equipment" (35). In two of these sectors the coefficient of variation significantly exceeds the benchmark: "radio, TV and communication" and "office, accounting and machinery". One possible explanation is that price dispersion in these sectors reflects the firms' power and higher ability to discriminate between different markets given the technology intensive and highly differentiated nature of these products.

Among the services sectors, the highest degree of price dispersion is observed in "electricity, gas and water supply" (E), "insurance and pension funding" (66), "financial intermediation" (65) and "other business activities" (74). In the electricity and gas sector most of the price dispersion is likely to reflect differences in local taxation (which is country-specific and varies widely from one country to another). Other factors such as cross-country differences in terms of the sources of electricity generation may also play a role. In "financial intermediation" and "insurance and pension funding" price dispersion reflects the fact that integration of financial markets is still far from complete, but also that the characteristics of financial products vary across countries. Arguably the high price dispersion in the "insurance and pension funding" sector can also be partly due to differences in pension systems, which would imply differences in the use of individual insurance and pension funding schemes across countries. Finally, the important entry barriers in the "other business activities" sector would explain the large price dispersion found in this sector.

5. Identification of poorly integrated sectors

On the basis of the four indicators considered we have tentatively classified the sectors in three main categories: sectors that can be considered as being relatively poorly integrated, i.e. the sectors (marked ** in table 4) where several indicators point to insufficient integration, sectors (marked *) for which we cannot exclude problems of integration on the basis of at least one of the indicators used and sectors for which there are no indications of problems on the basis of indicators used. However, further in depth and qualitative analyses of each of the considered sectors would be required to confirm these classifications.

An Analysis of the Possible Causes of Product Market Malfunctioning in the EU

Table 4: Signs of integration problems among selected sectors

SECTORS	Market thickness	Intra-EU Import penetration	Total import penetration	Share of cross-border M&A deals over total	Price dispersion	Signs of integration problems
22 - Painting, publishing and reproduction	0.92	0.10	0.14	17.0	0.019	**
25 - Rubber and plastics	0.98	0.30	0.42	33.2	0.012	*
27 - Basic metals	0.92	0.34	0.55	32.6	n.a	-
28 - Fabricated metal	0.97	0.14	0.20	27.6	0.013	**
29 - Machinery	0.98	0.38	0.58	n.a	0.012	-
30 - Office, accounting and computing machinery	0.95	0.69	1.60	27.3	0.044	*
31 - Electrical machinery and apparatus	0.93	0.55	0.86	27.5	0.014	*
32 - Radio, TV & communication equipment	0.91	0.58	1.28	27.9	0.060	*
34 - Motor vehicles, trailers and semi-trailers	0.94	0.52	0.67	28.3	0.025	*
35 - Other transport equipment	0.78	0.32	0.73	n.a.	0.019	**
36 - Furniture, other manufacturing goods n.e.c.	0.98	0.33	0.67	21.4	0.016	-
37 - Recycling	n.a	n.a	n.a	n.a	n.a	-
E - Electricity, gas and water supply	0.16	0.04	0.06	23.5	0.052	**
50 - Sale, maintenance and repair of motor vehicles	n.a	n.a	n.a	26.2	0.012	-
51 - Wholesale trade	n.a	n.a	n.a	25.5	n.a	-
52 - Retail trade	n.a	n.a	n.a	15.2		**
H - Hotels & restaurants	n.a	n.a	n.a	15.3	0.028	*
60 - Inland transport	n.a	n.a	n.a	28.8	0.031	-
63 - Supporting & auxiliary transport act.	n.a	n.a	n.a	27.7	0.033	*
64 - Post & telecommunications	n.a	n.a	n.a	29.3	0.025	-
65 - Financial intermediation	n.a	n.a	n.a	23.4	0.040	**
66 - Insurance and pension funds	n.a	n.a	n.a	22.4	0.046	**
74 - Other business activities	0.34	0.00	0.00	22.5	0.039	**
EU average all manufacturing	0.89	0.38	0.71	28.7	0.018 *	
EU average all services	0.46	0.06	0.06	23.8	0.032	

Note: * The values refer to the median for services and manufacturing respectively; The shaded numbers represent, for a given indicator, the sectors that were selected as having problems according to that indicator.

First, when considering the evolution in the period between 1995 and 2006, we find that, whatever the indicator used to measure market integration, the degree of integration has increased in both the manufacturing and services sectors.

Second, many of the services sectors selected in the screening show indications of integration problems, confirming the belief that they are less tradable than manufacturing and suggesting that non-tariff and other entry barriers remain in these sectors. Five of the services sectors selected in the screening have clear indications of integration problems: "electricity, gas and water supply" (E), "retail trade" (52), "financial intermediation" (65), "insurance and pension funding" (66) and "other business activities" (74). The low values of the market thickness and import penetration indicators in the "electricity and gas" sector are due to the lack of cross border physical infrastructure necessary that hamper trade in electricity and gas. Prices in this sector remain importantly influenced by local taxation and by the different degree of liberalisation in the different countries. In retail trade and business services, entry and legal barriers continue to limit the integration of markets. However, in the latter the scope of integration is also hampered by the home bias in domestic demand due to cultural and linguistic affinities. In the "financial intermediation" and "insurance and pension funding" sectors regulation remains an important barrier to integration.

There are also some indications of integration problems in "hotels and restaurants" (H), and "supporting and auxiliary transport activities" (63). In the latter sector, evidence points to significant public procurement barriers to integration.

Third, despite the evidence pointing to a lower degree of integration in services than in manufacturing, there are still some manufacturing sectors which appear as poorly integrated: "printing, publishing and reproduction" (22), "fabricated metal" (28) and "other transport equipment" (35). In the publishing sector there is only a small share of domestic demand supplied by foreign output and the share of cross-border M&A deals as well as price dispersion are below their respective benchmarks. This reveals that markets within this sector remain fragmented. However, the scope for policy intervention is limited due to the presence of cultural and language barriers. In the "fabricated metal" sector the variety of products traded and the degree of price dispersion are above the benchmark. However, the trade flows and the M&A activity remain relatively limited. While there is evidence pointing to significant technical barriers to trade, transport costs also play a role in keeping markets segmented as production in the sectors is generally heavy. Nearly all of the indicators available in the "other transport" sector point to significant market segmentation (the only exception being the total import penetration indicator which is only slightly above the benchmark), which may be partially due to the low degree of competition in public procurement in the sub-sectors linked to defence or aerospace.

IV. Competition

1. Motivation for the analysis

In general, effective competition pressure is an essential element for the good functioning of markets. Competition can lead to an overall positive impact on economic performance and to higher social welfare as firms aiming to safeguard or increase their customer base are driven to increase their efficiency and to offer products at lower prices and better quality than their rivals.[39] The objective of this section is thus to identify, among the sectors filtered out at the screening stage, those in which market malfunctioning can be associated with indications of insufficient competition pressure.

The analysis presented in this section rests on the definition and application of a methodology aimed at measuring the intensity of competition in the 23 sectors, which have been identified as being important while showing signs of market malfunctioning in the screening. However, this is an inherently difficult task. Effective competition is a very broad and multidimensional concept which cannot be fully assessed by a set of indicators. Moreover measuring competition pressure in the current exercise is further complicated due to the lack of data at the market level. Therefore the aim of this exercise is to find indications of problems and to provide potential insight into different dimensions of competition rather than to offer definite conclusions. In particular, no finding of this section can be interpreted as indicating an infringement or the absence of an infringement of any provision of EC or national competition law.

2. Methodology used for the analysis

The horizontal analysis that is developed in this section is based on a set of indicators reflecting the fact that effective competition is a multidimensional concept which cannot be fully captured by a single measure.

Indeed, competition assessments of particular markets (e.g. analysis of "relevant markets" as defined under EC competition law in merger or antitrust cases[40]) require an in-depth knowledge of the characteristics of the market including a thorough understanding of the behavioural relationships of the agents present

---

[39] The pursuit of profitability should incite firms to compensate the mutually exerted downward pressure on prices by reducing their costs. Such cost reductions (efficiency gains) can arise through four different channels: i) improvements in allocative efficiency as resources are allocated to their most efficient use; ii) improvement in productive efficiency as firms are given added incentives to use their inputs in the most efficient way iii) a reduction of the "managerial slack" (so-called "X-inefficiency"), and iv) improvements in dynamic efficiency as individual firms are led to invest and innovate more in new products and production technologies.

[40] Commission notice on the definition of the relevant market for the purposes of Community competition law, OJ C 372, 9.12.1997.

therein (between competitors, vertical relations, the relationship between suppliers and customers, etc), which goes beyond the scope of this exercise. Hence, the option chosen for this analysis was to use four types of indicators that aim at capturing different dimensions of competition, and to consider them in combination. These different dimensions reflect elements of market structure (measured by market concentration), performance (price-cost margin), conduct (turbulence indicators), as well as a policy dimension (number of competition law infringements).

A number of caveats should be put forward at this stage. First, the indicators retained (e.g. mark-ups and concentration) while standard in the literature are nonetheless theoretically ambiguous and may sometimes contradict each other. Second, while the competition indicators that are used should in theory refer to "relevant markets" as defined under EC competition law, due to data constrains the analysis will be done at the level of sector of activity[41]. Data on markets generally only become available as a result of specific market investigations, which are well beyond the scope of this exercise. Third, while the data are usually provided at a common geographic level for all sectors (e.g. national or EU), this often does not coincide with the "true" geographical markets, which can be wider or narrower[42].

To identify sectors with weak competition we first consider each of the adopted indicators in isolation. However, it is important to be aware that the conclusions drawn from the individual indicators depend on the benchmark chosen. While perfect competition would be the ideal benchmark, it is unrealistic in practice. Due to the existence of sunk costs and imperfect information, the notion of workable competition is in principle a more realistic approach to define a benchmark. It implicitly recognises for example that positive price-cost margins may be essential to cover fixed costs and that these margins may vary between industries. In this light a simpler and more pragmatic approach has been applied in this exercise. Wherever data availability allows it, the level of competition in a sector will be judged against the US benchmark (i.e. by comparing the EU indicator with the US indicator). When this is not possible due to lack of comparable US data the cross-sectoral average is taken as the benchmark[43].

---

[41] Indeed, a single sector may in fact either include several product or geographic markets or be narrower.

[42] For example, computing an "EU-wide" indicator of, say, market share for sectors that have been identified as having possible "integration-problems" in section 2, may only be of limited relevance. For the sake of completeness, we will nonetheless do so.

[43] We distinguish between manufacturing and services sectors using the average of the two groups as benchmarks. Only regarding competition law infringements we do not make this distinction.

Box 5 - Indicators and data used

1. Mark-ups (or price-cost margins)

- **Definition:** ratio of the difference between price and marginal cost over price (see Christopoulou and Vermeulen, 2007).

- **Interpretation:** The indicator is presented as the differential between the EU and the US. Positive values imply that the mark-ups in the sector are higher in the EU than in the US. We make the general assumption that mark-ups are normally decreasing with the intensity of competition and are thus indicative of the degree of competition. There are however important limitations with the interpretation of the mark-ups in the context of the current exercise given that are theoretically market-specific, since they are affected by market specific characteristics such as the importance of sunk costs and the degree of business risk, notably of R&D-intensive activities[44].

Moreover it is difficult to distinguish to what extent high mark-ups signal a low degree of competition in (low risk) markets and to which extent they reflect the result of successful firm strategies in a competitive and risky market where R&D investment and therefore some degree of market power is necessary[45].

- **Source of data:** The data used to compute mark-ups are taken from Christopoulou and Vermeulen (2007), which estimates mark-ups for 50 sectors in 8 euro area countries and the US over the period 1981-2004. The estimates are obtained by applying the methodology developed by Roeger (1995) to the EUKLEMS data. The assumptions on which this estimation is based are profit maximization, cost minimization and constant returns to scale.

2. Degree of market concentration

- **Definition:** The indicator retained to measure the degree of market concentration is the eight-firm concentration ratio (C8), i.e. the cumulative market share of the eight largest firms in a sector.

---

[44] R&D intensive activities are associated with higher mark-ups due to the higher differentiation of production (and therefore market power) which will allow firms to recover the costs of innovating.

[45] Limitations of more practical nature should also be taken into account when interpreting mark-ups, which are computed in this exercise as the difference between the price and average cost, see Christopoulou and Vermeulen (2007). Given the latter are not entirely exogenous, a fall in mark ups can actually be driven by an increase in average costs associated with strategies to raise barriers to entry rather than a reflection of an increase in the competitive pressure.

The market share of company j in sector i is defined as the ratio of the company's turnover (reported at market prices) in sector i to total sector turnover (i.e. the sum of the turnover of all the companies in the sector)

- **Interpretation:** A high degree of concentration may, under specific circumstances, be interpreted as providing an indication of the existence of market power and therefore as an indication of low competition[46]. The two adopted benchmarks are the cross sectoral average for manufacturing sectors and for services sectors.

- **Source of data:** The indicator is computed with data from the Orbis database for the year 2005.

3. Market turbulence

- **Definition:** The indicator retained to measure the degree of market concentration is the "total number of different firms index" (TNF), which following the methodology used in London Economics (2007) is defined as the ratio of the number of firms that have belonged to the group of the 8 largest firms in the years between 2002 and 2005 over the maximum number of different firms (32) that could have potentially been included in this group in this period. A more direct approach to measure turbulence would be the tracking of entry/exit rates and of the volatility of market shares. Entry rates measure the importance of entry barriers and the degree of contestability of the market while exit rates can be interpreted as an indicator of the selection process associated with elimination of the least efficient firms[47]. However, data for entry-exit rates are limited in terms of geographic and sectoral coverage and data on the volatility of market shares would only be available in the course of investigation of specific markets (e.g. in specific merger and antitrust cases under competition law)[48].

- **Interpretation:** A value close to 1 would mean a higher number of entries and exits of firms in the C8 which would suggest significant competitive pressure.

---

[46] However, in the absence of substantial entry barriers potential competitors may exert a sufficient force to limit market power of the firms in the market.

[47] As noted above, it is possible that in some (contestable) markets entry rates are low because the mere threat of entry causes the incumbent firms to maintain prices and output at competitive levels, thus pre-empting entry.

[48] An analysis of turbulence based on production shares of the main firms in 67 manufacturing sectors in the EU15 is available in Veugelers. (2004). The results suggest that levels of concentration are generally quite stable, despite the significant turbulence often observed within the top market players in each industry. The usefulness of this analysis for the current exercise is limited given the higher level of sectoral aggregation and the incomplete geographical coverage of the data used.

> As the indicator is presented as the differential between the EU and the US a negative number signals a lower level of turbulence (entry/exit in the C8) in EU than in the US.
>
> - **Source of data:** The data are extracted from the Orbis financial database.
>
> **4. Infringements to competition law**
>
> - **Definition:** The number of infringements to EC competition law, using data on the number of antitrust cases in which the Commission took a decision between 1999 and 2006 finding an infringement of Article 81 or 82 of the EC Treaty.
>
> - **Interpretation:** While the identification of breaches of competition law in the past is not in itself an accurate indication of current or future competition problems, it can nonetheless provide indications of which sectors may be more prone to problems of that sort. The benchmark used for this indicator is the EU cross-sectoral average.
>
> - **Source of data:**
>
> The data used are from the anti trust cases dataset of the European Commission[49].

Finally, given that each of the considered indicators can only provide a partial assessment of competition pressure in a given sector in order to draw more general conclusions we conclude the analysis with an horizontal overview of all the indicators. In doing this we can identify sectors where on the basis of the latter there are important indications of competition problems (i.e. when most indicators point to that same conclusion) and sectors where there are no indications of problems. Furthermore, special attention is given to the indicator based on mark-ups, which – among the indicators available to us – reflects the degree of price competition intensity best. Finally, we will also identify sectors where the indicators used do not lead to any clear cut diagnostic (i.e. cases where there will be indicators pointing to different conclusions). These will be regarded as sectors where, at least at this stage, one cannot exclude the existence of competition problems.

3. Main findings

Table 5 lists the sectors that have shown signs of market malfunctioning and identifies those where these are most likely to be associated with insufficient competition pressure.

---

[49] The data can be downloaded from: http://ec.europa.eu/comm/competition/antitrust/cases/index.html.

Table 5: Signs of competition problems among selected sectors

SECTORS		EU-US mark-up differential	Market concentration (C8)	Turbulence (TNF)	Number of antitrust cases	Signs of competition problems
22	Printing, ….	-0.11	21.14	0.06	17	*
25	Rubber and plastics	-0.01	29.62	0.03	4	-
27	Basic metals	0.11	33.26	0.03	7	**
28	Fabricated metal	-0.04	24.07	0.00	0	-
29	Machinery	-0.12	32.37	-0.06	12	*
30	Office, account. and comp. mach. (***)	-0.02	59.15	0.09	5	*
31	Electrical machinery	-0.01	17.26	0.13	2	-
32	Radio, TV and comm. equip.	-0.09	38.50	-0.03	4	*
34	Motor vehicles, trailers,	0.14	51.09	0.00	4	**
35	Other transp. equip.	-1.7	47.29	0.06	4	*
36	Furniture	-0.02	16.40	0.09	7	*
37	Recycling	n.a	31.47	0.00	1	-
E	Electricity, gas and water supply	-0.13	28.15	-0.13	10	**
50	Sale, maint. and rep. of motor vehicles	0.39	8.72	0.03	4	*
51	Wholesale trade	0.04	16.29	0.25	3	*
52	Retail trade	0.23	22.55	0.13	2	*
H	Hotels & restaurants	0.11	30.83	0.06	0	**
60	Inland transport -	-0.08	28.59	0.03	2	*
63	Sup. and auxiliary transport activities	0.11	18.87	0.09	6	**
64	Post &telecoms	0.10	39.44	-0.03	15	**
65	Financial intermediation	0.17	14.34	0.06	8	**
66	Insurance,…	0.19	20.62	0.25	2	*
74	Other business activities	0.18	11.73	0.19	3	*
Benchmarks		US	Average manufacturing (34.56) Average services (26.67)	US	Average (5.07)	

Degree of market power

Given that mark-ups are affected by sector/market specificities (due for example to sunk cost), cross-country comparisons are clearly more informative than cross-sector comparisons[50]. In this light, the mark ups data for the euro area are benchmarked against the US. While this option is not meant to signal US mark-up as "optimal", it can nonetheless be considered as an appropriate benchmark in the sense that it gives an indication of what could actually be achievable in terms of mark-up (and competition intensity) in a market of similar size.

The differences between mark-ups in the euro area and in the US for each sector are reported in table 5. A positive value (i.e. a higher mark-up in the euro-area than in the US) is interpreted as a sign of relatively low competition (or high market power) in the EU. In 11 out of the 23 sectors that were selected in the screening phase, the mark-up is higher in the euro area than in the US.

Moreover, it seems that higher mark-ups in the euro area are more frequently observed in the services sectors. In only 2 services sectors only (out of the 11 selected in the screening) are mark-ups lower in the euro-area than in the US, namely "electricity, gas and water supply" (E); and "inland transport" (60). Among the manufacturing sectors, the "basic metals" (27), and the "motor vehicles" (54) sectors are characterised by higher mark-ups in the euro area[51].

Degree of market concentration

The indicator of market concentration shown in this table is the eight-firm concentration ratio (C8) which is computed for each sector in the EU. The obtained values are then benchmarked against the averages for the manufacturing and services sectors respectively. Values higher than the adopted benchmarks are interpreted as indications of relatively low degree of competition[52]. Among the 23 sectors considered, eight show signs of relatively high concentration. Four of these sectors are manufacturing sectors, namely "office accounting and computer machinery" (30), "radio TV and communication equipment" (32), "motor vehicles trailers and semi trailers" (34) and "other transport equipment" (35). The remaining four belong to the services sectors, namely "electricity, gas and water supply" (E), "hotel and restaurants" (H), "inland transport" (60) and "post and

---

[50] For example, the cross-industry average mark-up in the euro area is 1.53, whereas in the US it is 1.45 (not reported in the table). However, these averages mask important heterogeneity across sectors.
[51] It should be noticed that in the "motor vehicles" sector, the differential in mark ups vis-à-vis the US that is found in Christopoulou and Vermeulen (2007) is mainly driven by an unusually low estimated profit margin in the US rather than being evidence of a particularly high margin in the EU.
[52] It should be recognised however that there may be good reasons why market concentration can differ across industries. Due to data constraints, the comparison between the EU and the US cannot be made.

telecommunications" (64). The sectors with relatively high values for C8 also exhibit relatively high values in terms of the HHI.

Turbulence in the market

The turbulence indicator retained for this table is the total number of different firms index (TNF), which is computed for each sector in the EU and the US. A sector is considered to show signs of malfunctioning if the TNF in the EU is lower than the TNF in the same sector in the US. Within the group of 23 sectors listed in the table, four sectors seem to be characterised by lower turbulence in the EU, namely "machinery" (29), "radio, TV, communication equipment" (32), "electricity, gas and water supply" (E), and "post and telecommunications" (64). While these four sectors are evenly distributed across manufacturing and services, it should be noted that the services sectors belong to network industries, which are still in a phase of market opening and where entry barriers are high.

It should also be noted, that in most sectors turbulence among the largest eight firms is generally low in both the EU and the US. The findings from the "in-out index" (IOI) confirm those obtained with the TNF.

Infractions to competition

The last individual indicator considered is the number of antitrust cases by sector. For this indicator the benchmark adopted is the average for all sectors given that a priori there is no valid justification to differentiate between services and manufacturing sectors in this respect. In total, 8 sectors reported more occurrences of cases than the average, being therefore considered as potentially problematic for the purposes of this monitoring exercise. The two sectors with the highest number of cases are "printing and publishing reproduction" (22) with 17 cases and "post and telecommunications" (64) with 15 occurrences.

4. Identification of sectors with weak competition

In this section we have analysed the 23 sectors selected in the screening in view of finding indications of weak competition. Each indicator was scrutinised individually but in order to classify a sector as "malfunctioning" from a competition point of view we now consider the four types of indicators (mark-up, concentration, turbulence and number of antitrust cases) in combination.

As indicated above, we tentatively classify the sectors into three categories based on the four types of indicators: *i)* sectors for which there are strong indications of competition problems (marked in table 5 with **); *ii)* sectors for which we cannot exclude the hypothesis of competitions problems despite contradictory indications given by some indicators (marked in table 5 with *); and, *iii)* sectors for which there are no compelling signs of problems in terms of competition, as revealed by this methodology. Sectors are deemed to have strong competition problems (**), either if at least three indicators point to weak competition (shaded in the table above), or if two indicators point to weak competition, one of them being the mark-up. This is justified by the importance we attach to mark-up. Sectors for which we cannot exclude competition problems (*) are those where one or two (excluding the mark-up) indicators signal a low degree of competition. However, further in depth and qualitative analyses of each sectors would be required to confirm these classifications.

On this basis, out of the 23 sectors under analysis seven can be classified as showing strong indications of problems namely "basic metals" (27), "motor vehicles, trailers, and semi-trailers"(34), "electricity, gas and water supply" (E), "hotels and restaurants" (H) "supporting and auxiliary transport activities" (63), "post and telecommunications" (64) and "financial intermediation" (65).

Overall it seems that problems of competition are more likely to be observed in the services sectors. Indeed, five of the seven sectors classified as showing strong indications of competition problems are services sectors. This can largely be explained by the high mark-ups in these sectors relative to the US - the only exceptions being "electricity, gas and water supply" and "inland transport".

On the basis of the adopted indicators we do not find any indication of weak competition in only four sectors: "rubber and plastics" (25), "fabricated metal" (28), "electrical machinery and apparatus" (31) and "recycling" (37). In contrast, in seven sectors of the 22 sectors that were not selected in the screening, we found important indications of competition problems, namely "wearing apparel, dressing and dying of fur" (18), "wood and of wood and cork" (20), "coke, refined petroleum and nuclear fuel" (23), "water transport" (61), "air transport" (62), "research and development" (73), and "other service activities" (93).

Finally, despite the observed signs of competition problems that we found it seems that there has been a slight intensification of competition pressure in many sectors the EU over the last years. While the opportunity to carry out a detailed dynamic analysis is limited we find that for example mark-ups in the EU for the sectors, for which data are available have been mostly decreasing (-0.06 on average), between the period 1981-1992 and the period 1993 to 2004. Furthermore, we can observed the evolution of the two indicators of market concentration (C8 and HHI) from 2002 to 2005 and in both cases there is a decrease in concentration levels in the EU in many sectors.

V. Innovation

1. Motivation for the analysis

A well-integrated, competitive and dynamic Single Market helps to create an innovation-friendly environment in Europe, which supports long-run competitiveness and sustainable economic growth. Despite being relatively close to the world productivity frontier, the EU has not reached its potential in terms of innovative capacity (see Griffith and Harrison, 2004). The relatively poor performance in terms of innovation creation and technology adoption may be explained by a wide range of policy and institutional factors. Indeed, innovation is a complex process characterised by the interaction between different actors (firms, universities, banks, venture capitalists, governmental agencies and consumers) which operate within a specific institutional framework (laws, rules, regulations, norms and standards) shaped by a wide spectrum of public policies (Edquist, 2001).

In recent years, innovation policies have mainly focused on the enforcement of intellectual property rights (IPRs) and competition as tools for sustaining the creation and the diffusion of technological change across firms. Indeed, IPRs do not generate proper incentives for firms to invest in innovative activities if they fail to ensure that innovation is properly rewarded and preserved (Jaffe, 1988). Interactions between IPRs, incentives for knowledge creation and the structure of product markets in which the innovation takes place need to be considered when defining appropriate policies (Gilbert and Newbery, 1982). For example, competition policies have aimed at the design of the correct market structure to support innovation by recognising the existence of important differences across sectors in the dynamic interaction between firm size, market structure and innovation (Scherer, 1992).

Several sectoral specific components - such as the extent of scale economies, capital intensity, and the degree of a sector's technological content - affect innovation processes, inputs and outputs and the interaction between the actors which lead to technological change (Doms et al., 1995). Ideally, one would like to measure the performance of the entire innovation system as a whole (Malerba, 2002), namely the systemic evaluation of all the dimensions which are encouraging technological change rather than the separate assessments of each specific component.

However, this task is very difficult because of the complexity which characterises the innovation system itself and the heterogeneity of the different dimensions concerned. Even though the measures of the individual elements cannot describe the performance of the entire system, all of them combined may give some insights on how the system is actually performing (Carlsson *et al.*, 2002).

An important sectoral distinction applies to services versus manufacturing sectors. Indeed, the growing structural specialisation of industrialised economies towards services sectors implies that their innovative performance will be a crucial determinant of long run growth in Europe. Services sectors are often perceived as being less innovative than manufacturing, because R&D spending and the number of patents obtained by services firms is relatively low.

However, these two indicators are somewhat misleading since innovation in services tends to take the form of incremental changes introduced to processes and procedures. Moreover, the conceptual tools developed to study (technological) innovation in manufacturing are not as effective when applied to the services, since the latter are characterised by the prevalence of incremental, non-technological, process and organisational innovation (OECD, 2005a). Further work is needed to better capture the innovative capacity of services sectors.

2. Methodology used for the analysis

The analysis of innovation performance at the EU sector level faces important constraints related to both the measurement of innovative activities and the quality of available data. Internationally comparable measures of technological change are particularly hard to find for some variables; in turn, this makes difficult a comparative assessment of overall innovation systems at the sectoral level. This analysis will focus on a limited number of innovation inputs, outputs and outcomes for which sector-level data are available.

Innovative inputs refer to the investment performed by firms aimed at introducing technological innovations. The most common measures of input are R&D investment, R&D personnel, and other investment in tangible and intangible knowledge assets such as technologically new equipment and know-how. Innovative outputs refer to the direct result of the innovative activity such as scientific publications, patents, technologically new or improved product, process and services. Finally, innovative outcomes indicate the broader economic result obtained by a firm thanks to the performed innovative activity such as greater market shares, a higher total factor productivity (TFP) growth, and other related measures of economic performance.

The three input measures used in the analysis below reflect R&D intensity, namely the share of R&D spending in value added, as well as investment in new technologies and human capital (approximated by the contributions of ICT and labour quality, respectively, to the growth of value added in the sector). Two output/outcome measures were identified: patent applications and the contribution of total factor productivity (TFP) to the growth of value added in the sector.

Not all these indicators are available for services: information on R&D intensity and the number of patent applications with the European Patent Office (EPO) are available only for EU and US manufacturing sectors but not for services.

The sectoral performance in terms of these two measures of innovation has been evaluated by taking a simple EU/US ratio. A ratio lower than one in terms of the R&D variable indicates, therefore, a relatively poor performance of EU compared to US in that specific sector. On the contrary, we use the aggregate ratio of EU/US manufacturing applications at the EPO as a benchmark for the patents variable in order to adjust for the built-in home advantage bias towards EU. A sectoral value lower than the aggregate ratio will, therefore, indicates a relative weakness of the EU in terms of patenting activity in that sector.

> **Box 6: Growth accounting framework in the EUKLEMS**
>
> An extended growth accounting framework is used to disentangle at the sectoral level the contributions to value added growth of capital and labour according to ICT and skill intensity, respectively. A distinction is made between ICT capital and non-ICT capital, on the one hand, and the quantity (in terms of hours) and quality (in terms of labour composition) of labour, on the other hand. As a result, the measure of TFP calculated better reflects the impact of "pure" disembodied technological change on value added growth.
>
> The analysis is carried out in the following way. First, we compare the determinants of aggregate growth in manufacturing and in services for the EU and the US and we identify the determinants of the EU-US productivity gap. The gap indicates the difference between the growth rates of the variables in the EU and in the US. Growth accounting variables are expressed in terms of logarithms. Data are presented in terms of annual growth rates for the EU and the US in the period 1996-2004. Second, we repeat the analysis for each sector at the NACE 2 digit level. To assess the performance of the different sectors in the EU, we use the contribution to growth in the US of the different production factors as benchmarks.
>
> Unfortunately, data are not available for all the two-digit NACE sectors. The EUKLEMS database provides a complete set of information on the growth accounting indicators at a macro-sector aggregation and only partial information on some 2 and 3 digit sectors. However, it is still possible to obtain a complete data series at the 2 digit level by assuming a constant structure of the production function within macro sectors.

The data on investment in human capital, ICT as well as on TFP growth have been computed using an extended growth accounting approach developed in the context of the EU-KLEMS project (see box 6)[53]. This data source provides comparable information on economic growth, productivity, employment creation, capital formation and technological change at the industry level for all EU and other major industrialised countries.

---

[53] We use data revised in March 2007, which are available on http://www.euklems.net/. The analysis is based on a subsample of 20 manufacturing and service sectors for which there are comparable data between EU and US in the period 1996-2004. An outlier analysis has been performed on the dataset. In particular, the extreme observations have been removed from the sample to ensure data consistency.

An Analysis of the Possible Causes of Product Market Malfunctioning in the EU

Box 7 - Indicators and data used

1. R&D intensity

- **Definition:** The ratio of the share of business expenditure on R&D in the value added a given sector in EU over the share of business R&D in value added of the same sector in the US, namely $(R\&D_{EU}/VA_{EU}) / (R\&D_{US}/VA_{US})$.

- **Interpretation:** R&D expenditure represents the most common indicator of innovative input (Griliches, 1979). In this analysis it is used as a proxy of firms' efforts to develop new technologies or to adapt existing ones. When the computed ratio assumes values lower than 1 this is taken as an indication that R&D investments by EU firms are trailing those made by US firms.

- **Source of data:** Data are drawn from EUROSTAT and refer to 2003, the last year for which data are available. The data for the EU cover BE, CZ, DK, DE, EL, ES, FR, IE, IT, HU, NL, PL, FI, SE, UK.

2. Quality of labour

- **Definition:** The contribution to value added growth of changes in the composition of the labour force according to three skill-related (high, medium, low) categories of workers. It is computed as the difference between EU and US annual average growth rates over the period 1996-2004.

- **Interpretation:** The upgrading of skills of the labour force is used as a proxy for technological change in the sense that it reflects the increased ability of workers to take up and develop new technologies. A negative value for this variable indicates that the EU is underperforming *vis-à-vis* the US.

- **Source of data:** Data are drawn from the EUKLEMS database. Data for the EU refer to AU, BE, DK, ES, FI, FR, UK, DE, IT, NL.

3. ICT

- **Definition:** the contribution to value added growth of ICT investment in office and computing equipment, communication equipment and software. It is computed as the difference between EU and US annual average growth rates over the period 1996-2004.

- **Interpretation:** ICT investment is a measure of innovative input and it represents a proxy of embodied technological change, such as for example a technological improvement in the design or quality of new capital goods or intermediate inputs. A negative value for this variable indicates that the EU is underperforming *vis-à-vis* the US.

- **Source of data:** Data are drawn from the EUKLEMS database. Data for the EU refer to AU, BE, DK, ES, FI, FR, UK, DE, IT, NL.

4. TFP

- **Definition:** The difference between EU and US TFF annual average growth rates over the period 1996-2004.

- **Interpretation:** TFP is a common (although imperfect) proxy for innovation output namely regarding disembodied technological change, i.e. technological change which is not incorporated in any specific production factor[54]. A negative value for this variable indicates that the EU is underperforming *vis-à-vis* the US

- **Source of data:** Data are drawn from the EUKLEMS database. Data for the EU refer to AU, BE, DK, ES, FI, FR, UK, DE, IT, NL.

5. EPO patents

- **Definition:** The ratio of the number of EU and US patent applications at the European Patent Office filed by EU and US agents in 2003.

- **Interpretation:** Patents are used as indicator of innovation outputs which are associated with introduction of new products in the market place. When the computed ratio assumes values lower than 1 this is taken as an indication that by EU firms are trailing US firms. We use as a benchmark, the aggregate cross sectoral ratio of EU/US patent applications at the EPO, which implies - by construction - the so-called home advantage bias in favour of the EU. However, this bias is not relevant for this analysis since we compare the relative innovative performance across different EU sectors (and not EU versus US).

- **Source of data:** Data for the EU refer to EU27 and cover only manufacturing sectors. No patent data are available for services. Data for sector 29 refer only to subsector 291.

3. Main findings

The empirical analysis of the innovation performance at the EU sectoral level will be based on three indicators of innovation input and two indicators of inno-

---

[54] Within a traditional growth accounting approach with no adjustment for the quality of production capital, TFP growth measures both disembodied and embodied technological progress. When adjustments are made to the capital stock (as in the case of EUKLEMS data), TFP encompasses only disembodied technological change. However, the neoclassical assumptions of perfect competition and constant returns to scale are crucial for the equalisation of TFP growth and technological progress. Indeed, non-technological factors such as adjustment costs, non-competitive market structure, scale and cyclical effects, and measurement errors all affect the TFP indicator since it is obtained as a "residual" of the growth accounting exercise, namely as the component of value added growth unexplained by the growth of the two conventional production factors, capital and labour.

An Analysis of the Possible Causes of Product Market Malfunctioning in the EU 71

vation output. On this basis table 6 identifies the sectors for which there are indications that the signs of market malfunctioning can be associated to weaknesses in terms of innovation.

Table 6: Signs of innovation problems among the selected sectors

SECTORS	INPUT			OUTPUT/OUTCOME		Sign of innovative problems
	R&D Intensity	Quality of Labour	ICT^2	TFP^2	EPO patents	
	RATIO	DIFF.	DIFF.	DIFF.	RATIO	
MANUFACTURING	**0.73**	**-0.15**	**-0.16**	**-2.01**	**1.66**	
22 - Publishing, printing	0.25	0.32	-0.40	-1.03	1.46	**
25 - Rubber and plastics	1.15	0.03	0.37	-19.70	2.62	*
27 - Basic metals	1.43	-1.97	-0.48	-0.69	2.23	**
28 - Fabricated metal	0.77	1.08	0.07	-2.32	3.12	**
29 - Machinery	0.94	-0.41	-0.38	-1.61	2.99	**
30 - Office machinery	0.37	2.95	1.45	-43.36	1.33	**
31 - Electrical machinery	1.02	-0.27	-0.60	-7.93	1.96	**
32 - Radio, TV and comm. equip.	1.07	-1.55	0.09	-7.94	1.39	**
34 - Motor vehicles	1.30	0.20	-0.02	-5.17	3.25	*
35 - Other transp. equipment	n.a.	-0.03	0.72	-1.99	2.33	*
36 - Furniture	0.53	n.a	n.a	n.a	2.21	-
37 - Recycling		n.a	n.a	n.a	n.a	n.a
SERVICES	**n.a**	**-0.10**	**-0.13**	**-0.22**	**n.a.**	
E - Electricity, gas and water supply	n.a.	-0.14	-0.06	1.93	n.a	*
50 - Sale, maint. & repair of motor vehicles	n.a	0.03	-0.30	-5.55	n.a	**
51 - Wholesale trade	n.a	-0.49	-0.98	-1.04	n.a	**
52 - Retail trade	n.a	-0.23	-0.11	-3.86	n.a	**
H - Hotels & restaurants	n.a	0.09	-0.30	-1.22	n.a	**
60 - Inland transport	n.a	-0.33	-0.34	0.59	n.a	*
63 - Sup. transport act.	n.a	-0.62	-2.45	7.31	n.a	*
64 - Post and telecoms	n.a	0.01	-0.87	5.62	n.a	*
65 - Financial intermed.	n.a	0.19	1.02	-3.74	n.a	*
66 - Insurance	n.a	-0.66	-2.36	0.94	n.a	*
74 - Other business activities	n.a	-0.30	-0.44	-1.28	n.a	**

Note: The shaded numbers represent, for a given indicator, the sectors that were selected as having problems according to that indicator. Averages at the aggregate level are computed across the sectors for which data are available.

Innovation inputs

The innovative performance of the EU economy appears overall weaker than in the US. Aggregate values for manufacturing and service sectors show – for all the adopted indicators of innovative input – the occurrence of a gap between the EU and the US.

On average, R&D intensity in EU manufacturing sectors reaches a level equivalent to 73% of that in US manufacturing. The largest EU-US gap in terms of R&D intensity can be observed in the office machinery sector, which is one of the most R&D intensive sectors overall. In this sector the EU-US ratio of R&D intensity is 0.37. Only in the publishing and printing sector is this ratio lower (i.e. 0.22). Overall, the EU performance in terms of R&D intensity is relatively weak in 5 out of 10 manufacturing sectors.

The negative sign of the growth accounting input variables (quality of labour and ICT) confirm the lower performance of European sectors compared to the US. Although these two indicators show a very similar pattern at the aggregated level for manufacturing and services, the sectoral distribution of the EU/US gap varies accordingly to the chosen indicator. In particular, regarding "quality of labour" the EU shows signs of underperformance in 12 out of 20 sectors (5 in the manufacturing and 7 in services) while it performs relatively poorly in terms of ICT capital growth in 15 out of 21 sectors (5 in the manufacturing and 10 in services).The largest gap in the "quality of labour" indicator emerges in two manufacturing sectors "basic metals" (27) and "radio, TV and communication equipment" (32) due to an opposite effect of this variable on value added growth in the EU and in the US. Two services sectors namely "supporting transport activities" (63) and "insurance" (66) show the largest gaps in terms of ICT growth. This evidence seems to confirm the idea that there a need to promote diffusion of ICT technologies in European service sectors.

To sum up, EU performance in terms of R&D intensity, ICT investment and quality of labour is relatively weak in many of the sectors considered. This evidence seems to suggest that there is room for improvement in the EU.

Nonetheless the analysis of the evolution of these indicators over time reveals that the gap between EU and US has been reduced in the period 2001-2004 compared to the previous years 1996-2000 in most of the manufacturing sectors (8 out of 10 for the "quality of labour" indicator and 7 out of 11 for the ICT variable) and in some service sectors (7 out of 10 for the "quality of labour" indicator and 4 out of 11 for the ICT variable).

Innovation outputs and outcomes

The comparison of economy-wide aggregate data reveals a disappointing performance of EU sectors in terms of TFP growth. The gap EU/US is a relevant issue in manufacturing (10 out of 10 sectors) whereas the outcome for services highlights a very heterogeneous performance across sectors (there is a relatively slower rate of TFP growth in 6 out of 11 service sectors). Moreover, the differential in TFP is much higher than the comparable indicators (labour quality and

ICT) on the innovative input side. This suggests that the knowledge existing and created within the EU is not easily translated into higher sustained economic growth. The broader difference with the US in terms of TFP suggests that there is room for market and institutional reforms aimed at increasing the diffusion of knowledge and the adoption of new technologies among European firms. Furthermore, the gap in TFP growth appears to be especially large in those manufacturing sectors with a higher technological content, i.e. sectors of "office machinery" (30), "electrical machinery" (31) and "radio, TV and communication equipment" (32) and in some services using ICT extensively, i.e., wholesale and retail trade and business services. A very different pattern over time distinguishes the evolution of TFP growth in manufacturing and services. Indeed, most manufacturing sectors (8 out of 10) have reduced their gap with the US in the period 2001-2004 compared to the previous years 1996-2000, while only 2 out of 11 sectors have witnessed a similar result.

Finally, patent data shows signs of underperformance in 3 out of 11 manufacturing sectors. Among these sectors, the poor performance of sector "office machinery" (30) confirms our previous finding in terms of R&D intensity and suggests therefore the existence of a fundamental weakness in the R&D-patent performance of this sector.

4. Identification of sectors with limited innovation

On the basis of the indicators used we tentatively distinguish three groups of sectors, namely sectors which do not show any indications of problems in terms of innovation , and sectors where there are indications of moderate (*) and serious (**) concerns related to their innovative process. A star is assigned to a sector which appear weak in at least either one input or output indicator compared to the benchmark adopted for that specific variable. Two stars are given to sectors with problems in both input and output indicators. A further qualitative evaluation of the results would contribute to a more precise identification of the different groups of sectors.

The overall picture indicates that Europe does not perform well in terms of innovation performance compared to the US. We find room for improvement both in terms of research – based on the analysis on R&D investments and patent applications – as well as in terms of technological usage, diffusion and translation into higher economic growth – based on the analysis of the growth accounting indicators. Moreover, this investigation has depicted the relative contribution of different innovation indicators to economic growth and knowledge creation in the EU and in the US.

Innovation problems are detected in all the selected sectors, with the exception of the furniture and recycling sectors, for which only limited data were available. In 11 out of the 23 selected sectors (6 manufacturing sectors and 5 services sectors), a combination of problems regarding innovation input and output can be found and in all the other sectors, there is at least some evidence of problems regarding input or output. Moreover, it is particularly problematic that many of the sectors where there are clear indications of innovation problems are producer of ICT goods like office and computing machinery, electrical machinery and communication equipment. Moreover, the services sectors identified, such as wholesale and retail trade and business services, use ICT intensively.

Overall Assessment

This section aims at presenting the overall assessment of the potential causes of market malfunctioning in the EU based on the indicator analyses presented above. Table 7 below summarises the findings of the analysis across the four dimensions. Sectors are classified into three groups: those – marked with ** – presenting indications of serious problems because several indicators point to this conclusion, those – marked with *– where the presumption of problems cannot be rejected because of at least one of the indicators considered and those where there is no evidence of problems on the basis of indicators used. Given the shortcomings of a horizontal analysis of this nature and the fact that at this stage the focus is still on sector level data and publicly available indicators, these findings should necessarily be taken as preliminary.

Nonetheless, they offer useful information which complements the screening device carried out in the first stage of the market monitoring exercise. Thereby, the current analysis can be regarded as a robustness check of the screening results on two grounds.

First, it allows the identification of sectors that have been selected in the screening stage but which do not show signs of problems regarding regulation, integration, competition and innovation. In this case, the inclusion of these sectors in the selection could be questioned. However, this does not seem to be the case. Overall, the analysis of the causes of market malfunctioning confirms the selection made at the screening stage. All the sectors selected by the screening show signs of problems in at least one of the domains analysed. Moreover in 10 of these sectors there are indications of problems in all four domains (2/3 of these being services sectors).

Second, as the indicators used for this analysis have been computed for all the manufacturing and services sectors of the economy, it is also possible to check whether there are sectors which have not been selected in the screening stage but for which there are strong indications of problems in terms of regulation, integration, competition and innovation. On the basis of these indicators this seems to be the case for only two sectors, namely "coke, refined petroleum and nuclear fuel" and "air transport".

The sector "coke, refined petroleum and nuclear fuel" (23) presents indications of serious problems of integration (low degree of market thickness and import penetration), competition (higher mark ups than US, high levels of concentration and low turbulence in the market) and innovation (lower R&D intensity, ICT investment, quality of labour and TFP growth than in the US). Regarding the sector "air transport" (62) there are some indications of problems with competition (higher mark-ups than the US and high levels of concentration relative to that of other services sectors) and innovation (lower TFP growth and ICT investment than in the US). In both sectors there are some indications of over-regulation of firms' activities in 2003 (the most recent year for which data are available). These findings should be further scrutinised on the basis of more recent, qualitative information. If the indications of problems are validated these two sectors could also benefit from closer market monitoring.[55]

The analysis presented in this note can also be used to construct general and comprehensive hypotheses concerning the nature of market (mal)functioning from the supply-side point of view in specific sectors and to draw some tentative conclusions regarding the scope for policy intervention. Such hypotheses, which should be completed with additional information regarding demand-side issues to fully take consumer welfare considerations into account, would then serve as starting points for the analyses to be done in subsequent more in-depth market monitoring exercises.

Our analysis suggests that over regulation is a cross cutting affecting all but three of the sectors that have been scrutinised. This raises the question of to which extent many of the problems that we identify in these sectors in terms of integration, competition and innovation are driven by inadequate policy inputs. Thus the analysis of the impact of regulatory framework faced by firms in a given sector/market and the interactions of rules and regulations with market openness and cross border integration, competition environment and market-based incentives to innovate should be given centre stage in the subsequent in-depth market monitoring exercises.

---

[55] These sectors have not been selected in the screening stage because their direct contribution to growth and employment is not substantial and they did not appear to contribute significantly to the adjustment capacity of the European economy. Moreover no productivity growth gap with the US between 1995 and 2004 was observed for the sector of "cork, refined petroleum and nuclear fuel". By contrast, the "air transport" (62) show problems in terms of labour productivity, which is the economic indicator for market malfunctioning adopted for the first screening.

Table 7: Summary overview of the causes for market malfunctioning

SECTORS	POLICY ENVIRONMENT	MARKET PERFORMANCE		
	Regulation	Integration	Competition	Innovation
22 - Printing, publishing and reproduction	*	**	*	**
25 - Rubber and plastics	*	*	-	*
27 - Basic metals	*	-	**	**
28 - Fabricated metal	*	**	-	**
29 – Machinery	-	-	*	**
30 - Office, accounting and computing machinery	-	*	*	**
31 - Electrical machinery and apparatus	*	*	-	**
32 - Radio, TV and comm. equipment	*	*	*	**
34 - Motor vehicles, trailers and semi-trailers	-	*	**	*
35 - Other transport equipment	*	**	*	*
36 - Furniture, other manufactured goods	*	-	*	-
37 – Recycling	*	n.a.	-	n.a.
E - Electricity, gas and water supply	**	**	**	*
50 - Sale, maintenance and repair of motor vehicles	**	-	*	**
51 - Wholesale trade	**	-	*	**
52 - Retail trade	**	**	*	**
H - Hotels and restaurants	*	*	**	**
60 - Inland transport	**	-	*	*
63 - Supporting and aux. transport activities	**	*	**	*
64 - Post and telecom.	*	-	**	*
65 - Financial intermediation	*	**	**	*
66 - Insurance and pension funding	*	**	*	*
74 - Other business activities	**	**	*	**

The lack of innovation appears also to be associated with market malfunctioning in almost all of the sectors identified. The exceptions are the sector "furniture and other manufacturing activities" (36) and "recycling" (for which no data were available). Furthermore it is the domain where more indications of serious problems have been found: more specifically in 11 out of the 23 sectors. Many of these sectors producers of ICT goods like "office, accounting and competing machinery", "electrical machinery and apparatus", and "radio, TV and communication equipment", as well as ICT-intensive services sectors like "retail trade" and "other business sectors".

In contrast with innovation where indications of serious problems seem to be evenly distributed across manufacturing and services, the indications of serious problems related to lack of integration and insufficient competition seem to be relatively more concentrated in the services sectors. In particular, there are indications of weak integration and competition in electricity and gas, retail trade, transport, posts and telecommunications, financial and business services[56].

These findings broadly support the view that the emphasis put by Member States on reforms in the area of R&D and innovation as the right strategy. According to the MICREF database (see box 8) most of the reform measures enacted by Member States (30% of all implemented measures) in the recent past were in this area. Such measures refer mainly to the development of national research and innovation strategies and policies, increasing public R&D spending, enhancing the diffusion of technology and the use of ICT. However, given the remaining problems regarding integration and competition in services, it is somewhat disappointing that Members States have been much less active in the implementation of the reform measures in these areas (just 6% and 3% of the total number of measures respectively). The measures in the area of competition concerned reforms to increase the powers and means of competition authorities, to better control state aids and to improve the regulation in specific sectors. With respect to market integration the reported measures relate mostly to the modernisation of public procurement, and the implementation of specific EU directives concerning the Internal Market.

While the MICREF database focuses on the measures taken by the Member States it is not clear cut that this is the appropriate level of governance for policy intervention in all the sectors scrutinised. This depends on the characteristics of the sectors and on the nature of the problems that affecting the functioning of markets. Retail trade and network industries such as electricity and gas supply provide clear examples of two sectors that are affected by problems of similar nature (both are over regulated and show low levels of market integration), but for which the scope for policy intervention at the level of Member States and at the Community level varies significantly.

---

[56] Notice, that before drawing any policy conclusions relating to "other business services" it is necessary to carry out more analyses at a more disaggregated level given the heterogeneity of the different activities that it includes.

> **Box 8: Summary description of MICREF database**
>
> The objective of the database on microeconomic reforms (MICREF), which has been developed by the Commission (DG ECFIN and JRC) in collaboration with Member States, is to help monitor and analyse the process of the implementation of structural reforms in product markets and thereby to improve the quality policy design and the surveillance of its impact across EU Member States.
>
> MICREF organises and presents product market reform measures undertaken by the EU Member States in a systematic way with a set of descriptive features of the actions undertaken, while placing the initiatives described in the National Reform Programmes into the appropriate historical context. The main value added of MICREF in relation to other databases currently used to analyse microeconomic reforms is that it explores the qualitative dimension of the data as well as their dynamic nature.
>
> The database is organised around three major economic dimensions: *i*) open and competitive markets; *ii*) business environment and entrepreneurship, and *iii*) knowledge-based economy. These dimensions correspond to 7 policy fields: market integration; competition policy; sector-specific regulation; start-up conditions; improving the (small) business environment; R&D and innovation; and education. The different policy actions are then classified according to each of the 7 policy fields.
>
> The principal data source for MICREF are the reports on the implementation of the National Reform Programmes; additional information is drawn from international data sources and Commission reports in order to achieve a complete overview of the measures taken within each specific policy area.

In retail trade the low level of integration and innovation are probably associated with the regulatory framework that often create barriers to the entry of new firms in the market and slow down the expansion of existing ones. Such regulations mainly target (i) *the location and availability of the service provision* (restrictions on type, size and location of stores, restricted and discriminatory opening hours, etc.); (ii) *advertising and marketing rules* (there are often limits on promotions, loyalty schemes, selling below cost, restrictions on specific products or advertising, etc.); and (iii) *labour market issues* (limited flexibility of employees, setting of minimum wages, etc). They vary widely across Member States and are very often introduced by regional and even local authorities[57].

---

[57] It should be nevertheless pointed out that some regulations (such as the Unfair Commercial Practices Directive) are necessary to guarantee informed choice and empowerment of consumers and are therefore beneficial to the functioning of markets.

The scope for policy intervention at the Community level is therefore limited and such regulatory barriers can best be tackled by each Member State[58].

Network industries in the EU, such as the electricity and gas sector, are currently ongoing a transition phase from state-run national monopolistic markets to an EU-wide competitive market. Despite this liberalisation process, their singular economic features, i.e. the presence of an essential facility and the resulting issue of network access, warrant the continuing presence of sector-specific regulation. The introduction of effective competition can be pursued by measures taken at the Member State level (e.g. market opening or the degree of vertical unbundling) but it is also closely related to promoting access of energy suppliers to markets in neighbouring countries. This requires not only a sufficient level of cross-border interconnection, but also a set of common rules: measures that clearly require intervention at the EU level. Indeed, the "energy package" adopted by the Commission in September 2007 foresees a number of measures to enhance competition in the electricity and gas sectors, notably by strengthening the position of the regulatory authorities, improving cross-border coordination in order to create more integrated markets (for example through the creation of an agency for the cooperation of energy regulators) and providing for a sharper vertical separation between infrastructure management and supply activities.

Finally, it is also important to be aware that there is not necessarily scope for policy intervention in all sectors. In sectors like "printing, publishing and reproduction" (22) and "fabricated metal", there is limited scope for policy intervention to promote further integration as it is naturally determined to a large extent by the cultural and linguistic affinities/differences and high transport costs respectively. By contrast, in other transport equipment, the home bias in public procurement may still play an important role, while in financial services, insurance and other business services the legal barriers to entry that were in place until recently may explain to a large extent the current situation. Regarding network industries we find indications that the remaining problems sectors are of diverse nature requiring different kinds of policy interventions.

---

[58] A recent study by Viviano (2007) illustrates well this point using as an example the experience of two Italian regions Abruzzo and Marche. These two otherwise similar regions have opted for two different regulatory approaches in the retail sector: Abruzzo set tight restrictions on the opening of large stores, while Marche did not impose substantial entry regulations. The results show that in latter the share of retail trade in total employment increased by 0.8 percentage points more than in the former. Fiercer competition also, promoted innovation. The latter however can be further promoted with measures targeted for example at facilitating the uptake of ICT where the Community can play a complementary role to that of national authorities.

In the case of post and telecommunications, the problems seem to be closely related to insufficient competition pressure and therefore policy intervention should aim at reducing barriers to entry and at improving the consumers' access to information. In electricity, gas, the problems seem to be more closely associated with insufficient integration and therefore policy intervention may be more necessary to tackle inadequate investment in cross-border network infrastructure.

Next Steps

To conclude it is important to set this exercise in the wider context of the market monitoring approach to policymaking that the Commission is promoting. Thereby this exercise, which will be complemented by a detailed analysis of demand-side issues that affect market functioning in the scrutinised sectors, will serve as a basis for a multi-annual programme of in-depth market monitoring exercises.

In this light the next steps are twofold: *i*) to start to the in-depth market monitoring exercises featuring some of the sectors that have been scrutinised thus far, and *ii*) to extend the screening and the analysis of the causes of market malfunctioning of the selected sectors to the level of each Member States. The Commission services have already started to implement in-depth market monitoring investigations in two sectors, namely retail trade and electrical machinery. The in-depth analysis of these sectors will be made in ad-hoc working groups which bring together staff from all the interested services. The final output of each ad-hoc working group is expected in the first half of 2009 and will include a presentation of the policy implications of the findings.

The analysis made at the EU level may be complemented by similar exercises at the level of each Member State, involving a national screening and an analysis of the causes of market malfunctioning at the national level. The Commission services would like to work in close collaboration with the Member States in this area. A national screening would help Member States in identifying areas that create bottlenecks for national growth and adjustment. Moreover, from a Community perspective, it would be useful to investigate whether the problems affecting EU market functioning have a national dimension. This should not come unexpected since the industrial structure and the characteristics of sectors differ from one Member State to another. Finally, such an investigation would allow defining policy actions at the national level which can complement the actions eventually proposed by the Commission services on the basis of its own market monitoring exercise. This last point is particularly important given that has we argued earlier the burden of policy intervention can fall either on the Union or the Member States depending on the sectors and market that are being considered.

References

Ades, A.F. and Glaser E.L., (1999). "Evidence on Growth, Increasing Returns, and the Extent of the Market". *Quarterly Journal of Economics*. MIT Press. Vol. 114(3), pp. 1025-1045. August.

Aghion, P. and Griffith R., (2006). *Competition and Growth*. MIT Press. Cambridge.

Alesina, A., Spolaore E. and Wacziarg R., (2000). "Economic Integration and Political Disintegration". *American Economic Review*. Vol. 90(5), pp. 1276-1296. December.

Arnold J., Nicoletti, G. and Scarpetta S., (2007). "Product Market Policies, Allocative Efficiency and Productivity: A Cross Country Analysis". *OECD unpublished research paper*.

Bernard, A.B., Eaton, J., Jensen J.B. and Kortum, S., (2003). "Plants and Productivity in International Trade". *American Economic Review*. 93(4), pp. 1268-1290.

Carlsson, B., Jacobsson, S., Holmén, M. and Rickne A., (2002). "Innovation Systems: Analytical and Methodological Issues", *Research Policy*. Vol. 31.

Cincera, M. and Galgau O., (2005). "Impact of Market Entry and Exit on EU Productivity and Growth Performance", *European Economy Economic Papers* No. 222. European Commission. Brussels.

Christopoulou R. and Vermeulen P., (2007). "Mark-ups in the Euro-area and the US over the Period 1981-2004: A Comparison of 50 Sectors". *European Central Bank Working Paper*, European Central Bank. Frankfurt.

Conway, P., Janod V. and Nicoletti G., (2005). "Product Market Regulation in OECD Countries, 1998 to 2003". *OECD Economics Department Working Paper*. No. 419. OECD. Paris.

Conway, P. and G. Nicoletti (2006). "Product Market Regulation in the Non-manufacturing Sectors of OECD Countries: Measurement and Highlights". *OECD Economics Department Working Papers* No. 530. OECD. Paris.

Dierx A., Ilzkovitz, F. and Sekkat, K., eds. (2004). *European Integration and the Functioning of Product Markets*. Edward Elgar. London.

Dierx, A., Ilzkovitz, F. and Schmidt, J.H., (2007). "Competition, Regulatory Costs and Economic Growth", unpublished.

Doms, M., Dunne, T. and Roberts M.J., (1995). "The Role of Technology Use in the Survival and Growth of Manufacturing Plants". *International Journal of Industrial Organization*. Vol. 13, pp. 523-542.

Drejer, I. (2004), "Identifying Innovation in Surveys of Services: a Schumpeterian Perspective". *Research Policy*. Vol. 33, pp. 551-562.

Edquist, C., (2001). "Innovation Policy - A Systemic Approach". In: B. Lundvall, and D. Archibugi (eds.). *Major Socio-Economic Trends and European Innovation Policy*. Oxford University Press. Oxford.

European Commission, (2003). Chapter 2 - Drivers of Productivity Growth - An Economy-wide and Industrial Level Perspective. In: *The EU Economy: 2003 Review*. European Commission. Brussels.

European Commission, (2007a). "Guiding Principles for Product Markets and Sector Monitoring". *European Economy Occasional Papers*. No.34. Brussels.

European Commission, (2007b)."Implementing the New Methodology for Product Market and Sector Monitoring: Results of a First Sector Screening", *European Commission Staff Working Document*. Brussels.

European Commission, (2007c). *Monitoring Industrial Research: Analysis of the 2006 EU Industrial R&D Investment Scoreboard*. European Commission. Luxembourg.

Gilbert, R. J. and Newbery D.M.G., (1982). "Pre-emptive Patenting and the Persistence of Monopoly". *American Economic Review*. Vol. 72, pp. 514-526.

Griffith, R. and Harrison R., (2004). "The Link between Product Market Reform and Macroeconomic Performance". *European Economy Economic Papers*. No. 209. European Commission. Brussels.

Griffith, R., Harrison R. and Simpson H., (2006). "The Link between Product Market Reform, Innovation and EU Macroeconomic Performance". *European Economy Economic Paper* No. 243. European Commission. Brussels.

Griliches, Z., (1990). "Patent Statistics as Economic Indicators: A Survey". *Journal of Economic Literature*. Vol. 28. No. 4.

Griliches, Z., (1979). "Issues in Assessing the Contribution of Research and Development to Productivity Growth". *Bell Journal of Economics*. Vol. 10, pp. 92-116.

Harrison, A.E., (1994). "Productivity, Imperfect Competition and Trade Reform: Theory and Evidence". *Journal of International Economics*. No. 36, pp. 53-73.

Hipp, C. and Grupp H., (2005). "Innovation in the Service Sector: The demand of Service-specific Innovation Measurement Concepts". *Research Policy*. Vol. 34. No. 4, pp. 517-535.

Hollanders, H. and Arundel A., (2005). *European Sector Innovation Scoreboards*. European Commission. Brussels.

Howells, J. and Tether B., (2004). *Innovations in Services: Issues at Stake and Trends*. Centre for Research on Innovation and Competition. University of Manchester.

Ilzkovitz, F., Dierx, A., Kovacs, V. and Sousa N., (2007). "Steps towards a Deeper Economic Integration: The Internal Market in the 21st Century", *European Economy Economic Papers*. No.271. European Commission. Brussels.

Jaffe, A.B., (1988). "Demand and Supply Influences in R&D Intensity and Productivity Growth". *Review of Economics and Statistics*. Vol. 70, pp. 431-437.

Kanerva, M., Hollanders H. and Arundel A., (2006). "Can we Measure and Compare Innovation in Services", 2006 *TrendChart Report*. European Commission, Brussels.

Knetter, M. and Slaughter M., (1999). "Measuring Product Market Integration". *NBER Working Paper* No. W6969.

London Economics, (2007). *Identification of Industrial Sectors with Weak Competition: Analysis of Causes and Impacts*. Report to the DG Enterprise and Industry of the European Commission.

Malerba, F. (2002). "Sectoral Systems of Innovation and Production". *Research Policy*. Vol. 31. No. 2.

Nås, S.O., (2007). "Measuring Innovation Processes". Paper presented at the 32nd CEIES Seminar *Innovation Indicators-More Than Technology?*. Århus 5-6 February.

Nicoletti, G., Scarpetta S. and Boylaud O., (2000). "Summary Indicators of Product Market Regulation with an Extension to Employment Protection Legislation". *OECD Economics Department Working Paper*. No.226. Paris.

Nicoletti, G. and Scarpetta S., (2003). "Regulation, Productivity and Growth: OECD Evidence". *Economic Policy*. No.36. April.

OECD, (1997). *The OECD Report on Regulatory Reform: Synthesis*. OECD. Paris.

OECD, (2001). *Innovation and productivity in services*. OECD. Paris.

OECD, (2004). *Compendium of Patent Statistics*. OECD. Paris.

OECD, (2005a). *Promoting Innovation in Services*. OECD. Paris.

OECD and EUROSTAT, (2005b). *Oslo Manual: Guidelines for Collecting and Interpreting Innovation Data*. 3rd edition. OECD. Paris.

OECD, (2006). *Compendium of Patent Statistics*. OECD. Paris.

Pavcnik, N., (2002). "Trade Liberalization, Exit and Productivity Improvements: Evidence from Chilean Plants". *Review of Economic Studies*. Vol.69. January, pp. 245-76.

Roeger, W., (1995). "Can Imperfect Competition Explain the Difference between Primal and Dual Productivity Measures? Estimates for US Manufacturing". *Journal of Political Economy*. No. 103, pp. 316-330.

Salter, A. and B.S. Tether (2006), "Innovation in Services- through the Looking glass of Innovation Studies", background paper for Advanced Institute of Management (AIM) Research's Grand Challenge on Service Science

Scarpetta, S., Hemmings, P Tressel T. and Woo J., (2002). "The Role of Policy and Institutions for Productivity and Firm Dynamics: Evidence from Micro and Industry Data". *Economics Department Working Paper*. No.15. OECD. Paris.

Scherer, F.M., (1992). "Schumpeter and Plausible Capitalism". *Journal of Economic Literature*. Vol. 30, pp. 1416-1433.

Tether, B.S. and Metcalfe J.S., (2004). "Services and Systems of Innovation". In: F. Malerba (ed.) *Sectoral Systems of Innovation: Concepts, Issues and Analyses of Six Major Sectors in Europe*. Cambridge University Press. Cambridge.

Tybout, J.R., (2003). "Plant and Firm-Level Evidence on "New" Trade Theories", in J. Harrigan and K. Choi (eds.) *Handbook of International Trade*. New York. Blackwell Publishig. New York, pp. 388-415.

Veugelers, R., (2004). "Industrial Concentration, Market Integration and Efficiency in the European Union". In: A. Dierx, F. Ilzkovitz and K. Sekkat (eds) *European integration and the functioning of product markets*. Edward Elgar. London.

Viviano, E., (2007). "Entry Regulations and Labour Market Outcomes: Evidence from the Italian Retail Trade Sector". *Bank of Italy Economic Research Department*.

ANNEX 1: Main characteristics of sector selected in the screening stage

Sector's code	Sector's name	Contribution to total employment	Contribution to total value added	Productivity growth 1995-2004	Interlinkages (*)	ICT (**)	Economically important	Important for adjustment
22	Printing, etc	1.0	1.0	14.3	F	U		X
25	Rubber and plastics	0.8	1.0	32.3	F		X	
27	Basic metals	0.5	0.7	28.9	F		X	
28	Fabricated metal	1.9	1.8	19.3	F/I		X	
29	**Machinery**	**1.7**	**2.1**	**25.1**	**B/I**	**U**	**X**	**X**
30	Office, acc. .etc	0.1	0.1	64.2	I	P		X
31	**Electrical machinery**	**0.8**	**0.9**	**24.7**	**I**	**P**	**X**	**X**
32	**Radio, TV, comm. eq.**	**0.4**	**0.5**	**154.2**	**I**	**P**	**X**	**X**
34	Motor vehicles	1.1	1.4	26.7	B/I		X	
35	O. transport equip.	0.4	0.4	35.8	I	U		X
36	Furniture,.	1.1	0.8	10.1	I	U		X
37	Recycling				F	U		X
E	Elect., gas & water	0.7	2.2	52.9	F		X	
50	Sale, ... of motor vehicles	2.2	1.7	7.2	B		X	
51	**Wholesale trade**	**4.4**	**3.6**	**27.2**	**F/B**	**U**	**X**	**X**
52	**Retail trade**	**8.5**	**4.3**	**14.6**	**F/B**	**U**	**X**	**X**
H	Hotels and restaurants	4.5	2.2	-1.3	B		X	
60	Inland transport -	2.7	2.6	27.6	F		X	
63	Supp. aux. transp. act.	1.3	1.8	-2.0	F		X	
64	**Post and telecom.**	**1.4**	**2.4**	**121.1**	**F**	**P**	**X**	**X**
65	**Financial intermed.**	**1.7**	**4.1**	**46.7**	**F**	**U**	**X**	**X**
66	**Insurance**	**0.5**	**1.0**	**-13.4**	**B**	**U**	**X**	**X**
74	**O. business activities**	**8.8**	**7.0**	**-7.7**	**F**	**U**	**X**	**X**
	Total contribution	46.0	44.0					

(*)"B" stands for backward interlinkages, "F" for forward interlinkages and "I" for investment.

(**) "P" stands for ICT – producing sector and "U" for ICT – using sectors.

ANNEX 2: OECD Non - Manufacturing Regulation Indicators in 2003

SECTORS	EU*		US	
Electricity, gas and water (E)	Electricity: 1.6		Electricity: 2.3	
	Gas: 3.3		Gas: 0.4	
Wholesale and retail trade (50-51-52)	2.5		2.6	
Transport and storage (60-61-62-63)	Rail: 3.6		Rail: 3.0	
	Road: 1.8		Road: 0.5	
	Airlines: 2.2		Airlines: 0	
Post and telecommunications (64)	Post: 2.9		Post: 3.7	
	Telecoms: 1.4		Telecoms: 0.2	
Renting of machinery and equipment and other business activities (71-72-73-74)	2.2	Accounting: 2.4	1.8	Accounting: 1.7
		Architect: 1.8		Architect: 1.7
		Engineer: 1.6		Engineer: 1.9
		Legal: 2.8		Legal: 1.8

This indicator is constructed on the basis of the same methodology as the economy-wide indicators for product market regulation: higher values mean that more restrictions are imposed on competition in the sector. It is bound between 0 and 6. For more detailed information regarding the methodology for the computation of these indicators see Conway and Nicoletti (2006), "Product market regulation in the non-manufacturing sectors of OECD countries: Measurement and highlights", OECD Economics Department Working Papers No. 530.

* The EU average covers only 19 OECD Members (FR, UK, DE, NL, BE, DK, SE, IE, IT, GR, ES, PT, LU, FI, AT, CZ, HU, PL, SK) and use the US as a benchmark.

Chapter 3

Liberalizing Trade in Services
A New Agenda for Growth and Jobs in Europe?

Suparna Karmakar[1]

Abstract

Development economists' cautious approach to services trade as a viable engine of growth has been expressed through both theoretical and empirical analysis. Their skepticism stems from the relatively jobless nature of service sector growth, especially in tradable service sectors in developing countries. On the other hand, the increasing importance of the cross-border supply of services has evoked strong emotions on both sides of the Atlantic. Given that services have become an important component of sustaining competitiveness and productivity growth, a new evaluation of the dynamic gains from an open services regime has become crucial.

This paper evaluates the benefits of increasing unilateral globalization in service sectors, the role of unilateral policy initiatives and multilateral trade negotiations in opening markets, and assesses the prospects for countries to further their growth and employment objectives by pursuing a liberal cross-border service trade regime. The paper draws its lessons and conclusions from an analysis of recent Indian development experience, highlighting the potential for knowledge spillovers and innovation to the rest of the economy from a liberal service trade regime in key input services. The analysis considers the particular role of liberal international trade in services for enhancing high-skill high-wage employment in the non-traded sectors of the economy. The lessons from this analysis appear to be of particular relevance to policymakers concerned about sustaining the competitiveness of their domestic economy.

Introduction

Development economists' disfavor with services trade as a viable engine of growth and employment generation has been expressed through both theoretical and empirical analysis. Their well documented skepticism emanates from evidence of the relatively jobless nature of service sector growth, in particular in the tradable service sectors in developing countries. Economic history indicates

---

[1] Senior Fellow, ICRIER, New Delhi, India, e-mail: suparna@icrier.res.in.

that growth in developing countries has normally been led by the manufacturing sector.[2] Even in the developed world, the recent trend has been one of increasing protectionism in services, and more proximate causes of job losses like weak domestic demand, rapid productivity growth in competing countries and strong currencies in the developed world (Baily and Lawrence, 2005) have been overlooked in the urgency to portray the increasing trade in services as the cause of all economic ills. Unfortunately, liberalizing services is now regarded as a zero-sum-game by the developed world. However, given that services have become an important component of sustaining competitiveness and productivity growth, and with the rise in intra-industry trade in infrastructure services such as information and communication technology (ICT) and finance, a new empirical evaluation of the above hypotheses has become crucial.

Services today are the premier engine of growth in most economies. In developed countries, the service sector contributes over 80 percent of domestic GDP, and over 70 percent of employment (OECD, 2005). Since the turn of this century, even in the developing world, services have been contributing upwards of 50 percent of GDP, and have been the principal source of domestic employment, especially in employment-intensive services such as tourism, hospitality, transportation, construction and wholesale and retail trade. Because services are crucial inputs into all economic activity, potential gains from service sector liberalization are much greater than those for industrial goods. Inefficient and high-cost intermediate "backbone" or input services affect the competitiveness and productivity of the firms in all sectors of the economy, impeding further growth and investment in the economy.[3]

In the past couple of decades, there has been a tremendous expansion of cross-border investments in service industries by transnational companies (TNCs).[4] In 2005, services accounted for about two-thirds of FDI inflows worldwide (up from 49 percent in 1990), and for half of FDI inflows in developing countries. The increase in FDI in recent years has also led to rising employment in foreign affiliates of TNCs. Data from the OECD Scoreboard indicate that employment in foreign-owned affiliates (as a share of total employment in the country) ranges from 10 to 50 percent, and the new member states of the European Union are particular beneficiaries of such investment.[5] But while global merchandise

---

[2] For a detailed literature survey, see Ros (2000); Joshi (2004).

[3] O'Mahony et al. (2003) found that one of the main causes of the relative productivity slowdown in Europe compared with the United States is that European ICT-using services, such as wholesale and retail, have slower productivity growth than comparable sectors in the US.

[4] The World Investment Report 2007 estimates that the foreign capital stock of TNCs (i.e. the total assets of foreign affiliates) rose by 20 percent in 2006.

[5] Almost 30 percent of manufacturing and services employees in Poland are employed with the foreign affiliates established in the country.

trade flows have increased significantly over the last few decades, at about 20 percent of total merchandise and commercial services trade by value, trade in commercial services has remained significantly lower when compared with its share in global output. Services markets seem to be largely protected in all countries.

In 2006, world commercial services trade (excluding intra-EU25 trade) was at US$ 4.00 trillion,[6] growing at a rate of 12.5 percent, with this growth (albeit from a low base) being driven largely by sharp increases in cross-border trade in services and across a large number of service sub-sectors. A recent analysis by *McKinsey Quarterly* (Davis and Stephenson, 2006) estimated that global cross-border service trade as a percentage of global GDP would reach 30 percent by 2015, from 18 percent in 1990.

One of the most commented trends in recent years has been the increasing importance of cross-border supply of services, or offshoring. This has caused concern among developed country policymakers about its implications for unemployment. But available evidence indicates that this trade is still relatively miniscule, and the economic loss and employment impact attributed to it is largely overplayed. The WTO Secretariat in 2003 had estimated offshored IT software and business process outsourcing (BPO, also known as IT-enabled services, or ITeS) services, at just 2.5 percent of world commercial services exports (valued at US$ 45 billion, and essentially comprised of Mode 1 and Mode 2 trade) and at a meager 0.125 percent of global GDP. According to the McKinsey Global Institute analysis, of the full US$ 1.45 to 1.47 of value created globally from every offshored US dollar spent, the United States captures US$ 1.12 to 1.14, while the receiving country gets only 33 cents on average. *The European Restructuring Monitor 2007* reports that in the four years between 2003 and 2006, services offshoring accounted for approximately 10 percent of cases of industrial restructuring and 8 percent of announced job losses in the EU.

It needs to be recalled here that international trade in services is not a new trend. Transportation and communication (services that bridge the physical distance between the buyer and seller of goods), tourism, education (students going abroad to study), and temporary (immigrant) workers in foreign countries (including plantation/mining/construction workers) have been the most notable and oft traded services in the past several centuries. In most research reports, however, services were deemed non-tradable because of the high transaction costs (measured in time, distance or otherwise) that prevented the close interface

---

[6] International Trade Statistics 2007, p. 15. Reported circumstantial information on commercial presence through foreign affiliates abroad (Mode 3) indicates that such sales are rising faster than the traditional trade in services. Estimates suggest that Mode 3 is an important (if not dominant) mode of delivery for trade in services.

between the buyer and seller deemed necessary for trade in services to occur Mann, 2004).

In other words, traditionally, trade in services occurred primarily through investment or commercial establishment in foreign countries and by movement of labour to provide essential services.[7] The new feature of our time therefore is the increased tradability of services by means of cross-border trade, a result of innovation in ICT technology[8] and existing regulatory impediments on the free movement of foreign service providers, which caused a large number of erstwhile domestically provided services to be undertaken on an arm's length basis. That said, it is also important to remember that the enhanced offshore tradability will potentially impact less than a fourth of the total universe of services and affect at most 20 percent of total employment in services. The vast majority of services jobs are in services that are essentially produced and consumed locally and cannot be offshored; the services of retailers, restaurants, hotels, leisure and hospitality, tourism and travel, electricians, and carpenters, as well as personal care services, for example, are unlikely to ever be provided on an arm's length basis.

Given the above, an objective understanding is how the dynamic gains from a liberal services regime get translated into higher growth, productivity and employment, and finally international competitiveness is important for dispelling myths. While the recent past has seen a large body of work identifying the gains from liberalization vis-à-vis productivity, employment impact and welfare effects, they mostly model the productivity growth and welfare effects of relaxing regulatory barriers in services,[9] and favour increases in regional competition.

---

[7] An important point to note here is that not all remittances from labor working abroad can be counted as trade receipts under GATS. As per the current scope in GATS, only services by high-skill temporary foreign providers that are provided via the movement of natural persons across national borders are considered as trade under the fourth mode of GATS. GATS Mode 4 does *not* apply to skilled and unskilled natural persons seeking citizenship, residence or employment on a permanent basis.

[8] In particular the evolution of internet technology and IT software enabled technological unbundling of complex service processes. This allowed firms to splinter certain portions of the erstwhile non-tradable services into smaller jobs and hire outside providers for enhanced efficiency and better supply-chain management in services.

[9] Robinson et al (1999) suggest that global welfare gains from a 50 percent cut in protection in service sectors is five times larger than that from non-service trade. Stern (2005) calculated that free trade in services could result in a global welfare gain of US$ 1.7 trillion. An estimate by Catherine Mann (2004) indicates that offshoring in the US IT industry led to an annual productivity increase of 0.3 percentage points between 1995 and 2002, which translated into a cumulative effect of US$ 230 billion in additional GDP. In the EU, researchers at the CBP Netherlands Bureau for Economic Policy Analysis in the Hague, Copenhagen Economics, and the Institute for the Study of Labor (IZA) in Bonn have undertaken studies on productivity growth and welfare effects and found that in a

This paper evaluates the benefits of increasing unilateral integration in service sectors, the efficacy of unilateral policy initiatives vis-à-vis multilateral trade negotiations in opening markets, and assesses the prospects for countries to further their growth and employment objectives by pursuing a liberal cross-border service trade regime.

The paper is organized as follows. The following section analyzes the recent Indian development experience, highlighting the extant growth and productivity spillovers to the rest of the economy from a liberal service trade regime in key infrastructure sectors such as IT, ITeS, telecommunications and financial services. This section also identifies the regulatory regime that supported the above growth experience, highlighting in particular the role of the liberal international trade in services in enhancing high-skill high-wage employment in the non-traded sectors of the economy. The lessons from this analysis are elucidated in the final section, especially the dynamic gains from learning and knowledge spillovers to the rest of the economy, which brings out the imperatives of particular relevance to European policymakers concerned about sustaining the growth and competitiveness of their domestic economy. A key conclusion is that a deregulated and liberal service sector infuses competition in the domestic economy and helps create the enabling environment for dynamic productivity and knowledge gains, which in turn help economies move up the value chain in tradable sectors.

Services in India: A Growth Engine for the Economy

1. Current State of Play

India's growth experience of the past decade and a half has been rather unique. Unlike in most developing countries, the service sector has become the most important sector of the Indian economy not only in terms of its contribution to the nation's GDP growth, but also in employment creation and generating export revenues. India now ranks among the 10 fastest growing economies in the world, growing at over 8.5 percent in the last four years, and the services sector has been the key driver of this growth for over a decade. In the five years between 2002-2003 and 2006-2007, India's service sector contributed approximately 68.6 percent of the overall average real GDP growth (Service Value

---

regime where the Services Directive is implemented, trade in commercial services is expected to go up by 30 to 62 percent, and enforcement of mutual recognition, under the Country of Origin Principle (CoOP), would contribute about 10 percent to the total welfare effects.

Added); in 2006-2007, growing at 11.2 percent year on year, services (excluding construction) constituted 54.9 percent of Indian GDP.[10]

Notably, service sector growth in India is broad-based, and cross-sectoral complementarities and synergies are strengthening the overall performance of the sector, given that some high-growth services constitute important inputs for both manufacturing and services growth and productivity. For example, the communications sub-sector has grown at over 15 percent since the 1980s. Consequently, the shares of services sub-sectors dependent on advanced IT and telecommunications technology also increased. Financial services also benefited from such synergies. Available data show that business services (sub-sector of "other services" in the National Account Statistics, Government of India, and consisting of mostly IT software and ITeS) have been the fastest growing sub-sector since the 1990s, attaining a growth rate of about 20 percent year on year.[11]

The second notable fact is that services have been an important source of employment generation in a country beset by problems emanating from a rigid labor law regime. At present, services account for about 26 percent of total organized sector employment in the country, while contributing a little over 55 percent to the national GDP, which has led to concerns about jobless growth in this high-growth sector. But a sectoral disaggregation of the employed work force shows that four services categories (excluding construction) contributed 16.8 million to new employment, or 23.4 percent to the total incremental employment generated in the five-year period between 1999-2000 and 2004-2005 (gross incremental employment in the period was around 60.82 million). Despite the low overall elasticity of employment in India (at just 0.48), the latest NSSO (2004-2005, based on the 61st Round Survey) data show that employment elasticity is reasonably high (and increasing) in certain service categories, with financing, insurance, real estate and business services registering an elasticity of employment of 0.94, followed by construction sector employment elasticity at 0.88 (details in Table 1 below).

---

[10] Author's calculation from Central Statistical Organization estimates of GDP (at factor cost; 1999-2000 prices); http://mospi.nic.in/pressnote_31may07.htm.
[11] *Economic Survey*, various issues, and NASSCOM *Annual Report*, 2004-05.

Table 1: Employment statistics (disaggregated)

	Sectoral Share (%) 1999-2000	Sectoral Share (%) 2004-05	Elasticity
Agriculture, forestry & fishing	59.8	58.4	1.52
Mining & quarrying	0.6	0.6	0.82
Manufacturing	12.1	11.7	0.34
Electricity, gas and water supply	0.3	0.3	0.33
Construction	4.4	5.6	0.88
Trade, hotels & restaurants	9.4	10.3	0.59
Transport, storage & communications	3.7	3.8	0.27
Financing, insurance, real estate and business services	1.3	1.5	0.94
Community, social and personal services	8.4	7.8	0.28
Total	100	100	0.48

Source: Rangarajan et al., 2007; data from NSSO 2004-2005, based on 61st Round Survey.

Drawing ready inferences from the official data may be misleading because it is believed that a significant portion of the Indian population currently accounted for under agriculture/rural employment is working in unorganized service sectors in both rural and urban areas,[12] in particular in trade, hotels and transport (which added 10 million incremental organized sector workforce in 1999-2000 and 2004-2005); business services; and the informal community, social and personal services sector (which added 2.47 million incremental organized workforce in the five years), but the employment share of this last sector is declining in the formal sector, as indicated in Table 1 above. The official Economic Census for 2005 indicated that of an estimated 100.9 million people employed in 41.8 million establishments (25.54 million in rural and 16.29 million in urban areas) in India, the manufacturing sector employed 25.5 million and farming 9.2 million; the remaining are employed in the services sector, of which retail services accounted for 25.1 million employed.

Alongside tourism, ITeS is a mega-employer in India and a source of well paying white-collar jobs for the country's multitude of skilled graduates. The recent spurt in net employment in the ITeS, or Business Process Outsourcing (BPO), sectors has seen employment of almost 100,000-150,000 employees every year

---

[12] Assessment based on information on the employment-generation potential of unorganized service sectors. At a recent ICRIER conference on *Productivity Growth in a Globalizing Economy: Implications for Business and Policy*, India's chief statistician Dr. Pronab Sen said, "The NSSO data suggests that almost 50 percent of the income in rural areas is coming from non-agriculture sources." But because of inefficiencies in the data collection mechanism, this does not show up on official statistics.

for the past several years. Figure 1 below highlights the rapid employment growth in India's IT and ITeS/BPO sectors where the employed workforce is projected to reach 2.3 million by 2010. According to NASSCOM estimates, the number of total knowledge professionals employed in the Indian IT-BPO sector increased from 284,000 in 1999-2000 to nearly 2 million in 2007-2008.

Contrary to popular perception, India's IT sector is no longer largely export oriented. The domestically focused segment saw employment rise at a healthy 223 percent from the 2000 levels, and under the present global economic conditions this share is likely to rise significantly in the near future. Several Indian manufacturing and service companies have started outsourcing the non-core activities, in particular the IT, HR, accounting and financial services, resulting in a high growth of demand in ICT and ICT-using services (details in Table 2).

Table 2: Knowledge Professionals Employed in the Indian IT-BPO Sector (in thousands)

	1999-00	2000-01	2001-02	2002-03	2003-04	2004-05	2005-06	2006-07	2007-08
Software (exports sector)	110	162	170	205	296	390	513	690	865
Software (domestic sector)	132	198	146	285	318	352	365	378	427
BPO	42	70	106	180	216	316	415	553	704
Total	**284**	**430**	**522**	**670**	**830**	**1058**	**1293**	**1621**	**1996**

Source: NASSCOM Strategic Review 2008.

Lastly, and most significantly, particularly from the global integration perspective, India has emerged as one of the leading exporters of commercial services in the world. Data in Table 2 above indicates that in India's best known service sectors, namely IT software and BPO, export-demand-led employment generation increased by 686 percent and 1,576 percent respectively between 2000 and 2008. India's service trade (net) inflows continue to offset to a large extent the country's growing trade deficit; in 2005-2006, India's commercial service exports constituted around 37 percent of the country's global exports (goods and services). As we will note later, this increased integration with the world economy generated not only revenues but also dynamic knowledge spillovers and productivity gains, which permeated intra-sectorally and also to the rest of the economy.

Figure 1: Rapid growth in employment in India's IT & ITeS industry

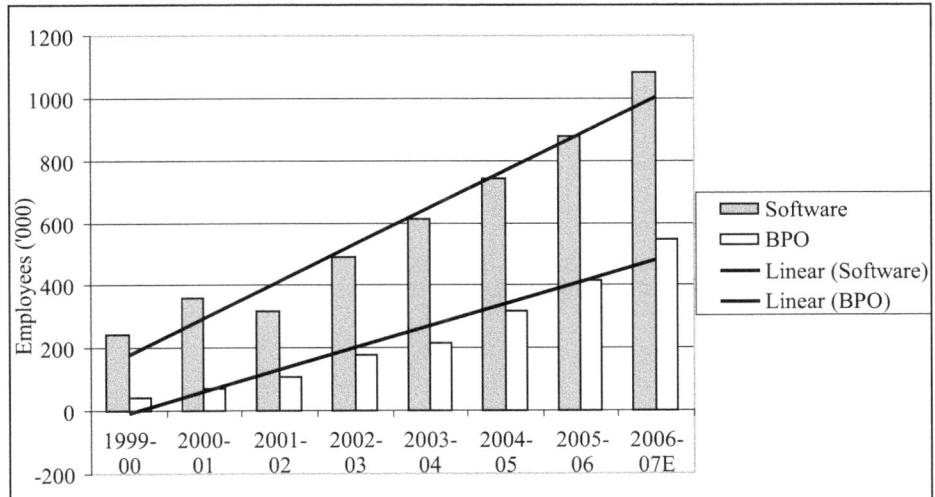

Source: Author's calculations based on data from NASSCOM 2007

India's exports of commercial services have been among the fastest growing globally in the past 15 years, and grew at over 17 percent per annum in the 1990s, with the world average at 5.6 percent. Between 2001 and 2006, India's exports of commercial services grew at over 30 percent on average, while the world average was 10 percent. In 2006, India exported US$ 73.8 billion worth of commercial services, an equivalent of 2.7 percent of global service trade (estimated at around US$ 4 trillion), and was ranked 10th in the global commercial service exporters list;[13] in 1997, the country's share in global trade was only 18 percent.

Table 3 highlights India's performance in exports of commercial services in the present decade.

---

[13] While the dynamic growth of India's commercial exports is widely reported—particularly with regard to software services (comprising computer services, IT-enabled services and business process outsourcing)—the dynamic expansion of its services imports attracts less attention even though the growth rate in 2006 exceeded that of exports. According to the most recent World Trade Organization figures, India was a net exporter of commercial services in 2006, though its commercial services imports grew by a hefty 40 percent in 2006 and were only about 5 percent short of its commercial services exports.

Table 3: Exports of commercial services

	2000	2001	2002	2003	2004	2005	2006
Global exports (US$ billion)	1,493.8	1,498.0	1,607.8	1,842.2	2,210.9	2,451.9	2,710.8
India's exports (US$ billion)	16.0	16.8	19.1	23.1	37.2	54.4	72.8
RoG (y-o-y) of India's exports (%)		4.8	13.8	20.7	61.0	46.4	33.8
India's share in world exports (%)	1.1	1.1	1.2	1.3	1.7	2.2	2.7

Source: Author's calculations based on data from *International Trade Statistics*, WTO, several issues.

Statistical analyses indicate that India continues to exhibit a strong revealed comparative advantage (RCA[14]) in services relative to goods. India's service sector competitiveness is reflected in its increasing global market share; RCA in services has been rising sharply since the mid-1990s, thus increasing the gap with the goods sector drastically in the past decade. Computation of RCA for the three categories of commercial services shows that, while in transportation and travel services, India's competitive position has been on the decline, it has been sharply rising in other commercial services (Figure 2).[15] As has already been noted, India has substantial exports in these areas, mainly on account of computer services and other business services. Between 1996 and 2000, India's RCA in business services grew a whopping 327 percent. The recent trend of increased specialization of India's exports of services in a selected set of sub-sectors within the services sector reflects the change in the composition of exports.

India's service exports have been growing at a rate two-and-a-half times faster than the services sector catering to the domestic market. As a result, India's service sector growth can be described as export-driven. India's growth in services can largely be attributed to the information technology (IT) boom, in which India has emerged as a world leader.

---

[14] Calculations based on Bela Balassa's Revealed Comparative Advantage (RCA) Index. An index value of RCA > 1 indicates competitiveness.

[15] Author's calculation based on data from the IMF Balance of Payments Statistics. Also see Karmakar (2005) Appendix Table 1 for related sector-specific details on market access and competitiveness.

Figure 2: Trends in India's services RCA

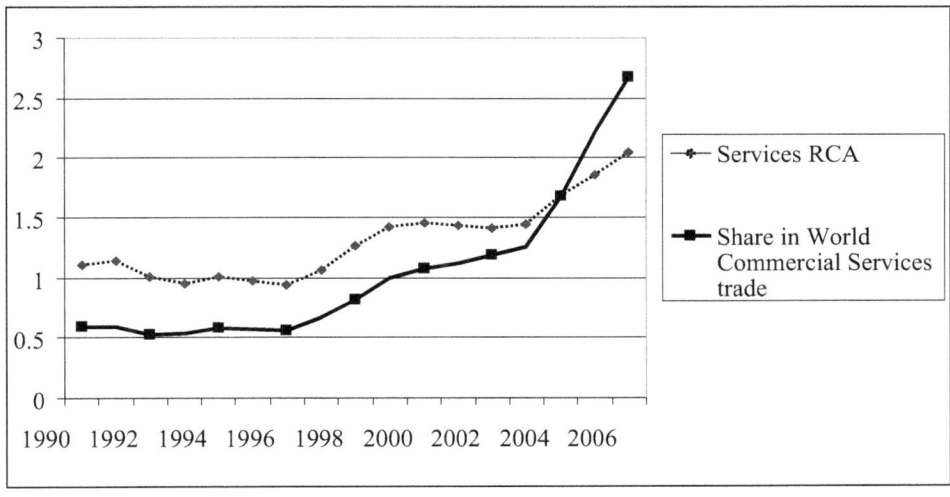

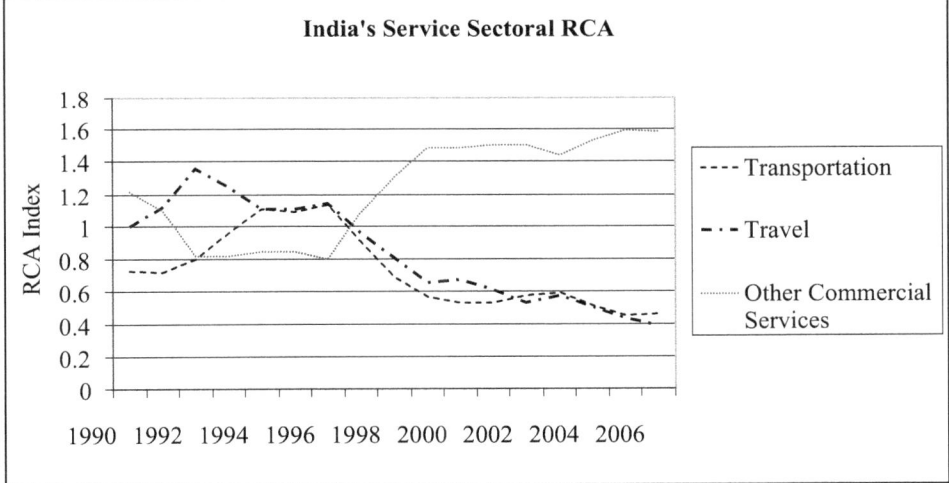

Source: Calculated from WTO International Trade and Tariff Database, Statistical Program – Time Series, accessed January 2008.

India accounted for 65 percent of the global market in offshore IT services and 46 percent of the global BPO market in 2004-2005. The World Bank estimates that, while developed countries still dominate global services trade, with a share of 80 percent between 1994 and 2003 and an annual growth rate of 50-60 percent year on year, exports of business services (essentially IT and BPO services) rose by 700 percent in India. The major segments driving India's IT and ITeS market are: customer care (call centers), finance and accounting, human resource management, payment and other administrative services, in addition to higher-end offerings such as process reengineering services and IT solutions, content development, logistics management, and legal services.

In 2006-2007, according to data from the Exim Bank of India, software and services exports grew by 33 percent to register revenues of US$ 31.4 billion; business services grew at a rate of 82.4 percent; engineering services and project exports registered revenues of US$ 4.9 billion, up 23 percent over the previous year; and financial services grew at a rate of 88.5 percent. India is also becoming a competitive destination for early-stage drug discovery, investigational new drug application (IND) and human clinical trials. India seems to be at the top of the ladder in the race for outsourcing opportunities in the global drug development and discovery market, which is growing at a rate of 13.37 percent and was expected to reach US$ 48 billion by the end of 2008. For the time being, India has a market share of 1.88 percent in this area, which leaves untapped the potential of the country's life sciences service industry.

As regards the view that the tremendous success of the Indian outsourcing industry is about to come to an end, current global economics and India's intrinsic and established competitive advantages seem to render that possibility unlikely. A recent study by Elixir Web Solutions has shown that India continues to hold an edge over China as the preferred outsourcing destination, in spite of the rising wage costs and employee crunch, because it commands global confidence to produce perfect turnaround time (TAT) for performing a task, especially receiving, completing and returning the assignment. It will take many years before other countries garner the combination of a stable legal system, language skills, track record of timely delivery, technical infrastructure and a work force capable of meeting increasing demands of judgment-based analytical skills of sophisticated customers. Interviews by Wharton analysts with executives in Silicon Valley and other high-tech centers in the US and venture capitalists evoked the answer: "Despite the difficulties, India still offers IT and engineering talent at a relative cost advantage..., so the country will retain its appeal as an offshoring destination."[16] Despite the pricing pressure and the rising rupee, over 60 percent of the world's Fortune 500 companies continue to outsource activities to India. Current global economic conditions also point to an increase in strategic outsourcing by multinational corporations (MNCs), which need to be leaner and more efficient in a slowing global regime.

The changing economics of outsourcing, along with the maturation of the industry, is making global IT sourcing a strategic imperative as opposed to merely a cost-arbitrage opportunity. And trade integration is increasingly being effected through investment and commercial presence, known as Mode 3 trade in the

---

[16] For details see India Knowledge @ Wharton (2007).

General Agreement on Trade in Services (GATS). With established competitive advantages and strength of their acquired domain knowledge over the years, Indian firms are now venturing outward and working at countering the emerging trend of nearshore outsourcing by MNCs through strategic acquisitions. A FICCI-Ernst & Young study also estimates that, in 2007 alone, Indian firms that set up shop in the US through greenfield units or via mergers and acquisitions (M&As) accounted for US$ 10.25 billion and created no less than 65,000 jobs; small and medium-sized enterprises (SMEs) alone have created over 35,000 jobs in the US in the past year. In 2006, Indian investors became a driving force in the M&A boom in Europe. In the UK in particular, India's image as one of a taker of British jobs through offshoring has changed to that of a creator of jobs. The relationship was increasingly marked by a new resonance—of Indian companies taking over British businesses and creating jobs in Britain, and British companies outsourcing low and high-end work to India to exploit India's strengths in intellectual property and low-cost economy.

Indian companies are also increasingly moving up the skills-value chain of outsourcing, in response to the increasing demands on global outsourcing providers to serve as innovation engines for corporations. Since the turn of the century, the spillovers from accumulated domain knowledge of the 1990s have been seen in the higher value and skilled offerings; Indian outsourcing providers are engaged in work across all levels of value and skill, with companies working industriously to change the product mix to ever higher proportions of high-value services.[17] To rapidly bridge the gaps in financial and administrative resources, companies are actively pursuing partnering strategies in multiple disciplines. For example, global outsourcing major Hinduja TMT forayed into the legal process outsourcing (LPO) segment by entering into a joint venture with the United Kingdom's business consultancy firm Centric and one of India's leading law firms, Fox Mandal Little. The new joint-venture company, Centric LPO, provides legal outsourcing services to multinational companies and international law firms. Reliance Life Sciences, a Reliance Group company, acquired UK-based GeneMedix Plc for 14.6 million pounds to enter the life sciences outsourcing market in Europe.

2. Dynamic Enablers—Deregulation and Reforms

This raises the following queries: (1) what were the enablers of the favorable situation that India finds itself in today, and (2) is it possible for other countries to emulate such success? As discussed above, a key feature of India's experience with trade has been the rapid growth of services exports. Over the past decade, merchandise exports have grown 145 percent but services exports have

---

[17] The revenue composition at the moment is 70 percent in low-end services and around 15 percent in high-value services: NASSCOM estimates.

grown by 275 percent. This high growth of services exports has been based on two distinct components. In the earlier period, invisibles revenues were primarily obtained through remittances from skilled Indians working outside India. In recent years, improvements in telecommunications have enabled India to be a part of global services supply chains. Export-oriented services production in India ranges from high volume production of low-end services such as basic accounting and call-center operations, all the way to services that require highly specialized and high-wage staff, like research and development. This is undertaken both through outsourcing to India-origin third party IT service providers and in the offshore units/JVs of parent MNCs. Large IT MNCs like IBM and Texas Instruments have been operating out of India since the 1980s, and have lately ramped up their capacity across their product value chain. To that extent, India's cross-border service exports consist to a large extent of insourced offshore activities of MNCs. For example, research laboratories of major US companies located in India (captive R&D units) have filed for over 1,000 patents with the US Patent and Trademark Office.

The abovementioned exponential growth in services in India—much as in most developing countries—was facilitated by a liberalized domestic policy regime and sector-specific promotional programs. Since the late 1980s, the government's focus has been on telecommunication and financial services liberalization, with the emphasis being on the introduction of market-driven reforms. It is important to note that India has moved much faster with unilateral reforms in key input-services sectors.

Reforms were undertaken in ensuring the development of a fiber-optic-based telecom network and other related telecommunications infrastructure, appropriate national educational policies (with focus on tertiary and technical education) and proper alignment of the nation's intellectual property regimes to encourage MNCs to offshore high-skill services to India. Several states also set up sectoral Export Processing Zones with special tax incentives (including tax holidays) and other infrastructure facilities to encourage companies to invest (UNCTAD, 2004; OECD, 2007). Successive national governments in India have provided a range of incentives as part of their investment promotion efforts. For example, tax exemptions under the Software Technology Park India (STPI) project helped nurture the fledgling and resource-scarce software sector in India by enabling businesses to plow back their profits, while not denying (post-establishment) National Treatment to foreign companies. Incentives also include government support with pilot facilities and other incubator functions for new service industries.

A second major area of focus in the economic reforms has been the financial sector. India has made good progress in building a sound regulatory framework for banking, insurance and securities markets. There is now a broad consensus that capital controls are ineffective when there is a large and free current account. There are simply too many opportunities for moving capital across the globe by over-invoicing, under-invoicing, transfer pricing by multinational corporations, and trade in gold. Hence India has steadily made progress on freeing up the capital account, particularly in the last five years. For foreign institutional investors, the country is 100 percent convertible. Indian firms can take up to 100 percent of their net worth out of the country. Domestic citizens can take up to US$ 25,000 out of the country, which is a lot when compared with the country's per capita income. Equity derivatives trading was launched in India in June 2000, and now has a daily turnover of US$ 4 billion. India's financial institutions are precious assets today, and will be key building blocks in the next steps of modernizing the financial sector and improving transparency and competition in the years to come.

Regulatory regimes were improved to make service sectors more competitive. The most critical regulatory reform has been in the telecommunications services. Domestic telecommunications firms have been able to grow and prosper in an almost control-free policy environment since the early 1990s, though the domestic market was opened up in phases to foreign presence as the ability and confidence of the domestic regulator to manage the market players enhanced over time.[18] In the second phase of reforms, know-how on advanced telecom infrastructure was gained by forming joint-ventures with MNC telecom firms. India today has multiple competing private sector telephone companies and internet service providers, with high-speed lines that reach into the outside world, with no large government effort at censorship or selective blocking of content. India is one of the world's first countries to shift to a "unified licensing," where the licensing is neutral to telecom technology. The effect of all of the above was that in a free competitive regime, the efficiency and productivity gains in India's telecom sector have been unprecedented. A direct effect of these reforms has been a drastic fall in the telecom costs. Today, mobile phone call and broadband connection charges in India are comparable to the rates in OECD countries. The falling tariffs of high-speed internet connections have enabled more services to be traded cross-border compared with what was possible via telephone or fax (in the health services sector, a surgeon can now consult on an operation or provide diagnostic services online) and increased the range of traders who can participate in cross-border trade (for example, by allowing greater participation of SMEs). The indirect effect of the telecom sector liberalization was that all the

---

[18] An outcome of the above policy is that India's overall teledensity reached 24.63 percent in January 2008, up from a meager 0.9 percent in 2001. Having prudential domestic regulations is a necessary precondition for developing economies to reap the benefits of liberalization.

ICT using service and manufacturing sectors increased their productivity and competitiveness.

As far as other emerging regulatory issues are concerned, IP issues stand out as critical determinants for facilitating cross-border services trade. Subsequent to the compliance with the WIPO and WTO mandated IP regimes, Indian service providers benefited from the existing liberal and planned multilateral legal regulatory regimes, and are keen to pre-empt future impediments by incorporating appropriate principles such as enactment of Consumer Protection Laws, Data Privacy Laws and Regimes for Digital Signatures and Security in accordance with the established international standards of ISO and IEC. Indian IT and BPO companies, in conjunction with their sectoral associations NASSCOM and Electronics and Computer Software Export Promotion Council (ESC), are actively promoting legislation and adoption of international standards such as ISO 18000 and ISO 24000 meant for ensuring quality of Management Systems, and the ISO/IEC 27000-family, the latest international standards for Information Security Management Systems. Even Indian pharmaceutical and biotech companies are steadfast in their commitment to the product patent regimes, transparency of financial reporting, business processes and quality management and compliance; as a result, the country has the largest number of USFDA approved plants outside the US.

There has been a powerful positive demonstration effect from the growing and dynamic services sector in India. Policymakers can see that reform and deregulation in one sector have led to growth, employment and productivity spillovers to other non-traded sectors of the economy. The employees of India's big IT-ITeS providers are enjoying higher salaries and are becoming more international in their outlook and consumer tastes. This has given rise to greater demands on the manufacturing, retail and logistics sectors to deliver and produce modern goods and services meeting international standards. A NASSCOM-CRISIL study (2006) estimates that for every job created in this sector, four jobs are being created elsewhere in the domestic economy. If this trend can be continued, employment opportunities can be expected to emerge across India's economy.

The resultant huge demand for new, qualified employees is in turn stretching India's education system, which already places huge competitive pressures on students wanting to attend the best ranked institutes and universities. The government is aware of the need for reform in education and skill development, and has instructed government institutions to facilitate training of skilled personnel in research, engineering and management disciplines. To increase the supply of high-skill technical professionals in the country, the Ministry of Human Resource Development (HRD) has allocated funds for the establishment of eight new Indian Institutes of Technology (IITs) and seven Indian Institutes of Management (IIMs), along with 30 Central "world-class universities" during the five-year period 2008-2012. The virtuous cycle of regulatory reforms and growth seems to have been firmly entrenched in the country with an understanding that the piecemeal deregulation of the 1970s and 1980s may have contributed to greater capacity utilization, but did not go far enough to improve India's international competitiveness. The present policy thrust of the government is on holistic regulatory and administrative reforms and enforcement.

Finally, the greater integration of their labor force into the global production system was an enabler and a dynamic trend in the emergence of developing countries as important offshoring destinations. While international labor movement from developing to developed countries is not new, a striking feature of the recent heightened participation of developing countries in the world has been the rising skill profile of their workers, in response to the rising demand and as a result of knowledge spillovers from expatriates. Educational levels in developing countries such as India increased significantly and meet the requirements of internationally traded newer services, and the supply of appropriately educated workers in some countries is not insubstantial. Recent studies[19] have shown that the availability of talent in some low-wage developing countries, especially India, already surpasses that in developed countries and accounts for more than twice as many university-educated young professionals who at the present moment cannot be absorbed in the domestic economy.

Businesses need specialized companies for their non-core software services, and the latter resort to global sourcing of labor given the limited availability of cost-effective specialized skills in developed countries. The developed country problems emanate not only from rising labor costs, but also slow productivity rises in services. Even the sectors which experienced rapid employment growth in OECD countries suffer from slow productivity growth. An ERM survey finds that due to the high degree of labor intensity in most service sectors, productivity growth is more difficult to achieve, especially in locally traded services. On the other hand, internationally traded services such as finance, CRS and telecommunications have experienced higher productivity growth rates. Typically, these sectors are exposed to international competition, which implies increased pressures to improve productivity. Yet, it has been found that those locally traded sectors that use internationally traded service inputs, benefit from transmitted efficiency gains. These trends provide a huge scope for demographically advantaged countries such as India to exploit their comparative advantages in labor-intensive services without displacing substantial labor in developed economies, and at the same time add to efficiency gains and reduction of costs in the latter. A further opening of markets for cross-border services, by providing the necessary boost to the global growth and productivity engine, could become a win-win situation for all.

---

[19] See reports by McKinsey Global Institute, Boston Consulting Group and Deutsche Bank.

3. Contribution of Multilateral Negotiations to Services Liberalization

It is also opportune to try to assess the role of GATS negotiations in the observed growth of services trade, and in particular on cross-border services supply. A recent analysis by the WTO Secretariat indicates that liberalization and privatization moves by WTO members in different service sectors have been "inspired by technical developments... and user dissatisfaction with prices and quality... GATS has not apparently proven a decisive factor in itself." (Adlung and Roy, 2007). Comparing the depth of commitments across different modes of service supply, the study by Adlung and Roy (2007) reveals that Mode 1 has attracted overall far fewer bindings as compared to Mode 3; among the committed sectors, Mode 1 is characterized by the highest share of non-bindings or "unbound" among the first three modes of service supply recognized by GATS. This is in spite of the actual trade occurring in a large number of sectors/sub-sectors that were earlier considered technologically impossible, as well as the dynamic spurt of the ICT sector where cross-border trade is becoming a major mode of delivery.

Even in bilateral and regional agreements on services, trade partners seem to have opted for the conservative mode when it came to making commitments, and the offers are limited to the so-called "GATS Plus" arrangement. A new study by Roy, Marchetti and Lim (2008) reviewed services commitments undertaken by 36 countries in 32 Preferential Trade Agreements (PTAs) completed since 2000; the countries involved in fact account for more than 80 percent of world services exports. Though *prima facie* the preferential commitments show great improvement, it appears that a large proportion of sector-specific commitments are under Mode 1, either "unbound" or without limitations ("none") and hence, the scope for improvements to existing commitments is low. For these 36 members, improvements to existing commitments in GATS offers seem to cover only 2 percent of sub-sectors on average, while the corresponding figure for improvements in PTAs compared to GATS offers is also low at under 4 percent. Therefore value added over GATS commitments is often limited under the PTAs.

It also emerges that developed countries other than the United States, Australia and Japan have not added significantly to the sectoral coverage contained in their GATS offers. For example, EU, Norway, Iceland, Switzerland, New Zealand and Liechtenstein are almost static. What is striking is that for these countries, the new GATS offers have also made rather insignificant additions as compared to GATS commitments. While it is true that the proportion of sub-sectors already covered in GATS is over 50 percent for all of the above mentioned countries, subsequent additions have not been significant given that wide gaps in commitments still remain. However, commitments in the PTAs in the two modes of cross-border trade have gone beyond GATS in a wide range of social sectors. With the exception of health services, where virtually no improvement has occurred under either GATS or PTAs, it is other social sectors such as education and environmental services that have seen significant additions to both existing commitments and new bindings in PTAs. In particular, in "other business services," the sector in which labor-abundant economies have a competitive advantage vis-à-vis cross-border trade potential, PTA commitments in agreements with the US show an improvement over the existing GATS commitments, but only for its trade partners. The United States, on the other hand, offers partial commitments and limited sectoral coverage, and actual policy restrictions remain the almost sole road block for full commitments (Chaudhuri and Karmakar, 2008). There is thus considerable scope for further liberalization.

It needs to be remembered that insofar as GATS follows a positive listing approach of liberalization in which members are also allowed to schedule most-favored nation (MFN) exemptions and limitations to market access, members impose several regulatory requirements on foreign service providers which at times amount to *de facto* barriers to trade. Therefore, the present liberalization experience in services, especially in developing countries such as India, has been more market-driven and unilateral rather than negotiation-driven multilateral tradeoffs. While, on the one hand, WTO members have benefited as service suppliers by liberalization of autonomous regimes in services, they continue to maintain several regulatory restrictions/requirements for market access for foreign service providers in their schedules of commitments on services in multilateral as well as preferential trade agreements.

An Open Services Regime: A New Agenda for Growth and Jobs in Europe?

So what are the lessons and way forward? However daunting politically, the key message from the above analysis seems that countries must not maintain high service sector barriers being paralyzed by the fear of job losses. Rather, a liberal and pro-competitive service regime can be a new source of growth and employment generation, as has been the experience of India. In a dynamic economy, continuous structural readjustments are but natural phenomena, and rather than resist change, countries must be open to benefit from the emergent opportunities. In the past couple of decades, India has created new skilled job opportunities specifically in those areas where government control and interventions were minimal; jobs were also created in areas not known of earlier and in informal service sectors, in response to the demands of the market economy.

Knowledge gained by employees in traded sectors helped the country move to higher-value service offerings, with spillovers into related high-skill service sectors. The gradual shift in the composition of offshore work is toward higher skilled and more sophisticated services like chip design, architecture, engineering and design, business consulting, pharmaceutical and biotechnology research, financial analysis, data mining, analytics and modeling, R&D services (such as product development and testing). Well paying jobs were also created in the non-traded service sectors of the economy (such as hospitality, retail and logistics) in response to the growth experience of the traded sectors. India's fifth Economic Census (2005) reported that during 1998-2005, retail trade alone accounted for 41.83 percent of job opportunities, with 14.95 million employed in the sector. Education, social and personal service activities claimed a share of 16.26 percent of the total employment generated. The positive role of the country's liberalized cross-border trade regime in services in this development can hardly be doubted.

The gains have not merely been in the economic sphere. The social welfare gains of the liberal services regime in the country extend to the efficiency of service provision unexpected in a developing country, which changed the contours of expectations and delivery modules even at the very lowest strata of the economy. The best example of this has been the opening up of the telecommunication service sector in India. Today, reforms and regulations in the largely open sector have enabled consumers in India to benefit from low call and broadband rates comparable to those in OECD countries, and customer service that rivals experiences in any developed country. This has not only benefited the upper echelons of society, but also brought newer economic gains and opportunities for the poorest. In contrast, the limitation of service sector competition in European countries is allowing service providers in the sector to extract monopoly charges and fees, while providing next to nothing by way of customer support to their huge base of consumers.

Even in education and other social sectors, the spillovers are evident. While in countries such as India and China service trade induced demand for skilled personnel has resulted in higher investment and innovation in educational service deliveries, OECD countries seem to be falling behind despite their initial advantageous position. The Euforia project (2004) aimed at understanding the limitations of the EU's knowledge society finds that the digital divide in EU member states is most apparent in the education sector. ICT diffusion among people in the 16-25 years age group is only about 25 percent of the whole population.

A competitive and open ICT regime could infuse more dynamism to this critical sector, as experienced in India. Even in business and professional services, a fast growing employer in the EU, greater integration with the rest of the world could generate dynamic gains from knowledge spillovers. As mentioned earlier, the ERM 2007 report concludes that the nature and extent of globalization have a limited impact on the overall restructuring and services job losses; on the other hand, resistance to openness is imposing severe productivity and competitiveness costs on both traded and non-traded services sectors in Europe. Even in the new member states, which have been benefiting from post-integration outsourcing from the EU-15, efficiency losses are mounting despite the present buoyancy in the labor market scenario, which may have deleterious consequences for their overall competitiveness and future growth prospects.

Therefore, a liberal service regime should be viewed as an opportunity to catalyze support for reforms to key service-sector infrastructures that are integral to broad-based economic and human development in the country. If a country can provide these broadly to its citizens, then the gain in productivity and employment growth, and other indicators of social and human development will far exceed revenues from exports. These broad-based gains come as a result of cheaper service inputs to all manner of productive activity, as well as to the transformation of business activities that result when resources are freed up to be used in new business endeavors throughout the economy. An open services regime seems to be the best option for sustaining growth, productivity and efficiency gains, and employment generation simultaneously with providing for consumer welfare gains. Given the dynamism of the wage-cost structure in most economies, in the absence of outsourcing or offshoring, consumers would have had to make do with less of customer support/service or pay more for automated support; companies were already increasingly using technology to replace many jobs rendered unviable within the US or the EU. Most studies are unfortunately underplaying these developed country consumer welfare gains. The 2005 Lisbon Agenda on Growth and Jobs needs to be extended to include a globally integrated service trade regime. Focusing only on investment in innovation and mobility of researchers may just fall short of the realization of the goals set by the Lisbon Agenda.

In the present weak global economic scenario, sustaining productivity advantages and international competitiveness is a necessary condition if the growth and employment prospects are to be improved and the emigration of high-skill and high-tech European services MNCs is to be reversed. The losses from factor endowment differences can be increasingly replaced by gains from intra-industry trade in services by the use of appropriate regulatory policies and reforms. The ERM report has identified that offshoring in Europe has largely concentrated in call centers, operational activities, administrative and financial operations, and back-office accounting functions. In a manpower deficient society, this helps facilitate intra-industry trade and make higher-skill activities financially viable at home. Through trade and investment, therefore, national service firms can be made more efficient and competitive, and scarce human resources released for the higher value added activities.

Rather than resisting the inevitable industrial restructuring, policymakers will be well advised to institute regulations and policies that reduce the adjustment costs of such restructuring. The first action should be to undertake structural reforms in their domestic economies and eliminate the fear of adjustments that globalization today requires of them. For this to happen, it is necessary to substantially enhance the education and skill levels of the majority of the work force in the long run, which would enable employees to benefit from international trade liberalization. In the short run, however, an expansion of the domestic safety nets to cushion the transitional costs of (trade-related) adjustment would be an appropriate policy choice. This would be more beneficial than the present policy of protecting inefficient service sectors/providers. At the multilateral negotiation platforms, countries could shed their cautious approach to cross-border supply and push for enhanced commitments along the lines of the GATS plurilateral requests on cross-border supply.

References

Adlung, R. and Roy, M. (2007). "Services Liberalization in the New Generation of Preferential Trade Agreements (PTAs). How Much Further Than the GATS?," *World Trade Review*. July.

Baliy, M. and Lawrence, R., (2005). "Don't Blame Trade for US Job Losses". *McKinsey Quarterly*. Vol. 1. January.

Chaudhuri, S. and Karmakar, S., (2008). "Cross-Border Trade in Services". In Juan A. Marchetti and Martin Roy (eds.). *Opening Markets for Trade in Services: Bilateral, Regional and Multilateral Approaches in the 21st Century*, CUP and WTO. Geneva.

Davis, I. and Stephenson, E., (2006). "Ten Trends to Watch in 2006". McKinsey Quarterly Web Exclusive. January.

Dossani, R., (2005). "Globalization and the Offshoring of Services: The Case of India". Brookings Trade Forum. pp. 241-267.

Elixir Web Solutions,(2007). "India Remains World's Favorite Outsourcing Destination". Media interaction by Elixir Partners Vipul Prakash and Jacob Samuel. Sept. 5, www.livemint.com.

European Restructuring Monitor, (2007). "European ERM Report 2007—Restructuring and Employment in the EU: The Impact of Globalization" and "Recent Restructuring Trends in the EU," reports of The European Foundation for the Improvement of Living and Working Conditions.

Government of India, *Economic Survey*, various issues.

India Brand Equity Foundation resources, (2007).
http://www.ibef.org/artdispview.aspx?in=51&art_id=17158&cat_id=116&page=3

India Knowledge @ Wharton: "Will Jobs Move Back to Silicon Valley from India? Don't Hold Your Breath...". 18 October 2007, http://www.ikw.in/

International Monetary Fund, (2007). *Country Report – India*. Washington D.C. February.

Jaumotte, F. and Tytell, I., (2007), "Globalization of Labor". *Finance & Development*. Vol. 44. No.2. June.

Jensen, B. and Kletzer, L., (2005). "Tradable Services: Understanding the Scope and Impact of Services Outsourcing". IIE Working Paper No. 05-9. Washington D.C.. September.

Joshi, S., (2004). "Tertiary Sector-Driven Growth in India—Impact on Employment and Poverty". *Economic and Political Weekly*. Special Article. India. 11 September.

Karmakar, S., (2005). "India–ASEAN Cooperation in Services—An Overview". ICRIER Working Paper 176. November.

Karnik, K. et al., (2006). "Globalization of Services: Facilitators and Barriers". background paper prepared for the Oxford University workshop on Grand Challenges in Services. May.

Kirkegaard, J.F., (2007). "Offshoring, Outsourcing, and Production Relocation—Labor-Market Effects in the OECD Countries and Developing Asia". Peterson Institute Working Paper. April, www.iie.com/publications/wp/wp07-2.pdf.

Kox, H. and Lejour, A., (2006). "Dynamic Effects of European Services Liberalization: More to Be Gained". In: *Globalization Challenges for Europe*. Secretariat of the Economic Council. Prime Minister's Office. Helsinki. Vol. 1.

Mann, C.L., (2004). "Globalization of Services: Why, How Much, and What to Do About It". IIE Publication. Washington D.C.

McKinsey Global Institute, (2005). "The Emerging Global Labor Market". June.

NASSCOM-CRISIL, (2006). "The Rising Tide – Output and Employment Linkages of IT-ITeS."

NASSCOM, (2006). "Factors and Policies Influencing the Expansion of Services Trade-Experiences of the Indian IT-BPO Sector". New Delhi. October. www.worldbank.org/INTRANETTRADE/Resources/WBI-Training/288464-1161888800183/S2b2_Singh_En.pdf .

NASSCOM. *Strategic Review 2008* and *Annual Report*. Various issues.

OECD, (2005). "Growth in Services Fostering Employment, Productivity and Innovation". Ministerial Meeting of the OECD Council.

OECD, (2007). *OECD Science, Technology and Industry: Scoreboard 2007*. OECD. Paris.

O'Mahony, M. and van Ark B. (eds.) (2003). *EU Productivity and Competitiveness: An Industry Perspective*. European Commission. Brussels.

Rangarajan, C. et al., (2007). "Revisiting Employment and Growth". ICRA Bulletin—Money & Finance. Vol. 3(2).

Robinson, S., Zhi W. and Will M., (2002). "Capturing the Implications of Services Trade Liberalization". *Economic Systems Research*. Vol. 14(1). Taylor and Francis Journals.

Ros, J., (2000). *Development Theory and the Economics of Growth*. Ann Arbor. University of Michigan Press.

Roy, M., Marchetti J. and Lim H., (2008). "The Race Towards Preferential Trade Agreements in Services: How Much Market Access is Really Achieved?". In: M. Panizzon, N. Pohl and P. Sauvé (eds.), *The Regulation of International Trade in Services*.

Stern, R., (2005). "The Places of Services in the World Economy". University of Michigan Discussion Paper No. 530. February.

UNCTAD, (2007). *World Investment Report*. Washington D.C.

World Bank, (2007). *Global Economic Prospects—Managing the Next Wave of Globalization*. Washington D.C.

WTO, (2005). *World Trade Report*. Thematic Essays C: "Offshoring Services: Recent Developments and Prospects".

WTO, (2007). *International Trade Statistics*. Washington D.C.

Chapter 4

Changes in the Competitiveness of Service Sectors in New EU Member States: The Role of Business Process Outsourcing

Magdolna Sass[1]

Abstract

With technological advancements, especially in the field of communication technology, fragmentation in services has been made possible. This has triggered a process of relocation of certain services activities to locations where they can be carried out at a lower cost and/or in better quality. Due to that process, coupled with the liberalization of services trade, especially among countries that are members of regional blocs, new countries have been increasingly appearing on the map of trade in services. The Visegrad countries, especially the Czech Republic, Hungary and Poland, have become hosts to various business services as a result of the relocation of these activities from other, higher-cost locations, especially from Western Europe. This paper makes an attempt to estimate the extent of that process, its main characteristics and its impact on the host economies, including various channels of spillovers, and impact on foreign trade in services and its balance, concentrating on developments in the three abovementioned countries.

The paper was written as part of a project entitled "Foreign Direct Investment in Central and Eastern Europe: What Kind of Competitiveness for the Visegrad Four?," and additional company interviews were made with the financial support of the Hungarian Research Fund (OTKA).

Introduction

The Czech Republic, Hungary and Poland are becoming increasingly important players as hosts of FDI in services, including services connected with the outsourcing of certain activities. In part, the increased role of these three countries is linked with the relocation of these activities from other European countries (EU15). This trend has attracted media attention in EU15 countries due to the job losses involved. However, little attention is being paid to countries on the receiving end. This paper tries to show the changing role of the three analyzed

---

[1] Senior research fellow, Institute of Economics of the Hungarian Academy of Sciences, Budapest, Hungary, email: sass@econ.core.hu, sass.magdolna@chello.hu.

countries in the services trade of the EU25, and their still limited contribution. Second, it shows the main developments in services outsourcing, and countries and locations covered by the process. Third, it shows the location advantages related to this specific type of FDI. Fourth, it lists the various channels through which these projects impact the local economy, and sets out to explain what this impact means to the three analyzed countries. This part of the paper is mainly based on the results of company interviews, because methodological and data problems revealed the importance of a bottom-up approach in trying to address questions connected with the development of business services in the analyzed countries. Fifth, some conclusions are drawn.

The research was undertaken as part of a project partly financed by the Visegrad Fund. Additional company interviews were made with the financial support of the Hungarian Research Fund, OTKA. The paper's findings are mainly based on interviews with Hungary-based companies; supplementary information is drawn from the results of interviews made as part of the abovementioned projects in the Czech Republic, Poland and Slovakia (for details, see the list of references).

Developments in services output and trade in the Czech Republic, Hungary and Poland

As we will see later, our knowledge of the development of services trade and FDI is limited by data and measurement problems. While acknowledging these limitations, we start our analysis by looking at the characteristic features of services trade and output in the Czech Republic, Hungary and Poland.

Table 1: Services trade of the selected countries and EU25, total (inside + outside EU25), million Euros

Export	2004	2005	2006
Czech Republic	7747.79	9469.36	10598.08
Hungary	8763.26	10288.41	10573.23
Poland	11316.63	13861.90	16349.50
EU25	881632.0	956963.9	1031834.0
Import			
Czech Republic	7228.38	8242.37	9378.24
Hungary	8525.27	9235.88	9282.21
Poland	10004.64	11537.66	14601.76
EU25	812095.60	876161.50	930959.50
Balance			
Czech Republic	519.41	1226.99	1219.84
Hungary	237.99	1052.53	1291.01
Poland	1311.99	2324.24	1747.74
EU25	69536.35	80802.39	100874.30

Source: Eurostat.

It is clear that the share of the analyzed countries in total inside-EU25 services trade flows is growing, and that their shares in the inside-EU services trade balance increased in the analyzed years. The analyzed countries' relative orientation toward EU25 markets is shown by the fact that their shares in inside-EU25 flows were slightly higher than for overall EU25 flows. Moreover, as Table 5 shows, the majority of their exports and imports are directed toward EU markets. It is also evident that most of their positive services trade balance is realized in their trade with EU-25 countries.

Table 2: Share of the analyzed countries in the total services trade of the EU25 (in %)

Export	2004	2005	2006
Czech Republic	0.88	0.99	1.03
Hungary	0.99	1.08	1.02
Poland	1.28	1.45	1.58
EU25	100	100	100
Import			
Czech Republic	0.89	0.94	1.01
Hungary	1.05	1.05	1.00
Poland	1.23	1.32	1.57
EU25	100	100	100
Balance			
Czech Republic	0.75	1.52	1.21
Hungary	0.34	1.30	1.28
Poland	1.89	2.88	1.73
EU25	100	100	100

Source: Eurostat.

The relatively short period for which data are available hinders deeper analysis. However, one can see that:

- As far as the big service categories (transportation, travel and other services) are concerned, the share of "other services" grew in all three countries;
- In the "other services" group, the share of "other business services" is the highest in all the analyzed countries (in 2006: Czech Republic—18%, Hungary—27%; Poland—18%); this share grew a few percentage points between 2004 and 2006;
- Among "other services," the second largest share in 2006 was claimed by: computer services in the Czech Republic (5.3%); personal, cultural and recreational services in Hungary (8%); and construction services in Poland (6%);
- In the "other business services" category, the highest (and growing) share is claimed by: "other miscellaneous business, professional and technical

services" in the Czech Republic and Poland; and "legal, accounting, management and public relations services" in Hungary;

- Specialization indices $((X-M)/(X+M)*100)$ and RCA compared with the EU25 were calculated for all aggregation levels for the three countries. RCAs did not change and did not reveal comparative advantages for the three countries at the highest level of aggregation for "other services" (they showed CA for transport and travel for the Czech Republic and Poland, and for travel for Hungary);

- At a lower level of aggregation, among other services, an RCA was shown for the Czech Republic and Hungary in communication services; for the Czech Republic in information services; and for Hungary in "personal, cultural and recreational services," "royalties and licenses," and "other business services."

- At an even lower level of aggregation, in the "other business services" category, Hungary had an RCA in legal, accounting, management and public relations services; all three countries had an RCA vis-á-vis the EU in advertising, market research and public opinion polling; Poland had an RCA in agricultural, mining and on-site processing services; and the Czech Republic and Poland had an RCA in "other miscellaneous business, professional and technical services" in 2006 (there was basically no significant change taking place between 2004 and 2006, for which years data were available).

Table 3: Export, import and balance of services trade, million Euros (inside EU25)

Export	2004	2005	2006
Czech Republic	5511.19	6787.89	7363.26
Hungary	5649.93	6735.50	7314.71
Poland	7934.08	9720.11	12207.70
EU25	515474.18	556372.25	593170.81
Import			
Czech Republic	4445.50	5680.52	6364.77
Hungary	5369.94	6044.23	6261.48
Poland	7457.37	8678.35	10839.60
EU25	490485.24	528139.19	560201.22
Balance			
Czech Republic	1065.69	1107.38	998.49
Hungary	280.00	691.27	1053.24
Poland	476.72	1041.76	1368.11
EU25	24988.95	28233.06	32969.59

Source: Eurostat.

Table 4: Share of selected countries in total EU25 services trade, % (inside-EU25 flows)

Export	2004	2005	2006
Czech Republic	1.07	1.22	1.24
Hungary	1.10	1.21	1.23
Poland	1.54	1.75	2.06
EU25	100	100	100
Import			
Czech Republic	0.91	1.08	1.14
Hungary	1.09	1.14	1.12
Poland	1.52	1.64	1.93
EU25	100	100	100

Source: Eurostat.

Overall, these countries significantly increased their exports of certain services, mainly to other member countries of the European Union. However, their market shares remain limited.

Table 5: Share of intra-EU services trade in the total services trade of the Czech Republic, Hungary and Poland (%)

Export	2004	2005	2006
Czech Republic	71.13	71.68	69.48
Hungary	64.47	65.47	69.18
Poland	70.11	70.12	74.67
EU25	58.47	58.14	57.49
Import			
Czech Republic	61.50	68.92	67.87
Hungary	62.99	65.44	67.46
Poland	74.54	75.22	74.23
EU25	60.40	60.28	60.17
Balance			
Czech Republic	205.17	90.25	81.85
Hungary	117.65	65.68	81.58
Poland	36.34	44.82	78.28
EU25	35.94	34.94	32.68

Source: Eurostat

Services outsourcing

1. Main characteristics

Along with the outsourcing/offshoring of low- and medium-skilled production processes in manufacturing, the relocation (offshore outsourcing) of certain production processes and specific services from developed to other developed or emerging/developing countries became increasingly widespread in the 1990s. Relocation is perceived as a process in which there is either a transfer of production capacities from another country or a capacity extension in one affiliate parallel with a capacity reduction in another, or there is a capacity extension in one affiliate, while other affiliates' capacities do not change. (This definition of relocation is in line with Veugelers, 2005.) Table 6 shows the categories used in describing these processes.

Table 6: Categories used in the analysis

Location of production	Internalized	Externalized (outsourcing)
Home country	Production kept in-house at home	Outsourcing (at home)
Foreign country (offshoring)	Intra-firm (captive) offshoring	Offshore outsourcing

Source: Based on UNCTAD, 2004, p. 148

The process has been induced by technological development. As a result of technology advances, the fragmentation, division, standardization and algorithmization of services processes have been made possible, along with the evaluation of certain service process components, digitalization, and coding of information. This trend is similar to the fragmentation process in manufacturing, but on the basis of available evidence this fragmentation can go deeper in services processes. After such fragmentation, certain service processes can be separated and carried out in locations where this work can be cheaper, more efficient and better in terms of quality. As a result, certain services have become tradable internationally. Information and communication technologies have led to a situation in which services dealing with information have been made tradable. It is now possible to produce certain services in faraway locations and consume them in another faraway location at the same time.

Moreover, as a result of the development of information technology, the same type of service activities has become standardized for more than one manufacturing and/or services activities. For the same reasons, certain services have become transportable. New products have appeared that act as "mediators" (for example, CDs, software) in services trade. Moreover, the outsourcing of services has been helped by the ongoing uni-, bi- and multilateral liberalization of services trade, even if the level of liberalization of services is lower than that of manufacturing goods (UNCTAD, 2004).

At the company level, the process started in the 1990s, when, because of more intense competition, the outsourcing of non-core activities, either into one's own firm or independent firms, became the dominant trend. Technological change contributed to this process in an indirect way; it encouraged companies to reduce their costs and improve their competitiveness through outsourcing non-core business. Companies carrying out non-core activities were placed in a competitive environment, a move that was expected to help increase efficiency and reduce costs. While cost reduction was the main aim, other targets were also addressed. Other aims included an improved quality of services, timely provision of services, better risk management, access to special skills, and improved planning. The freeing of internal resources resulting from the outsourcing of non-core activities enabled companies to concentrate on their core business. This process started in the United States and gradually spread to other companies in developed and developing countries. However, not all services (non-core activities) were outsourced. As service activities became more important for the competitiveness of the company, corporate strategies determining plant locations and distribution of work between plants also changed. Parts of service activities started to be outsourced; other parts started to be concentrated in one or several plants. Services covered by the process have specific common characteristics.

They are:

1) labor intensive;

2) structured, describable with simple algorithms, and subject to standardization;

3) connected with information (for example, information processing);

4) in many cases, a certain form of telecommunication is used (for example, the internet);

5) routine work;

6) can be relatively easily measured and evaluated;

7) they are mass produced but can be provided from one location;

8) relatively low risk; the trust factor is not significant;

9) significant differences in wages (labor costs) between the home and host country for the service activity involved;

10) low costs of establishing a plant/office/location.

However, a growing number of service processes are involved in that process and the importance of certain characteristics (such as trust and wage differentials) seems to be decreasing. Table 7 lists service activities involved in the process of (offshore) outsourcing or (captive) offshoring.

It is obvious that these are very diverse activities, and the skill content of these activities varies from the least skill intensive (physical work, for example photocopying, transporting documents) to processes using the highest quality work force (for example, software development). Even in the case of the same activity, the skill content may be different depending on the real content of the activity. For example, a call center can provide basic information in one language, in multiple languages, and more comprehensive information in multiple languages.

There are various factors that envisage further growth in services outsourcing (and relocation). First of all, due to technological advances, the outsourcing of a growing number of service activities is now possible. In some cases, even the core business of companies is outsourced; in such a situation, only the head office remains, owning the brand name and coordinating various activities with a few dozen employees.

Second, a growing number of companies are joining the fray. Until recently, mainly large firms were interested in outsourcing; today many medium-sized and even small firms outsource various service activities (for example, many small companies outsource IT activities).

Table 7: Services offshoring: activities involved

IT services	IT services	Software development and implementation services, data processing and database services, IT support services, application development and maintenance, business intelligence and data warehousing, content management, e-procurement and B2B marketplaces, enterprise security, package implementation, system integration, SCM, enterprise application integration, total infrastructure outsourcing, Web services (internet content preparation, etc.), Web-hosting and application service providers (ASPs).
Business process services	Customer interaction services (Front office)	Sales support, membership management, claims, reservations for airlines and hotels, subscription renewal, customer services helpline, handling credit and billing problems, telemarketing and marketing research services.
	Back-office operations and services	Data entry and handling, data processing and database services, medical transcription, payment services, financial processing (financial information and data processing and handling), human resource processing services, payroll services, warehousing, logistics, inventory, supply chain services, ticketing, insurance claims adjudication, mortgage processing.
	Other professional and business services	Human resource services (hiring, benefit planning and payroll, etc.), finance and accounting services (including auditing, bookkeeping, taxation services, etc.), marketing services, product design and development.

Source: OECD, Information Technology Outlook, 2004, p. 90.

Third, new market players are joining the process, such as government bodies, agencies, public institutions, and nongovernmental organizations (NGOs). For example, various tax authorities from developed countries offshore-outsource certain activities (for example, data entry jobs).

Fourth, in connection with the two aforementioned processes, new countries participate in both the host and home "sides," because, as firms in emerging economies become more "international" and grow in size, they are encouraged to take part in the process. On the receiving end, as the absorbing capacity of host countries is gradually reduced (due to the rising costs and limited availability of labor with the required skills), and as new host countries build up the required physical and legal infrastructure and business environment, these latter countries can take up/over various activities. (There are even signs of a "flying geese" model among the new member states.)

Fifth, as companies (and consultants) gain more experience in this field, companies with failed attempts may try again, or companies that so far shied away, may try it, as empirical evidence shows (Gupta et al., 2006).

Sixth, (offshore) outsourcing has its dynamism; for example, it can serve new elements of the company strategy, not only cost reduction but also standardization, quality improvement, and so on.

2. Locations and countries covered by the process

The process of services outsourcing started in the United States and then spread to other English-speaking countries, first of all Britain. Countries (or rather companies) in continental Europe followed suit later; today they are in the process of catching up with the first movers. According to a Gartner forecast for 2008, in the United States, companies on average spend three times more on offshore outsourcing than their Western European counterparts, though the difference is shrinking. The dominance and first-mover advantage of the US can be traced in the fact that an overwhelming majority of companies specialized in services outsourcing have their headquarters in the US. These include EDS, IBM Global Services, GenPact, Convergys, Sitel, Sykes, and Accenture (the ownership background of this last company is not completely clear, but its North American affiliation is obvious).

On the receiving end, Ireland, India, Canada and Israel are the most important targets (UNCTAD, 2004). Ireland's market share in IT and business services may still be around 25 percent. An overwhelming majority of production is still located in developed countries, and in the relocation process developed countries are still the main targets. Thus, the market share of emerging and less developed countries, with the exception of India, is still much lower than one would think on the basis of media reports. According to a Gartner survey, in 2005, the total amount spent on services outsourcing was US$ 34 billion, of which US$ 3-3 billion went to Central and Eastern Europe, China, Southeast Asia, and Latin America.

Among less developed countries, India is traditionally the most important target, largely because it is an English-speaking country. The early start and important role of India in the process is underlined by the growing number of India-based companies, specialized in the outsourcing of services. Examples include Satyam, Tata, and Infosys. Besides India, "emerging" Asian economies such as China, Malaysia and Singapore are important relocation targets. Few data are available, but it is obvious that two-thirds of those employed in a foreign country in financial/banking outsourcing work in India (Mártonffy, 2007).

In Europe, traditionally, Ireland is the most important host country, but other "old" EU member countries also have a relatively high market share. These primarily include Great Britain, Portugal and Spain. Another characteristic feature of European processes is that, in many cases, local affiliates of US companies "move" production capacities in services outsourcing and relocations (see, for example, cases described in Hunya, Sass (2006), such as EDS and GE). European-owned companies move slower, and opt for services outsourcing more reluctantly.

In all, an overwhelming majority of services offshore outsourcing is realized between developed countries, though emerging economies, especially India, are becoming important players.

3. The Czech Republic, Hungary and Poland as host countries

A growing number of countries are joining in the services outsourcing process. As wages grow in traditional host countries, and as suitable labor becomes less available, and as other potential host countries develop their related infrastructure and business environment, new countries are being put on the map of services outsourcing.

The role of the new member states of the European Union is becoming more important. However, their market shares are still small, and even their role in relocations is limited. Because of methodological problems, it is not easy to prove this statement, but the following information can provide some insight. In Europe, there are 1,400-1,500 service centers, of which 150-180 can be found in Eastern and Central Europe, mainly in the Czech Republic, Hungary and Poland. It is important to note that the majority of the biggest projects goes to India, even from Europe. According to data by UNCTAD (2004), one-third of the services outsourcing projects of European multinational companies went to India; Western European countries (Ireland, Portugal, Spain and Britain) had a 29 percent share; and 22 percent of the projects went to Central and Eastern Europe, mainly to Hungary, Poland and Romania. Since then, the Czech Republic has caught up with the other two countries. Because larger projects go to India, this country' share can be close to 50 percent. According to McKinsey & Company (2006), the share of the Eastern and Central European region in global business services was a mere 1 percent. This means that the region is behind the leading Asian countries, but the belated start of European companies provides great growth potential in this respect. This is illustrated by the fact that, according to Deloitte (2007), one big multinational company employs three shared service centers on average, while 71 percent of the big European multinational companies own only one of them. According to a survey conducted by IBM and Oxford Intelligence (2004), Eastern and Central Europe, besides Ireland, is the location of pan-European service centers, which means companies in continental Europe are supplied from there. Moreover, as Table 8 will show later, it is apparent from the list of bigger projects in Hungary how US- and UK-based companies dominate the list of investors. Altogether, the role of Eastern and Central Europe is growing, though it is not as big as one could expect on the basis of information reported by the media. First of all, service centers servicing Europe are relocated and concentrated in the region, mainly by non-European (chiefly US-based) multinational companies.

In the analyzed countries, about 40-50 such projects per country have been carried out so far, including captive service centers. As far as the specialization of the analyzed countries is concerned, while Poland and Hungary have a wide range of activities, in the case of the Czech Republic specialization in IT-related activities can be found.

4. How to measure the process? Methodological problems

It is not easy to measure the real extent of the process and the change in the global composition and distribution of service activities. It is also not easy to determine how individual countries are involved in the process.

The first problem is caused by the need to define the services sector. Traditionally, the service sector was defined as output produced by human work, which is "destroyed" once that output is produced; this output is intangible and cannot be stored, and requires the physical proximity of the seller/provider and the buyer. However, these characteristics are becoming less valid, at least for certain service activities. Those activities for which these characteristics are ceasing to be valid are mainly those that are affected by outsourcing (and relocation). This calls the attention to the fact how different the activities which belong to the services sector are. Moreover, it is not easy, at the given level of aggregation, to determine which activities are involved.

Further problems are posed by the following factors:

1. (Relative) FDI data cannot be used to measure the extent of the process because the data are not detailed enough and the costs of setting up a related center (and so the volume of FDI) are negligible. These costs basically include the renting of business space, recruiting and training employees and buying the required equipment (mainly computers and office supplies).

2. Because of the different activities, labor requirements and size of outsourced service centers, the number of projects is not a reliable measure. Moreover, on the basis of company case studies, it is obvious that in offshore outsourcing or relocation, the same activity is carried out with a smaller number of employees in most other cases (Hunya, Sass, 2006). At the same time, detailed data on em-

ployees would give a good proxy, though these are not available in most of the cases.

3. Offshore outsourcing carried out in captive ways or by independent providers may be present in the same company, which makes measurement and comparisons problematic.

4. Categories used in data presentation, e.g. NACE, do not offer sufficiently detailed information on these activities; in many cases, the high level of aggregation hinders the analysis. For example, real estate, rental and business services are aggregated in one number.

5. Data on service exports would give a good proxy, but even for these there is a lack of detail, though Eurostat data enable international comparisons at a more detailed level. However, transfer prices distort the data in the same way as in manufacturing. Moreover, service export lines in the balance of payments are those that in many cases help companies repatriate their profits (for example, in the form of management fees or payment for cultural services), so even these data are unreliable regarding the real extent of services trade.

6. There are signs that some of these activities are recorded as manufacturing activities in terms of value added or jobs (Szalavetz, 2006).

It is also problematic to determine the share of relocations in services outsourcing; this can only be done on a case-by-case basis (for more details, see Hunya, Sass, 2006). "Customary" indicators such as FDI provide no information about that, and company interviews show that, even within one project, relocation and non-relocation elements can be mixed to a much greater extent than in manufacturing.

Location advantages from the point of view of services outsourcing

Location advantages determine which countries are chosen as hosts to new or relocated service centers. Location advantages for this kind of activities are similar to those of efficiency-oriented investments. They include the availability, at a lower cost, of factors of production that are used intensively in the production of the service involved. The key factor is skilled labor, coupled with knowledge of certain languages, though the skill requirement of the activities varies considerably. Because the products need to be transported to the place where they are consumed, quality telecommunication infrastructure (broadband) is an important location factor. In order to ensure smooth functioning of a service center, certain other services (including financial and other business services) must be available. Moreover, an enabling legal and regulatory environment with effective enforcement is important, and, in some cases, protection of intellectual property is indispensable. The availability of office space at competitive prices is also important. Geographical proximity is an advantage in some cases, together with the coincidence of time zones with the market served—though for certain activities a different time zone is required, which is an advantage for India.

The Czech Republic, Hungary and Poland have relative factor price advantages compared with more developed countries. They also have a "knowledge advantage" compared with other lower priced countries in terms of knowledge of "smaller" languages. They all have geographical proximity to Western European markets. In some cases, their relative proximity to South European, African and Middle East markets also matters. The necessary infrastructure is available in relatively good quality and at reasonable prices, as well as office space. The regulatory environment is fine; some elements are outstandingly good. EU membership can provide a good "trust" basis, which can be backed by the fact that, with the advent of their EU membership, Bulgaria, and especially Romania, started to attract this kind of projects in great numbers.

Among the countries analyzed in this paper, Poland stands out in size, which is reflected by the fact that the average size of projects in Poland seems to be bigger than in the other two countries. Geographical proximity puts the Czech Republic in an advantageous position, due to its central location in the region—though for some other projects with different geographical orientation, Hungary or Poland have this advantage. Moreover, the Czech Republic has been chosen in some cases for its best flight connections in the region.

Other factors play a determining role when choosing among the three countries. According to company interviews, these are the following:

- Earlier presence of the company in one of the three countries;
- Previous good (or bad) experience with the country;
- Choice is influenced by the relative dynamism and success of affiliates in the three countries;
- Special language requirements (For example, Hungary has an advantage because members of Hungarian minorities from neighboring countries taking up work in these centers speak at least two "small and exotic" languages; this factor can play a part in the other two countries as well);
- Active lobbying of the local affiliate;
- Quality of life, culture, English schooling etc. in the target city, especially in cases when expatriates are involved.

As far as the impact of investment incentives is concerned, company interviews show that it plays a minor role. Of 14 companies interviewed, only three received any type of financial or fiscal incentives. However, in all three countries, attracting regional headquarters and service centers is one of the most important targets of investment agencies. Incentives offered to this type of projects are relatively generous, though their generosity does not differ to a great extent among the countries in the region. Moreover, projects deemed to have strategic importance can receive additional "tailor-made" support from the government.

Table 8: Service centers receiving financial incentives in Hungary

Company	Home country	Location in Hungary	Number of jobs (actual or planned)
ExxonMobil	USA	Budapest	1200
IBM ISSC	USA	Budapest	1300
Diageo	United Kingdom	Budapest	600
Getronics	Netherlands	Budapest	510
Jabil	USA	Szombathely	719
SAP	Germany	Budapest	600
Tata	India	Budapest	450
Convergys	USA	Budapest	282
EDS	USA	Budapest, Szeged	1150
InBev	Belgium	Budapest	380
Budapest Bank	USA	Békéscsaba	530
Morgan Stanley	United Kingdom	Budapest	450
Citigroup	USA	Budapest	302
Vodafone	United Kingdom	Budapest	746
British Telecom	United Kingdom	Budapest, Debrecen	700
T-Systems	Germany	Budapest, Debrecen	1750

Source: ITDH.

There is information on the overall financial support granted to this type of projects in Hungary. The 16 companies in Table 8 received 9 billion HUF (around 35 million Euros) in financial support from the Hungarian government, which equals approximately 700,000 HUF (around 2,750 Euros) worth of support per job created (11,669 jobs). Other similar centers (their number can be between 25 and 35 and their average size is smaller than of those in the table) did not receive any financial support, though some of them were helped by the Hungarian investment agency through providing information or mediating between the company and the local municipality. Altogether, including captive centers, there can be more than 20,000 employees in Hungary working for such centers.

Impact on the host country

The (offshore) outsourcing of services activities offers advantages to both home and host countries. From the point of view of the host country, it has, for example, a job creation effect, which in many cases is based on employing skilled people; it may generate exports, improve company competitiveness by providing access to good quality services, and offer an opportunity to outsource certain services while focusing on core business.

From the point of view of the home country, the most important benefit can be an improvement in the competitiveness of the companies involved, and the opportunity provided by offshore outsourcing that freed resources may be used in more complex and more profitable activities requiring higher levels of skills. A cost reduction is obtained through reducing personnel costs, while concentrating certain activities in one location provides economies of scale as a benefit. However, temporary or permanent white-collar job losses are associated with services outsourcing. Because of this, the impact of offshore outsourcing of services has been widely researched and discussed in developed countries, while the impact on host countries has attracted far less attention.

On the basis of company interviews, the following main categories of impacts on host countries can be distinguished.

1. Job creation

Service center and regional headquarters projects have created a large number of medium- to high-skilled jobs in the analyzed countries. An overwhelming majority of the jobs is for white-collar workers (there was only one company among those interviewed in Hungary where a dozen or so blue-collar jobs were involved among the total number of 2,000 jobs created). The average age of employees is relatively low; there are many for whom this is the first job after graduation, which means that these projects have contributed to a reduction of unemployment among fresh graduates. Between 80 and 90 percent of employees have a university diploma, and most of them speak more than one foreign language. There is a gender aspect at the lower level of aggregation of services activities carried out in these centers: while engineers, software engineers and other IT-related employees are usually men, human resources managers and accountants are mainly women. The picture is more mixed for call center workers, though these are mostly women as well. Due to the strenuousness of certain jobs, coupled with the high demand for and relatively low supply of workers, a high attrition rate (employee turnover) characterizes the sector.

By now, in all three countries, companies in the sector face a shortage of properly trained employees. In one of the interviewed Hungarian companies, there are 200 vacancies among 2,000 positions. In Hungary and partly in the Czech Republic, this can be the reason why this kind of projects started to spread to the countryside. In Poland, the geographic distribution of these projects seems to be more equal than in the other two countries, where they are concentrated in the capital cities. In Hungary, especially university towns close to the border have recently attracted some important projects. In these locations, people with "small" languages from the other side of the border can be employed as an additional advantage. The abovementioned company with 200 vacancies now has a presence in 20 cities in Hungary.

2. Linkages and other local contacts

Companies' integration into the local economy depends on factors such as the type of activity, mode of entry (mainly greenfield, in some cases capacity extension), and demand for services offered.

Backward linkages are limited for companies operating in the sector. Local sourcing is confined to buying various services from local companies, such as cleaning, security services, catering, and certain training services; and to using local infrastructure, including telecommunications, electricity, and financial services (the two Hungarian companies that supplied information about the extent of local sourcing indicated a level of below 1 percent). There are only a few cases in which the core business of these companies is outsourced to local companies; one reason can be a temporary lack of capacity, another reason—one that may result in a more lasting relationship with a local company—is that mainly lower value added activities are outsourced to local companies. An alternative to this last practice is to relocate these activities to lower-wage neighboring countries.

As far as forward linkages are concerned, selling services to local companies is also at a relatively low level. Export intensity in terms of the ratio of export sales to local sales is close to 100 percent in most cases. In the case of captive centers, this is understandable: all services are exported except when the local affiliate is served, though the share of the latter is minimal in the two Hungarian captive cases. One Hungary-based company has a relatively low export/sales ratio, at 60%. In this case, one reason for the relatively high share of local sales may be the long history of that firm in the Hungarian market, which resulted in long-term contracts with big local companies in the 1990s, including privatized Hungarian companies and local affiliates of GE, Coca Cola, Thyssen-Krupp, ABN-AMRO, and Sony. The other two non-captive cases have almost 100 percent export/sales ratios.

Companies interviewed in the other two analyzed countries (Capik, 2008 and Trnik, 2008) also have a low level of local contacts, both on the backward and forward sides.

Thus the contribution of backward and forward linkages to the competitiveness of local companies is rather limited in these cases.

3. Impact on the business environment and infrastructure

Competition for employees is one of the main factors determining local activities and links among companies in the sector. Except for the captive cases, Hungarian companies interviewed as part of the project were all active participants in local business life, with membership and active participation in various local organizations (AmCham, Hungarian Chamber of Commerce, Hungarian Outsourcing Association). This was largely motivated by the fact that, as more companies appeared in Hungary in this sector, the availability of qualified employees became limited—and, in connection with that, wages started to move upward. One company actively lobbied for including certain jobs in an agreement with Romania and Bulgaria on the free flow of workers.

This problem encourages companies to establish ties with local universities and other education institutions. Companies approach students for temporary jobs and offer them jobs after graduation. One of the companies in Poland has even started a special training program for students. In Hungary, more "substantial" relationships, in terms of research and development cooperation between companies and universities, have been established whereby companies finance various university projects (four of five interviewed companies). The presence and problems of these companies highlighted the issue of missing educational categories, as a result of which, secondary-level training for future call-center employees were introduced in seven secondary schools in Hungary.

The analyzed companies use various measures to keep their employees. In addition to relatively high wages, other benefits, such as free meals and healthcare insurance, are given to employees, and social events and various training programs are organized for personal development and skill improvement.

Through their intense demand for local infrastructure and other services, these companies have contributed to an increased level of services offered. This primarily applies to telecommunications infrastructure and services in Hungary.

4. Spillovers through trained employees

One of the most important channels of local spillovers is through trained workers. These either go to work for local companies, or set up their own companies (or go to work in another local affiliate in the sector, due to the nascent shortage of adequately trained employees). In these cases, it is not only the special knowledge that is transferred to local companies, but also a kind of business culture and work ethic. This channel may contribute to raising the productivity of local companies.

This trend was especially important in one software engineering company in Hungary, where training is relatively long (between 1 and 2 years), and some former employees have set up their own small enterprise and carry out similar activities after having gained a foothold in the local market.

5. Balance-of-payment impacts: FDI, profit repatriation, services trade balance

As was already mentioned, these data are quite unreliable, though it is obvious that the activities in question impact the balance of payments. In Hungary, about 10 percent of total FDI arrived to business services.

No separate data are available on profit repatriation for these projects. Their overall contribution to the services trade balance can be evaluated as positive. Company-level data on export/sales ratios indicate a positive contribution in all cases.

6. Potential footlooseness

There are certain factors for and against the footlooseness of this type of projects. On one hand, low sunk costs when closing down a center, connected to low invested amounts (rented office space, buying office supplies and computer, recruitment and training of workers) and low integration and embeddedness in most of the cases into the local economy would increase the possibility of leaving a location that became too expensive. On the other hand, the "trust" factor in many activities and the fact that contracts are concluded for longer periods (5 to 10 years) reduce the mobility of the projects in the medium run. For captive centers, it is also easier to finance (cross-finance) losses from other activities, which makes them less sensitive to shorter-term changes in costs, and thus they can be considered as less footloose. Another factor that acts against footlooseness is that the majority of the interviewed companies deliberately replace their expatriates with local managers after a short period of time (1 to 2 years), and though the decision-making capacity and independence of the local management is limited, (basically no strategic decisions are made there), the local management's interests are clearly for keeping the activity in its current site.

The local history of the interviewed companies is relatively short (most of the companies were established after 2005, or there was a significant capacity extension after that date), so it is not easy to determine the level of their footlooseness. Among the Hungarian companies, there is one (non-captive) center in the case of which a special type of relocation is effectuated. With the EU membership of Romania, Hungarian capacities are not being extended any more, but new plants have been established in Cluj (Kolozsvár in Hungarian, part of Hungary before World War I) and Bucharest, and new activities are being concentrated in these new sites, though no transfer of existing activities from Hungary to Romania is taking place. It is expected though that with increasing wages in Hungary, some of the most labor-intensive activities will be transferred to Romania as well. All the other analyzed companies are at a stage of capacity extension, either through embracing new activities, or through hiring more employees for carrying out existing activities.

Footlooseness affects developments in the sector from another point of view: through relocations from other (more developed) countries. In the five Hungarian cases, one was a clear-cut relocation, mainly from Germany and the Netherlands. The two captive cases connected to manufacturing MNCs, involved relocation of existing activities through concentrating certain service activities in a newly opened Hungarian service center from various European affiliates. In one of the companies, three other European shared service centers were closed down and activities were transferred to Hungary. Thus, in these two cases, multiple locations in Europe were affected (basically all locations where these companies are present). Both companies are headquartered outside Europe. The service activities involved are finance, back-office and administration in one case, and accounting, finance and human resources management in the other case.

Conclusions

The Czech Republic, Hungary and Poland are increasingly involved in services process outsourcing as host countries. However, their share in the services trade of the European Union is still minimal though growing. These countries have clear-cut location advantages for attracting this type of projects. However, apart from the middle- to high-skilled job creation impact, these companies have limited contacts with the local economy.

References

Amiti, M., Wei S.-J., (2005). "Services Offshoring, Productivity and Employment: Evidence from the United States". *IMF Working Paper*. WP/05/238.

Banga, R., (2005). "Foreign Direct Investment in Services: Implications for Developing Countries". *Asia-Pacific Trade and Investment Review*. Vol. 1. No. 2. November, pp. 55-72.

Capik, P., (2008). *Outsourcing and Offshoring: New Trends in Service Sector Foreign Direct Investments in Poland*. Presentation at the project meeting "Foreign Direct Investment in Central and Eastern Europe: What Kind of Competitiveness for the Visegrad Four?". Hatfield. 8-10 February.

Craig, D. and Willmott, P., (2005). "Outsourcing Grows up". *The McKinsey Quarterly*. February.

Farrell, D., Rosenfeld J., (2005). *US Offshoring: Rethinking the Response*, McKinsey and Company.

Fifekova, M., (2008). *The Case of Slovakia*. Presentation at the project meeting "Foreign Direct Investment in Central and Eastern Europe: What Kind of Competitiveness for the Visegrad Four?". Hatfield, 8-10 February.

Futó P., (2005). *Az IKT technológiák által lehetővé tett outsourcing és offshoring tevékenységekMagyarországon* (Outsourcing and offshoring activities in Hungary enabled by ICT). Arios. Budapest. April.

Gagliardi, F., (2008). *The Outsourcing Decisions of a Global TNC: Case Study*. Presentation at the project meeting "Foreign Direct Investment in Central and Eastern Europe: What Kind of Competitiveness for the Visegrad Four?". Hatfield, 8-10 February.

Gupta, S., Puranam, P. and Srikanth, K., (2006). *Services Sourcing in the Banking and Financial Services Industries*. Capco. London Business School.

Gupta, S., (2006). *Financial Services Factory*. Capco. manuscript.

Hamar, J., (2005). "Üzleti szolgáltatások Magyarországon" (Business services in Hungary). *Közgazdasági Szemle*. LII. Évf. November, pp. 881.-904.

Kirkegaard, J.F., (2005). "Outsourcing and Offshoring: Pushing the European Model Over the Hill, Rather Than Off the Cliff!". *Working Paper* WP05-1, Institute for International Studies. Washington.

Hollinshead, G.., (2008). *Offshoring in the Financial Sector*. Presentation at the project meeting "Foreign Direct Investment in Central and Eastern Europe: What Kind of Competitiveness for the Visegrad Four?." Hatfield. 8-10 February.

Hunya, G.. and Sass M., (2005). "Coming and Going: Gains and Losses from Relocations Affecting Hungary", *WIIW Research Reports*. Wien.

Knowledge Wharton, (2004). *Offshoring Services: Which Are the World's Top Locations – and Why?* http://knowledge.wharton.upenn.edu/article.cfm?articleid=922

Mártonffy, A., (2007). "Pénzügyi offshoring" (Financial offshoring), *IT-Business*, 2007. augusztus 22., 26.o.

Sachwald, F., (2004). "The Impact of EU Enlargement on Firms' Strategies and the Location of Production in Europe". Tokyo Club Research Meeting, November.

Sass M., (2008). *Szolgáltatások relokációja – európai folyamatok* (Relocation of Services – European Developments). Európai Tükör.

Sass M., (2008). *Case Studies – Hungary*. Presentation at the project meeting "Foreign Direct Investment in Central and Eastern Europe: What Kind of Competitiveness for the Visegrad Four?". Hatfield. 8-10 February.

Schöller, D., (2007). "Service Offshoring and the Demand for Less-Skilled Labor: Evidence from Germany". *Hohenheimer Diskussionsbeitrage*. No. 287/2007. Universitat Hohenheim.

Szalavetz, A., (2006). "A piaci szolgáltatások és a gazdasági fejlődés" (Market services and economic development). Külgazdaság. L. évfolyam. 2006./1.

Trnik, M., (2008). *Services FDI in the Czech Republic*. Presentation at the project meeting "Foreign Direct Investment in Central and Eastern Europe: What Kind of Competitiveness for the Visegrad Four?". Hatfield. 8-10 February.

UNCTAD, (2004), *World Investment Report, 2004, The Shift Towards Services*. United Nations. Geneva.

UNCTC, (1989), *Foreign Direct Investment and Transnational Corporations in Services*. United Nations, New York..

Veugelers, H., (2005). *Delocalisation: A Challenge for the EU Economy?*. Paper presentation at a conference organized by IFRI and ECOSOC. Brussels, June 17.

Chapter 5

Investment Attractiveness of the Service Sector in Poland

Marzenna Anna Weresa[1]

Introduction

The aim of this chapter is to analyze foreign direct investment (FDI) flows and stocks in Poland located in the service sector. In this analysis we assume that the value of FDI flows and its growth rate reflects the country's attractiveness to foreign investment.

From a theoretical standpoint, FDI is a specific form of international capital movements. It is investment from overseas aimed at obtaining a direct influence over the productive activities of a firm. It involves either the organization of a wholly new company or the acquisition of all or part of the assets of an existing one.

The IMF and the OECD define FDI as investment, which provides the investor with an interest in a company operating in another country that ensures an effective influence over its management. For statistical purposes this is usually taken to be a shareholding of at least 10-25 percent. Aside from direct investment, foreign capital may be put into portfolio investment, that is, the acquisition of securities traded on the financial market. The subdivision into direct and portfolio investment is made chiefly because of the differences in the nature of the factors designating its level. Inflows of direct investment are determined by long-term considerations of the general economic situation in the host country and efficiency of production, while in portfolio investment the deciding factors are two elements: interest payable and rate of appreciation of the local currency.

From a theoretical point of view, FDI flows depend on various factors in both host and home countries. The most comprehensive concept explaining FDI is an eclectic approach to international production presented by John Dunning, which combines both micro and macroeconomic factors to explain FDI (Dunning, 1981).

There is no doubt that both the inflow and outflow of foreign capital are related to a country's economic performance. Therefore, a short analysis of FDI impact on

---

[1] Professor at the World Economy Research Institute, the Warsaw School of Economics, Poland, email: marzenna.weresa@sgh.waw.pl.

Poland's competitiveness will be provided as a background for considerations related to attractiveness of Poland's service sector to FDI flows.

Current trends in FDI flows in the service sector in Poland

Since the beginning of transition in Central and Eastern Europe and the opening of their economies, the inflow of foreign direct investment to this region has been continuously increasing. Integration with the EU facilitated this process. Foreign investors were attracted to Central and Eastern Europe not only because of these countries' GDP growth and growing and promising markets, but also by their anticipated membership in the European Union.

Since 1995, more than $20 billion has been invested in the region every year, while since 2004, the year of EU accession, investment has grown even more rapidly, reaching over $40 billion in 2005 and $76 billion in 2007 and $61 billion in 2008. However in 2009 it dropped to less than $20 billion as a result of global financial crisis (Table 1).

The inflow of FDI to Poland has been fluctuating in 2000-2009. In 2007 it amounted to $23.5 billion, which constituted nearly one third of the total inflow to the EU10. With this figure, Poland topped the list among EU10 countries[2] (Table 1). The current international financial crisis has had an impact on FDI flows: the inflow of foreign investment to Poland in 2008-2009 was much lower than in previous years, amounting to $14.7 billion in 2008, and $11.4 billion in 2009. While Poland experienced a sharp decrease in FDI inflows as a result of the global crisis, some other EU10 countries did not. Slovenia and Romania absorbed slightly higher amounts of foreign investment in 2008 compared with 2007, but this trend was not continued in 2009. Nevertheless, Poland maintained its leading role in the region in terms of investment attractiveness (Table 1).

Most of the FDI inflows into Poland come from EU countries. In 2008, capital from the EU constituted about 91% of the total inflow. Germany was the largest investor in 2008: German FDI constituted 16.2% of the total inflow into Poland. The Netherlands was second with 16.1%, and Luxembourg was third with 13.4%. Major non-EU investors in 2008 were Iceland (4.4%) and the United States. A disinvestment process (i.e. negative FDI inflow into Poland) was observed in 2008 in the case of many countries including South Korea, the Czech Republic, Lithuania, and Hong Kong (NBP, 2010, p. 18).

---

[2] The EU10 are the former communist countries that joined the European Union in 2004 (Poland, the Czech Republic, Slovakia, Hungary, Slovenia, Estonia, Latvia and Lithuania) and in 2007 (Bulgaria and Romania).

Table 1: FDI inflows into Poland and the EU10 in 2000-2009 ($ million)

Country	2000	2004	2005	2007	2008	2009
Poland	9343	12873	7724	23561	14689	11395
Czech Republic	4986	4974	10991	10444	6451	2725
Slovakia	1925	1261	1908	3581	3411	-50
Hungary	2764	4654	6699	7532	6088	-5575
Lithuania	379	773	1009	2015	1823	348
Latvia	413	699	632	2322	1261	72
Estonia	387	1049	2853	2725	1726	1680
Slovenia	136	827	496	1514	1924	-67
Romania	1037	6517	6388	9921	13909	6329
Bulgaria	1002	3443	2223	12388	9795	4467
Total inflow to EU10	22372	37070	40923	76003	61077	19812

Source: Author's elaboration based on UNCTAD, 2003, 2008, 2009 and 2010.

Poland is seen as an attractive country for FDI inflows. Its share in the total FDI inflow in into the EU10 has been relatively high. In 2008 it amounted to 24% (Figure 1).

Figure 1: The FDI inflow into Poland as a percentage of the total inflow to the EU10 in 2008

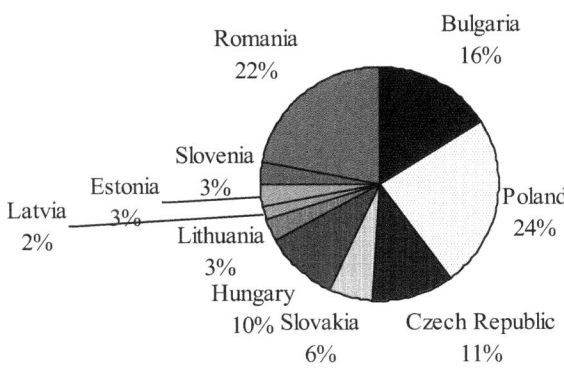

Source: Author's estimates based on UNCTAD data, 2009, p. 247.

Table 2: FDI inflow into service sector in Poland: years 2004, 2007 and 2008 compared (in million EUR and %)

Code	Branches of the service sector	2004		2007		2008	
		Million EUR	%	Million EUR	%	Million EUR	%
5095	**Total services**	5692.4	55.2	9597.7	57.9	6626.3	66.5
5295	**Trade and repairs**	1350.6	13.1	2158.0	13.0	1455.4	14.6
5500	**Hotels and restaurants**	-12.0	-0.1	108.2	0.7	-24.1	-0.2
6495	**Transport & communication,** of which:	1761.5	17.1	611.9	3.7	-500.7	-5.0
6000	Land transport	-488.3	-4.7	-15.1	-0.1	-70.2	-0.7
6110	Sea & coastal water transport	2.5	0.0	0.7	0.0	-41.6	-0.4
6200	Air transport	47.0	0.5	76.5	0.5	-168.5	-1.7
6420	Telecommunications	2126.1	20.6	485.9	2.9	-290.1	-2.9
6895	**Financial intermediation,** of which	1811.9	17.6	2495.0	15.0	3012.5	30.2
6510	Monetary intermediations	1062.4	10.3	1285.0	7.7	1598.3	16.0
6520	Other financial intermediations	241.4	2.3	546.4	3.3	644.5	6.5
6730	Insurance & activities auxiliary	449.4	4.4	398.8	2.4	648.2	6.5
7395	**Real estate & business act.,** of which:	923.3	9.0	4089.1	24.7	2605.2	26.1
7000	Real estate	672.3	6.5	1603.3	9.7	841.1	8.4
7200	Computer activities	-33.8	-0.3	-8.4	-0.1	115.0	1.2
7300	Research & development	-3.8	0.0	3.1	0.0	9.6	0.1
7400	Other business activities of which:	187.6	1.8	2406.3	14.5	1544.6	15.5
7410	- Business and management consultancy	124.2	1.2	2187.0	13.2	1464.6	14.7
7440	Promotion	8.9	0.1	133.5	0.8	21.1	0.2
9995	**Other services**	-142.9	-1.4	135.5	0.8	78.0	0.8
9999	**Total inflow to Poland**	10304.8	100.0	16582.1	100.0	9971.6	100.0

Source: Author's elaboration based on NBP data.

In the beginning of transition, privatization was a major source of capital inflows to Poland; privatization-related FDI peaked in 2000. In 2001-2008 an increasing number of greenfield projects began to compensate for the slowdown in privatization-related FDI inflows.

The structure of FDI inflow into Poland by sector has changed. The manufacturing sector, which absorbed a lot of the FDI in the beginning of the transition period, has lost its attractiveness recently in favor of the service sector. The breakdown of the FDI inflow by industry shows that since 2004, Polish services were the most attractive sector for FDI. In 2004-2008 its share in total FDI inflows changed from 55% to 66%. Further liberalization in the services sector coupled with privatization shaped this pattern. While finance has remained the top service industry, its attractiveness to FDI has declined. In 2000 "financial intermediation" accounted for 21% of the total FDI inflow into Poland, while in 2007 its share was only 15%. Surprisingly, in 2008 the share of financial intermediation grew again and constituted 30% of total FDI inflow into Poland. In 2004-2008 FDI inflows have expanded in business services and the transport, storage, and telecom industries. Trade has also grown in importance, its share in the FDI inflow doubling from 8% in 2000 to 15% in 2008 (Table 2).

Poland and other new EU member states are not only an attractive destination for foreign direct investment, but they have also become a source of capital outflows. While a country's attractiveness to FDI shows its locational advantages, capital invested by local enterprises abroad could be an indicator of the extent to which the ownership advantages of domestic firms are transferred to foreign countries in order to generate additional profits. Thus, outward investment could be treated as a test showing just how successful local businesses are in coping with global competition.

The outward movement of capital from the EU10 has been still much lower than the inward capital flow. In 2004-2006 Poland's investment abroad was increasing. However, in 2007, the value of Polish capital invested in other countries decreased from the previous year, a trend that continued in 2008 and 2009, which was a result of the global financial crisis. In 2004 Polish direct investment abroad amounted to $3.4 billion, while in 2006 it stood at $8.9 billion. In 2007 the outflow of direct investment from Poland was estimated at $5.4 billion and further decreased $2.9 billion in 2008. The decrease of Poland's investment outflow abroad was a result of declining equity capital investment, coupled with the withdrawal of profits. This trend appeared in 2007 and continued in 2008-2009. Nevertheless, in 2009, Poland was the largest foreign investor among EU10 countries; its investment abroad reached $2.9 billion (UNCTAD, 2010, p. 167).

In the 2005-2009 period, Poland's share in the total outflow of FDI from EU10 countries ranged from 32% in 2005 to 76% in 2006, reaching 33% in 2008 and nearly 40% in 2009.

In 2008, more than 75% of Poland's investment abroad was located in developed European countries, but compared with the preceding year the share of this region decreased by 20 percentage points. Nevertheless, developed European countries remained the most important destinations for Poland's investment abroad in 2008. The most popular destinations for Poland's FDI were the Netherlands and Luxembourg (each absorbing about 15% of total Polish FDI), Switzerland (7%), Germany (6.7%), and Norway (6.4%). Among Eastern European countries, the most attractive destinations for Poland's direct investment were Russia (6.5%) and Romania (6.4%), while the United States was the most popular non-European destination for Polish capital, absorbing 5.4% of the total outflow of Poland's FDI in 2008 (NBP, 2009, pp. 10-11). Notably, as a result of the financial crisis, in 2008 Polish enterprises decided to withdraw some capital from countries such as Sweden, the Czech Republic, Ukraine, Lithuania, and Latvia. In these countries, disinvestment of Polish capital was observed in 2008.

The service sector also dominated in the structure of Polish FDI abroad, constituting 69% of the total outflow in 2008 and 84% in 2008. The key service industries included business services (in particular accounting, consulting and management) and real estate (NBP, 2009, p. 22-23).

FDI stocks: Poland and other new EU member states compared

As a result of fluctuations in the inflows of FDI into Poland, the total inward stock of FDI in the country has been changing. By the end of 2008, the total inward stock exceeded $161 billion. However, Poland's share in the total capital invested in the EU10 decreased from 33.8% in 2000 to 29% in 2008.

In 2000-2008, the most dynamic increase in the FDI inward stock was noted in Romania and Bulgaria. The share of these countries in the total FDI stock in the EU10 nearly doubled, while the share of Poland, Hungary, and the Czech Republic, the most absorptive countries in terms of FDI in the 1990s, decreased. However, in 2008 Poland, Hungary, and the Czech Republic still accounted for a combined 60% of the total FDI inward stock in new EU member states (Table 3).

The service sector predominates in the structure of the FDI inward stock in Poland. Its share amounted to 60% of the total stock in 2008 and grew by 4 percentage points over 2004. Most FDI in the service sector has been of a market-seeking type and located in traditional sectors such as finance and trading, as well as in business-related industries (in particular accounting and management) or in industries that have only recently been liberalized, such as telecommunications (Figure 2).

Table 3: Inward FDI stock in Poland and other EU10 countries ($ million)

Country	1995	2000	2007	2008	Share in total stock in EU10 (in %)			
					1995	2000	2007	2008
Poland	**8528**	**34227**	**142110**	**161406**	**29.1**	**33.8**	**26.8**	**28.9**
Czech Republic	4100	21644	101074	114369	14.0	21.4	19.0	20.4
Slovakia	585	3733	40702	45933	2.0	3.7	7.7	8.2
Hungary	13027	2287	97397	63671	44.4	22.6	18.3	11.4
Lithuania	144	2334	14679	12847	0.5	2.3	2.8	2.3
Latvia	468	2084	10493	11447	1.6	2.1	2.0	2.0
Estonia	637	2645	16594	15962	2.2	2.6	3.1	2.9
Slovenia	529	2894	10350	15782	1.8	2.9	1.9	2.8
Romania	971	648	60921	71864	3.3	6.4	11.5	12.8
Bulgaria	352	2257	36508	46011	1.2	2.2	6.9	8.2
Total inward stock in EU10	29341	101168	530828	559292	100.0	100.0	100.0	100.0

Source: UNCTAD data.

Figure 2: FDI stock in the Polish service sector, 2004-2008 (million EUR)

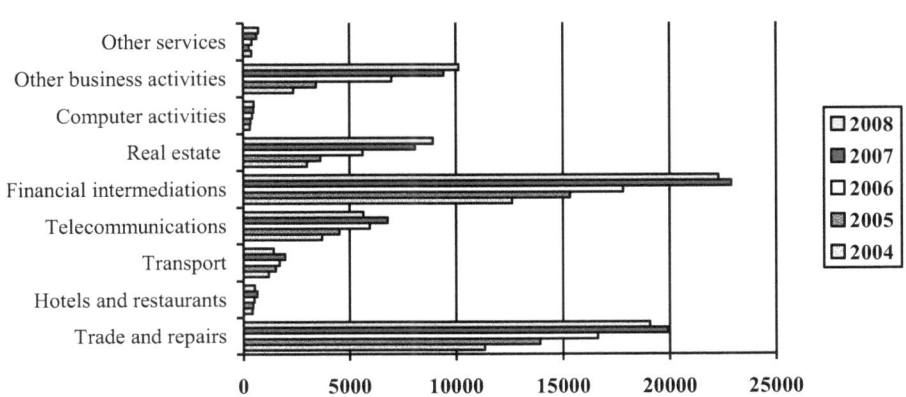

Source: Compiled by the author on the basis of NBP data.

In 2008 the total FDI inward stock in Poland's service sector amounted to 70 billion euro. Since Poland joined the EU in 2004 this value doubled. In 2004-2008 the highest increases of FDI stocks were noted in business services (in particular business consultancy, accounting and management) and real estate services. The shares of these types of services in the total FDI stock accumulated in Poland by the service sector increased by 7 percentage points and 5 percentage points respectively (Figure 3).

Figure 3: Structure of the inward FDI stock in the Polish service sector by industry: years 2004 and 2008 compared (in %)

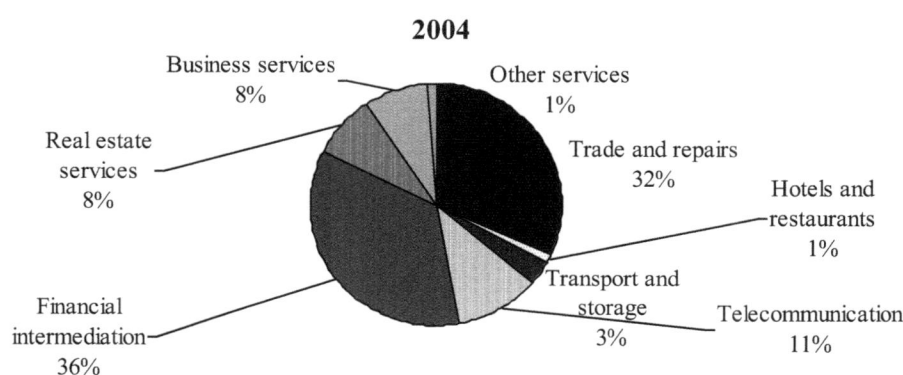

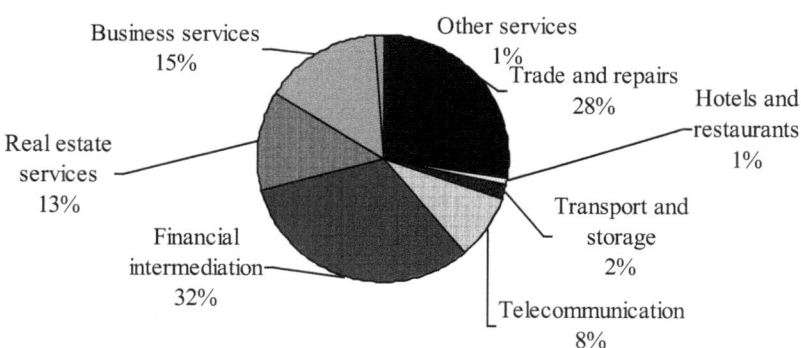

Source: Author's calculations based on NBP data, (NBP, 2008a and NBP, 2010).

Services have been also important target for Poland's investment abroad. Outward FDI stocks from Poland have been growing since 2004, making Poland the largest foreign investor from the EU10 (UNCTAD, 2008, p. 253 and Table 4).

Table 4: Outward FDI stock: Poland and other EU10 countries compared ($ million and %)

Countries	2000	2007	2008	Share in total outward stock in EU10 (in %)		
				2000	2007	2008
Poland	**1,018**	**19,644**	**21,814**	**27.1**	**31.5**	**37.1**
Czech Republic	738	6,971	9,913	12.8	11.2	16.9
Slovakia	325	1,609	1,901	3.2	2.6	3.2
Hungary	1,280	18,282	14,179	32.1	29.3	24.1
Lithuania	29	1,565	1,990	3.0	2.5	0.3
Latvia	24	776	1,066	1.1	1.2	1.8
Estonia	256	5,873	6,686	9.1	9.4	11.4
Slovenia	768	6,123	8,650	10.0	9.8	1.5
Romania	136	917	912	0.7	1.5	1.6
Bulgaria	85	599	1,248	0.9	1.0	2.1
Total outward stock from EU10	4,659	62,359	58,783	100.0	100.0	100.0

Source: Based on UNCTAD, 2007, pp. 255-258; UNCTAD, 2008, p 257; UNCTAD 2009, p. 251.

As far as Poland's investment in the service sector in concerned by the end of 2004 the outward stock of Polish capital invested abroad in the service sector amounted to 1.2 billion euro and it doubled by the end of 2008 reaching 3.3 billion euro. However, the share of the service sector in total Poland's outward investment located abroad decreased in 2004-2008 from 50.8% to 20.7%. There have been also significant changes in the branch structure of Poland's investment abroad in the service sector since Poland joined the EU.

In 2004 financial intermediation accounted for about 47% of the total Polish capital invested in the service sector abroad; trading activities attracted 26%, business services received 9%, while storage and telecommunications constituted 9%. Four years later, by the end of 2008, the share of financial intermediation in Poland's investment abroad located in the service sector decreased to 23%; trade and repairs accounted for 33% and the share of real estate services grew to 25% (Figure 4).

Figure 4: Breakdown by industry of Polish companies' outward investment stock in the service sector: years 2004 and 2008 compared (in %)

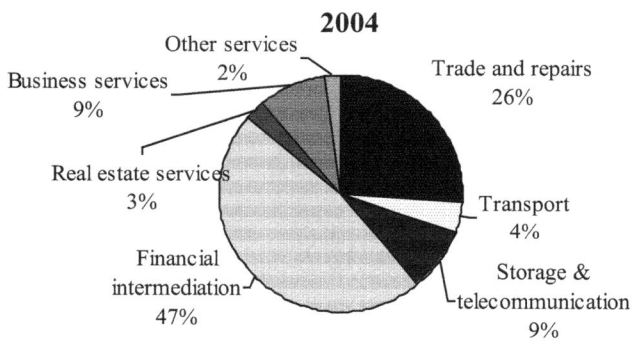

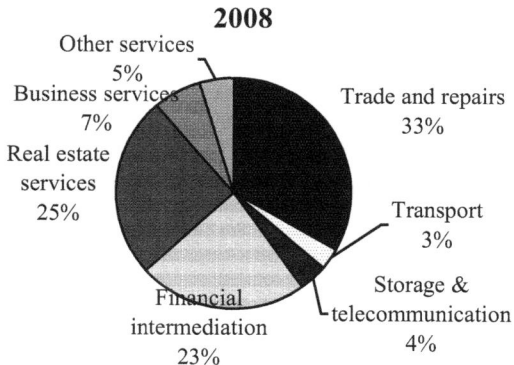

Source: Author's calculations based on NBP data, (NBP, 2008b).

Investment attractiveness of Polish services

As both inward and outward FDI stocks in Poland have been growing, it is worth comparing the investment attractiveness (IA) of individual industries. Investment attractiveness can be measured *ex post* by comparing a country's ratio of FDI flows invested in a particular industry related to the country's outward flows in the same industry, with the same ratio calculated for the whole FDI inflows and outflows of this country. Thus, the investment attractiveness (IA) index can be defined by the following equation:

$$IA = \frac{FDI\_IN_{ij}}{FDI\_OUT_{ij}} : \frac{\sum_j FDI\_IN_j}{\sum_j FDI\_OUT_j}$$

where:

FDI_IN_{ij} = inflow of FDI into industry *j* of country *i*

FDI_OUT_j = outflow of direct investment from country *i* to industry *j* located abroad

$\sum_j FDI\_IN_{ij}$ = total FDI inflow into country *i*

$\sum_j FDI\_OUT_{ij}$ = total outflow of direct investment from country *i*

Industries with an IA higher than 1 (IA>1) enjoyed a comparative advantage in attracting FDI in the analyzed period, while an IA lower than 1 but higher than 0 (0>IA<1) indicates that the industry did not possess a comparative advantage in attracting FDI. A special case occurs when disinvestment is observed in a particular industry in the analyzed period and when the IA is lower than 0. There are two possible interpretations of IA<0. One is when disinvestment is observed in the analyzed country, which implies the lack of a comparative advantage in attracting FDI to such an industry. The other case is when domestic capital is withdrawn from abroad, which means that this branch is relatively more attractive at home.

The Investment Attractiveness Indexes for various Polish industries, including the branches of the service sector are presented in Table 5.

The results of IA calculations confirm that most industries in Poland were relatively attractive for FDI in 2008 as their IA indexes were higher than 1 (Table 5). Looking from a sector perspective, it should be pointed out that attractiveness of different branches of manufacturing and services reflected in their IA indices varied significantly.

Table 5: Index of investment attractiveness (IA) for Polish industries in 2007-2008

Industries	IA Index 2007	IA Index 2008
Mining and quarrying	-0.370	0.082
- Extraction of petroleum and gas	-1.134	-0.026
Manufacturing	1.632	1.127
- Food products	1.829	0.769
- Textiles and wearing apparel	0.148	-0.100
- Wood, paper, publishing and printing	49.854	-0.261
- Refined petroleum & other treatment	0.001	-0.035
- Chemical products	1.256	-0.919
- Rubber and plastic products	3.440	0.975
- Metal products	12.645	0.515
- Mechanical products	2.620	1.100
- Office machinery and computers	184.775	6.943
- Radio, TV, communication equipment	33.093	3.635
- Motor vehicles	7.629	-0.574
- Other transport equipment	13.030	-1.618
Electricity, gas and water	0.320	2.510
Construction	1.917	-0.398
Trade and repairs	0.922	0.323
Hotels and restaurants	18.594	-1.375
Transport, storage and communication	9.633	19.609
- Land transport	-1.354	-28.043
- Sea and coastal water transport	0.206	1.511
- Telecommunications	55.669	-14.857
Financial intermediation	3.469	3.332
- Monetary intermediations	1.944	-12.185
- Insurance & activities auxiliary	2.723	4.530
Real estate & business activities	0.498	1.105
- Real estate	0.936	0.358
- Computer activities	-0.079	3.646
- Research & development	6.393	-6.392
- Other business activities	0.382	102.838
- Promotion	14.490	1.686
Other services	1.597	0.172
Other activities, non allocated	2.393	-0.068
Private purchases & sales of real estate	2.011	0.644

Source: Author's estimates based on NBP, 2008a and 2008b, 2009 and 2010.

In the service sector, the most attractive industries for FDI in 2008 were transport, storage and communication and some business services, including promotion and computer services. A lack of advantages for FDI in 2008 was observed for the following branches of the service sector in Poland: land transport, telecommunications, monetary intermediation, research and development services and hotels and restaurants.

A more detailed analysis of investment attractiveness data reveals that due to the economic crisis there were significant changes in investment attractiveness in 2008 compared to 2007 (Table 5). Some industries, such as telecommunications, monetary intermediation or hotel and restaurants that had been highly attractive in 2007 lost their comparative attractiveness for foreign investors in 2008. Furthermore, the analysis of long term trends in investment attractiveness of Polish industries for FDI allows concluding that since the second part of the 1990s the attractiveness of low-tech industries has been decreasing, while medium-high industries have become more attractive for foreign investors. The shifts in the IA of individual branches of Polish industry throughout the 1990s caused significant changes in the overall IA pattern. These changes are confirmed by a low correlation between IA indicators in 2000 and 2008 (Weresa, 2008).

FDI inflow and the development of the service sector in Poland

Given the growing stocks of FDI in Poland, it is worth examining the impact of foreign firms on a country's economic development as well as on the development of the service sector. This issue has been studied since the 1980s and the results of the research for different countries confirm that FDI and a country's economic performance are interrelated (Dunning and Narula, 1996; Lipsey, 2006; Narula 2009).

There are at least two general approaches that make it possible to assess the impact of FDI on growth and competitiveness. The first approach is an econometric analysis that links inward investment stock with various measures of economic performance, such as per capita GDP growth, level of schooling, per capita real income, and productivity growth. The main problem in assessing the impact of FDI on growth is that FDI is often associated with other growth-driving factors, and moreover, both growth and FDI are interrelated. On the one hand, FDI may accelerate the growth rate, while on the other a high growth rate is a determinant of the FDI inflow.

The other general approach to research on the relationship between FDI and competitiveness is based on a qualitative analysis of the externalities associated with FDI, such as technology transfer and learning spillovers.

In both approaches, some basic indicators have been identified that need to be taken into account when examining the role of FDI in shaping the competitiveness of a host country and development of different sectors. The most important ones are changes in the FDI-GDP ratio, the ratio of FDI flows to gross fixed capital formation, the share of foreign-owned companies in domestic investment outlays, and their role in foreign trade flows. These indicators will be analyzed for Poland in order to estimate the importance of FDI for Poland's economic development (Weresa, 2010).

In 2008, as a result of the global economic crisis, a downward trend in FDI flows was observed, which had an influence on the ratio of the inward investment stock to GDP. In Poland, as in other countries in the region, this ratio grew in the 2000-2007 period and fell in 2008 (Table 6). Furthermore, measured with the FDI/GDP ratio, Poland received less FDI than the EU average and less than its neighbors, i.e. the Czech Republic and Slovakia. Nevertheless, the importance of FDI for Poland's competitiveness cannot be neglected, as the inward FDI stock accounts for a third of Poland's GDP (Table 6).

Table 6: Inward FDI stocks in Poland and other new EU member states as a percentage of GDP, 2000 and 2008 compared

Country	2000	2007	2008
Poland	20.0	33.8	30.7
Czech Republic	38.2	57.7	52.7
Slovakia	23.3	53.6	48.4
Hungary	47.7	70.5	41.4
Lithuania	20.4	38.3	27.2
Latvia	26.6	38.6	33.9
Estonia	47.0	78.0	68.8
Slovenia	17.0	22.5	29.0
Romania	18.8	36.7	36.7
Bulgaria	21.5	92.3	92.2
EU27	25.6	40.9	35.1
World	18.1	27.9	24.5

Source: UNCTAD, 2008, pp. 261-262 and UNCTAD, 2009, pp. 255-256.

FDI has been an important source of additional capital supplementing local resources necessary for development, which is reflected in the share of the FDI inflow in fixed capital formation. In recent years, the inflow of foreign capital, measured as a percentage of gross fixed capital formation, has been swinging widely. In 2008, it decreased by 10 percentage points from 2007 to 14.4%, mainly due to the crisis in the world economy (Table 7). Surprisingly, this decline was higher than in most other new EU member states, except Latvia and Estonia, despite the fact that Poland was the only EU member state to maintain a positive growth rate in 2008 (UNCTAD, 2009, pp. 255-256).

Table 7: Inward and outward FDI flows into Poland as a percentage of gross fixed capital formation, 1990-2008

	1990-2000 annual average	2004	2005	2006	2007	2008
Poland						
Inward	11.8	28.4	18.7	29.1	24.7	14.4
Outward	-	1.8	6.1	13.2	5.2	3.1
EU						
Inward	12.0	8.6	18.2	19.4	23.4	13.0
Outward	15.9	13.4	22.2	23.0	33.1	21.6
World						
Inward	7.6	7.7	9.7	13.4	16.0	12.3
Outward	7.7	9.3	9.0	12.9	17.4	13.5

Source: UNCTAD, 2006, pp. 307-308, UNCTAD, 2009, pp. 255-256.

The role of FDI in Poland's development can also be assessed by analyzing the outlays of foreign investment enterprises on fixed assets (Weresa, 2010). According to the data of the Polish Central Statistical Office their outlays on fixed assets increased consistently in 2003-2008 (Figure 8). In 2008, they constituted 41.7% of total fixed asset outlays in Poland[3] (GUS, 2009, p. 55).

Figure 5: Fixed asset outlays by foreign investment enterprises in Poland, 2003-2008 (current prices)

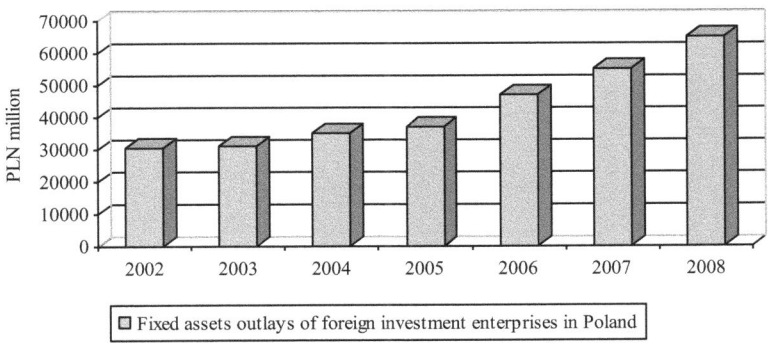

Source: Author's estimates based on GUS data.

---

[3] Businesses with 10 and more employees; balance-sheet data.

FDI inflows into Poland have also some influence on the development of the service sector. Despite of the economic crisis the number of new entities established by foreign investors in 2008 in the service sector in Poland was relatively high and majority of them were greenfield projects (Table 8). Service enterprises constituted about 70% of the total number of entities established in Poland with foreign capital involvement in 2008.

Table 8: Entities with foreign capital established in 2008 by NACE

NACE Sections	Number of entities established by foreign investors in 2008			Share of individual NACE sections in total (%)
	Total number	greenfields	by transformation	
Total	**1588**	**1320**	**268**	**100.0%**
Agriculture, hunting and forestry	21	17	4	1.3%
Industry	344	266	78	21.7%
mining and quarrying	11	10	1	0.7%
manufacturing	274	206	68	17.3%
electricity, gas and water supply	59	50	9	3.7%
Construction	111	97	14	7.0%
Trade and repair	391	351	40	24.6%
Hotels and restaurants	30	26	4	1.9%
Transport, storage and communication	74	58	16	4.7%
Financial intermediation	36	25	11	2.3%
Real estate, renting and business activities	528	441	87	33.2%
Education	9	6	3	0.6%
Health and social work	10	6	4	0.6%
Other community, social and personal service activities	34	27	7	2.1%

Source: Author's elaboration based on GUS data.

The highest number of new entities with foreign investors' involvement emerged in the service sector in the following NACE sections: "Real estate, renting and business activities" (528 entities) and "Trade and repair" (391 entities).

Furthermore, services constituted more than one third of total investment outlays of enterprises with foreign capital involvement in 2008, majority of which were outlays on fixed assets (Table 9).

Table 9: Outlays on fixed assets in Poland carried out by foreign investment enterprises in 2008 by NACE

NACE section	No. of entities	Investment outlays		The share of individual NACE sections in total investment outlays
		total	of which outlays on fixed assets	
		in mln PLN		in %
Total	**11630**	**81607.4**	**65198.3**	**100.0%**
Agriculture, hunting and forestry	333	459.9	274.6	0.6%
Industry	3918	33312.5	29610.8	40.8%
mining and quarrying	37	188.9	175.3	0.2%
manufacturing	3729	30120.4	26623.1	36.9%
electricity, gas and water supply	152	3003.2	2812.4	3.7%
Construction	571	3411.3	2918.3	4.2%
Trade and repair	3044	12070.9	9118.2	14.8%
Hotels and restaurants	197	1519.1	1461.9	1.9%
Transport, storage and communication	576	8540.8	7011.9	10.5%
Financial intermediation	193	5848.1	1288.7	7.2%
Real estate, renting and business activities	2530	14539.2	12082.1	17.8%
Education	45	21.4	19.0	0.0%
Health and social work	63	373.7	255.3	0.5%
Other community, social and personal service activities	160	1510.5	1157.5	1.9%

Source: Author's elaboration based on GUS data.

Apart from tangible assets, FDI brought new technology and know how to Poland's economy, leading to improvements in labor productivity, which grew by 60% in 2000-2008 (Ancyparowicz, 2009, p. 25). Moreover, FDI indirectly boosted innovation in Poland through learning spillovers that occurred as a result of either competition or collaboration. These positive effects, which helped upgrade domestic resources and capabilities and contributed to productivity increases, have been widely discussed in both theoretical and empirical studies (Narula, 2009; Ancyparowicz, 2009).

Wrapping up, we have to note that FDI has come to play an important role in Poland's economic performance, positively contributing to the country's competitiveness. FDI added to external financial resources for development, in particular by supplementing the domestic sources of financing investment. The role of FDI is reflected by a high and growing share of foreign-owned firms in investment outlays as well as by its impact on labor productivity. However, it has been stressed in many studies that these positive effects of FDI on productivity and the competitiveness of Poland's economy have been limited by insufficient linkages between foreign-owned enterprises and domestic firms.

Summary and conclusions

Poland has been maintaining its leading position among new EU member states in terms of the value and importance of FDI inflows and outflows. The inflows of FDI into Poland have been much higher than the outflows of Polish capital abroad. The structure of the inward FDI stock by sector has been evolving, with services playing a growing role. The service sector's share in the total FDI stock has reached nearly 60%. In 2007 the most attractive service industries in Poland include telecommunications, hotels and restaurants, promotion and R&D services.

The growing role of FDI in the service sector is important as it ensures an increase in the competitiveness of production sectors. Services play a crucial role in building competitive advantages in the whole economy as many services are important inputs into products that compete in both domestic and international markets. Service-sector FDI plays a growing role in a knowledge-based economy because information and communication technologies (ICT) enable services to be split into components, which can be located in different countries in order to produce them more efficiently. As a result, the offshoring of service activities becomes increasingly important. Recently this trend has been also observed in Poland, adding to the total inward FDI stock.

The positive shift in Poland's attractiveness for FDI in both services and medium/high-tech manufacturing shows that, step by step, Poland has been gaining comparative advantages in higher value-added sectors. However, in order to maintain this positive trend, more attention in economic policy should be paid to the development of human capital. Created assets are necessary for the country not only to attract FDI, but also to benefit from it (Narula, 2009).

References

Ancyparowicz, G., (2009). *Wpływ bezpośrednich inwestycji zagranicznych na wzrost polskiej gospodarki w okresie poakcesyjnym*. Central Statistical Office (GUS). Warsaw.

Dunning J.H. and Narula R., (1996), "The Investment Development Path Revisited: Some Emerging Issues". In: J.H. Dunning & R. Narula, (eds.) (1996), *Foreign Direct Investment and Governments: Catalysts for Economic Restructuring*. Routledge. London.

Lipsey, R., (2006). *Measuring the Impacts of FDI on Central and Eastern Europe*. NBER Working Paper No. 12808. Cambridge Mass.

Narula, R., (2009). *Multinational Firms. Globalisation and Innovation Systems: Policy Implications for New Member States of the EU*. Paper presented at the workshop Innovation for Competitiveness. INCOM Prague. Jan. 22-23.

NBP, (2007a). *Zagraniczne inwestycje bezpośrednie w Polsce w 2006 roku*. Departament Statystyki NBP. Warsaw.

NBP, (2007b). *Polskie inwestycje bezpośrednie za granicą w 2006 roku. Aneks Statystyczny*. Departament Statystyki NBP. Warsaw.

NBP, (2008a). *Zagraniczne inwestycje bezpośrednie w Polsce w 2007 roku*. Departament Statystyki NBP. Warsaw.

NBP, (2008b). *Polskie inwestycje bezpośrednie za granicą w 2007 roku*. Departament Statystyki NBP. Warsaw.

NBP, (2009). *Polskie inwestycje bezpośrednie za granicą w 2008 roku. Aneks Statystyczny*. Departament Statystyki NBP. Warsaw.

NBP, (2010). *Zagraniczne inwestycje bezpośrednie w Polsce w 2008 roku*. Departament Statystyki NBP. Warsaw.

UNCTAD, (2003). *World Investment Report*. United Nations. New York and Geneva.

UNCTAD, (2008). *World Investment Report*. United Nations. New York and Geneva.

UNCTAD, (2009). *World Investment Report*. United Nations, New York and Geneva.

UNCTAD, (2010). *World Investment Report*. United Nations, New York and Geneva.

Weresa, M.A., (2008). Foreign Direct Investment and the Competitiveness of Polish Manufacturing. In: M. Myant. T. Cox. (eds.) *Reinventing Poland: Economic and Political Transformation and Evolving National Identity*. Routledge. London. pp. 30-42.

Weresa, M.A., (ed.) (2010). *Poland: Competitiveness Report 2010. Focus on Clusters*. World Economy Research Institute. Warsaw School of Economics. Warsaw.

Chapter 6

The Development of the Service Sector in European Regions

Małgorzata Dziembała[1]

Introduction

In this age of a knowledge-based economy, the third sector, services, is of special importance. The Lisbon Strategy stressed the necessity of supporting the development of services (Presidency Conclusions, Lisbon European Council, 2000) because they contribute to the growth of national economies and help enhance the competitiveness of the European Union as a whole. Services are a source of innovative activity and innovation. In particular, this applies to business services, which employ considerable human resources. Business services are knowledge-intensive and provide the intangible assets (know-how, software, and organizational skills) which often become the key drivers of value creation. Business services are also subject to outsourcing.

Regions in which the service sector figures prominently and which have considerable human capital potential exhibit a significant competitive position. Specific areas of business activity are developing in individual EU regions, in a process that results from structural economic changes taking place in these regions, their geographical location and conditions, such as the proximity of consumers and the accessibility of skilled employees. This process also depends on a range of other factors (EC, 2007a, p. 14, p. 17).

This study presents the specialization of European regions in service activities, including business services, on the basis of an analysis of the structure of employment. Various regions of EU10[2] countries, including Poland, were the subject of detailed analysis because their economic structure has undergone transformation.[3] The paper examines selected aspects of innovation among service-sector enterprises in Polish provinces in 2004-2006.

---

[1] Research fellow, Karol Adamiecki University of Economics in Katowice, Poland, email: malgorzata.dziembala@ae.katowice.pl.
[2] The EU10 countries are the countries which joined the European Union in 2004 and 2007, i.e. Poland, the Czech Republic, Hungary, Lithuania, Latvia, Estonia, Slovenia, Slovakia, Bulgaria, and Romania.
[3] The selection of the regions was also determined by data availability.

Development of the services sector and its significance for national and regional economies

As globalization takes hold, services play an increasingly significant role. They constitute a highly diversified group that includes services linked with advanced technology, knowledge- and labor-intensive services, and also services in fields that require low-skilled employees (OECD, 2000, p. 7). The paper highlights specific trends in the service sector's development by distinguishing four stages of its development: primary stage (covering services that do not require high qualifications); growth stage (services requiring qualifications); stage of providing services to industry and of increased service consumption; and the stage of developing services based on advanced technology, including information and telecommunication services (Flejterski et al., 2005, p. 36). The service sector fulfills economic functions by providing services to manufacturing processes; it also has living, social, cultural, educational, administrative, organizational, scientific and research functions. (Flejterski et al., 2005, pp. 14-20).

As many factors influence demand for specific types of services, the service sector is evolving and its structure is changing. Demographic and social changes (including a demographic decline) should also be mentioned here. Economic changes imply an increase in demand for services, including those concerning communication, the flow of information, the assistance of specialists, and changes concerning politics and legislation. The process of European integration brings about specific changes in the sector. They are connected with factors such as liberalization of the methods of providing services. Research and development and BPO[4] services are undergoing progressive globalization (Flejterski et al., 2005, pp. 18-19, Szukalski, 1997, pp. 11-18, Dołęgowski, pp. 140-142).

Together with the development of the economy, the significance of the service sector is increasing, since the development of services is a kind of regularity of economic development and the level of services development is one of the indicators of social and economic progress; however, the concepts referring to the field of services cannot be examined in isolation as a problem in itself, but must be analyzed in close connection with general changes in the life of a particular society (Rylke, 1970, p. 26). Structural transformations are taking place in economies concurrently with economic development. This process has certain regularities, which are explained in the theory of three sectors developed by A. Fisher, C. Clarck, and J. Fourastié. The three sectors of the economy are agriculture, industry and services, and the researchers have also analyzed changes taking place in the structure of the economy as a whole. They have found that technical progress influences the results achieved in individual sectors of the economy. This is because each sector is characterized by a different susceptibility to

---

[4] Business Process Offshoring.

technical progress (lines of a high, medium and low level of reaction have been distinguished). This made it possible to identify the three sectors of the economy. Services were described as a sector with a natural, slight level of reaction to technical progress; industry was described as a sector displaying a high level of absorption of technical progress. However, developments in each sector are also influenced by changes in the structure of consumption demand, which corrects the influence of technical progress. Together with economic development, changes in the structure of consumption demand are taking place as the needs of sector 1 have to be met; after some time this process also occurs with regard to sector 2. Changes in employment tend to offset the existing disproportions. Employment in sector 1 is decreases in favor of sector 2, which is developing, and after the upper limit is achieved, services become a source of employment. J. Fourastié distinguished three phases of the development of civilization: agrarian (primary) civilization, transitional period, and tertiary civilization. Each phase shows changes in the contribution of individual sectors to overall employment, and in the last phase a certain regularity is established whereby services account for about 80% of the total work force, and industry and agriculture tie for the remaining 20%. This rule specifically applies to the most developed countries (Rogoziński 2000, pp. 91-114, Kwiatkowski, Kwiatkowska 2005, pp. 44-46). Challenging the typical scenario of economic development, a new role of industry has been indicated since an increase in industrial productivity results in an accelerated development of services new products in industry give rise to new needs and consequently new services (Rogoziński, 2000, p. 107). At the same time, the link between the two sectors was highlighted. In post-industrial societies, four sectors could be distinguished because the service sector was divided into traditional services and intellectual services, including information processing, research and development, and management (Flejterski, Wahl, 2003, p. 33).

The distribution of economic activity, including services, is not even. The effect of centripetal forces influences the concentration of economic activities, including those in the service sector. There are also centrifugal forces that lead to a spatial diversification of economic activity. Clusters that exist in various fields influence the location of companies and attract other businesses, including those active in the service sector (Misala, 2007, pp. 29-30). Integration processes influence the location of individual areas of economic activity and the relocation of labor-intensive production to outlying regions. However, these effects are not identical in all countries. In outlying regions, employment in industry has increased, while central regions have reported increased employment in the service sector. A process of specialization is in progress in the regions, which is diversified depending on the line of business. At the same time, concentration trends in the service sector have been less prominent than in industry (UKIE, 2006, pp. 156-158).

The development level of the service sector in a region influences the region's competitiveness. According to the European Commission, the regional diversification of GDP per capita is influenced by the structure of economic activity. There is a tendency whereby regions with a high concentration of employment in market services and/or industry are also regions where GDP per capita is high (EC, 1999, p. 80).

In the EU, employment in agriculture and industry has decreased, while the service sector has reported a long-lasting increase. The following types of services contribute to an increase in employment in the service sector: trading in real property, lease and business activity, health and social care, and education (EC, 2007c, p. 19).

Table 1: Value added and employment in EU regions by sector and development level in 2003 (% of total)

Regions according to GDP per capita in relation to the EU average	Agriculture	Industry	Construction	Basic market services	Business & financial services	Public services
Value added						
Below 50%	6.1	25.2	5.7	26.2	16.6	20.3
50-75%	4.9	19.5	7.5	23.3	20.6	24.1
75-100%	3.4	18.4	7.5	22.2	22.4	26.1
100%-115%	2.1	22.3	6.3	21.2	24.6	23.5
Over 115%	1.2	20.3	4.9	21.8	30.7	21.1
All regions	3.0	21.0	6.1	22.5	24.5	22.9
Employment						
Below 50%	17.1	24.1	5.7	23.0	7.5	22.0
50-75%	10.1	18.8	9.0	24.8	10.3	26.9
75-100%	4.8	16.3	8.7	25.9	12.1	32.2
100%-115%	3.7	18.3	7.1	25.9	14.2	30.7
Over 115%	2.1	18.2	6.0	26.0	18.7	29.0
All regions	6.0	18.8	7.1	25.5	13.8	28.7

Source: EC, 2007c, p. 32.

The regional diversification of GDP per capita is influenced by the structure of regional economies. There has been a relative concentration of low-value-added activities in regions that are less developed and characterized by a low level of income. In regions where GDP per capita is below 50% of the EU average (most of these regions are in new member states), value added is generated mainly by agriculture and industry. These regions are characterized by a relatively high proportion of those employed in agriculture (Table 1). Regions with a low level of development exhibit low productivity in all sectors. However, analyses show that value added has increased markedly in business and financial services as a result of changes taking place in industry and agriculture (Table 2).

Table 2: Growth of value added, employment and productivity by regional income groups in 1995-2003 (% per year)

Regions by GDP per capita in relation to the EU average	Agriculture	Industry	Construction	Basic market services	Business & financial services	Public services	Total
Gross value added							
Below 50%	-3.6	1.8	3.8	4.7	6.0	6.3	3.5
50-75%	-2.0	1.8	2.1	2.8	4.4	3.5	2.7
75-100%	-1.7	-0.1	3.4	2.3	3.6	3.0	2.1
100%-115%	-1.9	-0.2	3.1	2.7	3.7	2.8	2.2
Over 115%	-1.6	-0.2	1.2	1.9	3.5	2.4	1.9
All regions	-2.0	0.4	2.5	2.7	4.0	3.3	2.4
Employment							
Below 50%	-3.4	-2.6	-1.6	0.5	3.5	-0.2	-1.0
50-75%	-2.6	0.3	1.2	1.4	4.5	1.3	0.9
75-100%	-2.1	-0.5	1.9	1.5	4.1	1.5	1.2
100%-115%	-0.9	-0.9	1.5	1.6	3.9	1.7	1.3
Over 115%	-1.4	-1.1	0.4	1.4	4.0	1.4	1.3
All regions	-1.8	-0.9	0.8	1.3	4.0	1.3	0.9
Labor productivity							
Below 50%	-0.1	4.5	5.6	4.2	2.4	6.6	4.5
50-75%	0.7	1.5	0.9	1.4	-0.1	2.2	1.9
75-100%	0.4	0.4	1.5	0.8	-0.5	1.4	0.9
100%-115%	-1.0	0.7	1.6	1.0	-0.2	1.1	0.9
Over 115%	-0.2	0.9	0.8	0.6	-0.5	0.9	0.7
All regions	-0.1	1.3	1.8	1.3	0.0	2.0	1.5

Source: EC, 2007c, p. 35.

As the development of regions progresses, a movement of employment from traditional sectors to the service sector has been observed. The structure of economic activity in a region also depends on regional specialization (EC, 2007c, pp. 31-34).

Development of the service sector in European regions

The service sector's[5] contribution to the EU25's GDP increased from 60.5% in 1995 to 63.8% in 2005, and the sector's significance in national economies continues to grow (Alajääskö, 2006). In 2004, business services accounted for the largest number of almost 19 million non-financial sector enterprises in EU27 countries.[6]

Table 3: Service sector performance in EU27, 2004

Items	Enterprises		Value added		No. of employees		Average personnel costs, EUR 1000 per employee	Apparent labor productivity, EUR 1000 per person employed
	in 1000	Share (%)	EUR billion	Share (%)	in 1000	Share (%)		
Non-financial business economy* including:	**18900**	**100.0**	**5100**	**100.0**	**125000**	**100.0**	**27.6**	**40.9**
Motor trades	782	4.1	151	3.0	4 067	3.3	24.5	37.0
Wholesale trade	1 682	8.9	463	9.1	9 554	7.6	30.7	48.4
Retail trade & repair	3 735	19.8	384	7.5	16 970	13.6	17.6	22.6
Hotels & restaurants	1 605	8.5	163	3.2	8 652	6.9	14.9	18.9
Transport services	1 120	5.9	360	7.1	8 600	6.9	30.0	42.0
Communications	270	1.4	340	6.7	4 900	3.9	35.3	69.4
Business services	3 901	20.6	740	14.5	19 433	15.5	30.0	38.1
Real estate, R&D	1 072	5.7	304	6.0	3 500	2.8	31.0	87.0

Explanatory note: *NACE sections from C to I and K; excluding financial services; taking into account Eurostat estimations concerning confidential data.

Source: EC, 2007a, p. 10, *A Statistical Portrait*, 2008.

---

[5] Including the financial sector, covering sections G to P.
[6] The data come from the Structural Business Statistics; sections of the non-financial sector: C to K, concerning industry (NACE Sections C to E), construction: NACE Section F, and non-financial services: NACE Sections G to I and Section K, according to EC, 2007a, p. 1 and p. 10.

The business services sector produced the highest value added (alongside retail trade and repair) among all types of services with the largest number of employees[7] (Table 3).

Table 4: The most specialized EU27 regions by type of service, as % share of non- financial business economy employment in 2005* (according to NACE sections)

Items	Most specialized region		Mean share (%)	Standard deviation
	Name (NUTS code)	Share %		
Distributive trades (G)	Kentriki Makedonia (GR 12)	40.1	26.0	4.8
Motor trades (50)	Réunion (FR94)	6.8	3.7	0.9
Wholesale trade (51)	Attiki (GR30)	15.4	7.5	2.2
Retail trade & repair (52)	Kriti (GR43)	24.9	14.9	3.6
Hotels & restaurants (H)	Ionia Nisia (GR22)	29.8	7.9	4.4
Transport, storage & communication (I)	Åland (FI20)	50.4	9.2	3.9
Land transport & pipelines (60)	Bratislavsky kraj (SK01)	14.9	4.6	1.6
Water transport (61)	Åland (FI20)	41.3	0.4	2.5
Air transport (62)	Corse (FR83)	7.2	0.2	0.6
Supporting transport activities (63)	Bremen (DE50)	11.9	1.9	1.2
Post & telecommunications (64)	Köln (DEA2)	25.7	2.0	1.9
Real estate, renting, business activities (K)	Inner London (UKI1)	48.1	17.0	6.9
Real estate activities (70)	Latvija (LV)	5.4	1.9	0.9
Renting (71)	Hamburg (DE60)	1.7	0.5	0.3
Computer activities (72)	Berks., Bucks. and Oxon (UKJ1)	7.8	1.6	1.3
Research and development (73)	Oberbayern (DE21)	2.2	0.3	0.3
Other business activities (74)	Inner London (UKI1)	36.9	12.7	5.3

Explanatory note: * NACE sections from G to I and K.

Source: Johansson, 2008, p. 2.

---

[7] In 2000-2005, employment in industry decreased at an average annual rate of about 1.5%, which may have resulted from factors such as technological progress and outsourcing to other sectors. Alajääskö, 2007, p. 3.

The service sector is characterized by diversified productivity, which is in general lower than in industry (Dołęgowski 2002, p.141).[8] In relation to some regions, it is possible to indicate their specialization in individual types of services, taking into account their share in employment. Employment in non-financial sector services is concentrated in capital cities (in Inner London, for example, the service sector accounted for 88.9% of the total work force in 2004). A high concentration of services is also noted in the following regions: Noord Holland, Berlin, Région de Bruxelles-Capitale/Brussels Hoofdstedlijk Gewest, Île de France, Comunidad de Madrid, and Wien (EC, 2007a, p. 17). Various geographical, geological and location-related factors influence the specialization of regions in particular services (as well as industries) and their overall structure of economic activity. The development of specific services is also influenced by the geographical proximity of customers and the availability of employees with high qualifications. There are also clusters of businesses with specific specializations. In smaller regions, specialization is largely influenced by leading producers in the area (EC, 2007a, p. 17, EC, 2007b, p. 98). Regions specialized in particular kinds of services are listed in Table 4.

It is also possible to indicate the specialization of EU10 regions in individual types of services[9] (Table 5). In total, 50 NUTS 2 regions were analyzed.

---

[8] Productivity in the non-financial sector was EUR 40,900 per employed person, compared with EUR 49,000 in industry, EUR 38,200 in non-financial services, and EUR 33,000 in construction; at the same time, productivity was the highest in capital-intensive and high-tech sectors in 2004 (EC, 2007a, p. 22).

[9] Data from SBS data bases (Structural Business Statistics) published by Eurostat and containing a set of data concerning employment in sectors. It covers all sectors of the economy, excluding agriculture, public administration and non-market services. Employment "refers to persons in employment, i.e. those persons (paid or unpaid) working in a local unit and those working outside the unit while remaining part of it and being paid by it," according to Regions: Statistical Yearbook 2004, p. 79. See also: http://europa.eu.int/estatref/info/sdds/en/ebt/ebt_inlb_empl_sm.htm. Regional data presented in this study with reference to employment do not concern section J covering financial sectors. For more on methodology, see: EC, 2004a, pp. 79-80. Since the data for EU27 regions were incomplete, the scope of analysis was restricted to the regions of EU10 countries (lack of data concerning Malta and Cyprus); for Czech regions—data for 2004. Countries for which regions were not distinguished were also taken into consideration. The analysis did not cover the following Polish provinces (voivodeships): Podlaskie, Łódzkie and Lubelskie (due to lack of data). In the case of Warmińsko-Mazurskie province, due to a lack of data for 2005 for the mining & quarrying sector (which would make aggregation of data concerning the total number of persons employed in the region impossible), an extrapolation method was used. This note applies to data in Tables 5, 7 and 8. see: http://europa.eu.int/estatref/info/sdds/en/sbs/sbs_base.htm.

Table 5. Twenty leading EU10 regions in specific types of non-financial services in 2005 (as a percentage of non-financial business economy employment)

Distributive trades (G)		Hotels & restaurants (H)		Transport, storage & communication (I)		Real estate, renting, business activities (K)	
Regions	Share %	Regions	Share %	Regions	Share %	Regions	Share %
Małopolskie	33.23	Yugoiztochen	8.83	Bratislavský kraj	21.79	Praha	26.73
Świętokrzyskie	32.39	Severoiztochen	8.62	Mazowieckie	18.32	Közép-Magyarország	24.72
Mazowieckie	31.49	Praha	6.78	Közép-Magyarország	14.47	Bucuresti	21.00
Wielkopolskie	30.07	Severozapaden	6.18	Severoiztochen	13.96	Bratislavský kraj	17.58
Kujawsko-Pomorskie	29.96	Severozápad	5.93	Praha	13.94	Mazowieckie	17.00
Lithuania	29.17	Nyugat-Dunántúl	5.87	Yugoiztochen	13.21	Dolnośląskie	15.61
Zachodniopomorskie	28.98	Zachodniopomorskie	5.79	Latvia	12.87	Dél-Dunántúl	15.26
Latvia	28.61	Dél-Dunántúl	5.67	Severen tsentralen	12.64	Latvia	14.15
Podkarpackie	28.11	Slovenia	5.51	Stredné Slovensko	12.61	Estonia	14.15
Lubuskie	28.04	Yuzhen tsentralen	5.42	Sud-Est	12.03	Yugozapaden	13.65
Opolskie	27.92	Dél-Alföld	5.36	Bucuresti	11.80	Közép-Dunántúl	13.35
Warmińsko-Mazurskie	27.85	Yugozapaden	5.33	Yugozapaden	11.61	Dél-Alföld	12.97
Dolnośląskie	27.30	Közép-Magyarország	4.95	Estonia	11.14	Zachodniopomorskie	12.91
Pomorskie	27.00	Severen tsentralen	4.78	Lithuania	10.99	Małopolskie	12.72
Severoiztochen	26,71	Észak-Magyarország	4,66	Moravskoslezsko	10,60	Észak-Alföld	12,71
Közép-Magyarország	26.38	Severovýchod	4.61	Yuzhen tsentralen	10.32	Pomorskie	12.67
Bratislavský kraj	26.37	Észak-Alföld	4.61	Severozápad	10.10	Nyugat-Dunántúl	12.65
Bucuresti	26.24	Latvia	4.59	Pomorskie	9.56	Jihovýchod	12.20
Yugozapaden	26.12	Estonia	4.54	Zachodniopomorskie	9.48	Észak-Magyarország	11.99
Yugoiztochen	25.85	Jihozápad	4.50	Severozapaden	9.24%	Śląskie	11.90
Max	33.23		8.83		21.79		26.73
Min	15.34		1.64		3.48		4.02

Source: Own study based on Eurostat data.

The top 20 regions in distributive trade include 12 Polish provinces, among them Małopolskie and Świętokrzyskie, where the share of those employed in the sector exceeds 32%. Regions with capital cities are characterized by the highest proportion of those employed in transport and communication services. The same is true of Section K.

In this age of a global economy, services are also a source of knowledge. In 2003, a total of 545,000 enterprises dealt with knowledge-intensive services in EU27 countries, while the total number of high-tech industry businesses was 138,000. In 2006, those employed in knowledge-intensive services accounted for 32.6% of the total EU27 work force, and those employed in less knowledge-intensive services accounted for 33.6%. In Denmark, Luxemburg, the Netherlands, Finland, Sweden, and the United Kingdom, the knowledge-intensive services sector is well developed (EC, 2008b, p. 177, p. 183). An analysis of those employed in knowledge-intensive services in 2006 showed that the top 20 regions included five German regions. Among new member states, only Mazowieckie province was included on the list. The best regions in descending order were: Île de France (2.1 million people employed in the knowledge-intensive services, accounting for 46.1% of total employment in the region), Lombardia (1.4 million; 31.6%), Denmark (1.2 million; 43.8% of total employment), Outer London (51.9%), and Comunidad de Madrid. There were also Spanish, French, and German regions, one Italian region, Dutch regions, British regions and Poland's Mazowieckie province. In terms of the share of those employed in knowledge-intensive services, Stockholm tops the list, with 57% of total employment (EC, 2008b, p. 190).

Business services as a source of innovation in new EU member states

Employment in the service sector in OECD countries is growing due to the development of market services, including business services (OECD, 2005, p. 6). The concept of "business services" refers mainly to services provided to other enterprises. In 2004, about 86% of all business services in the EU were those provided to other enterprises (EC, 2007, p. 371).[10] The significance of the business services sector results from its functions in the economy. On the micro scale, it is expressed by increased effectiveness, productivity and international competitiveness of businesses; on the macro scale, business services boost economic growth and enhance the competitiveness of the economy. However, the sector is sensitive to business changes (Kuczewska, 2006, pp. 5-6, p. 16, p. 18). Its significance also results from the progressing outsourcing of these types of services, as a result of which enterprises can reduce their operating costs while

---

[10] A further 10% of services were provided to public sector entities, and the remaining 4% to households in 2004, according to Eurostat (EC, 2007a, p. 371).

focusing on their core business (sometimes an enterprise can outsource some of its basic services, such as recruitment). The possibility of outsourcing some services is offered by technological progress, including information and communication technologies, which increase the possibility of providing services over a distance (Alajääskö, 2006; EC, 2007b, p. 98). Business services are also treated as a factor contributing to the development of a knowledge-based economy. This especially applies to professional and technological services connected with other fields, such as advanced technology (Kuczewska 2006, p. 39).

The concept of "business services" covers a wide range of services, including computer, legal and accounting services, as well as monitoring, security and building maintenance and cleaning services. All these services require qualified personnel.[11] The contribution of individual types of activities in terms of value added varies; the highest contribution comes from legal services, accounting and management, followed by computer services (Table 6).

In 2004, the business services sector accounted for 15.5% of those employed in the non-financial economy in EU27 countries; the sector also generated 14.5% of value added (EC, 2007a, p. 372). Within this sector, the role of computer service development should be stressed; in 2004, Poland reported the largest number of employees in this sector compared with other new member states (*A Statistical Portrait*, 2008). In recent years, business services have been developing dynamically; in 1998-2006, employment in this sector increased by 43%. At the same time, computer services showed an almost 57% increase during this period, and employment in other services grew by 40% (EC, 2007b, pp. 103-104).

There are certain regularities in the specialization of regions in providing computer services. This type of activity is concentrated in northwestern and central Europe (specifically in regions in Scandinavia, Britain, Ireland and the Netherlands). At the same time, two clusters with a high concentration of computer services can be distinguished, one around London and the other in southern Germany. In general, this type of services is concentrated around capital cities, other big cities and in regions where capital cities are located. This last regularity applies to southwestern and eastern Europe (EC, 2007b, p. 100). An analysis of other business services shows that employment (and therefore specialization) is concentrated in big metropolitan areas. Capital cities are characterized by a high share of this type of services in total employment. Regions where capital cities are located tend to dominate in terms of total employment in Sections K 72 and K 74; the only exception is the Netherlands (EC 2007b, p.100).

---

[11] In further analyses, business services refer to sections K 72 and K 74, according to NACE.

Table 6: Business services (NACE Divisions K 72 and 74) in the EU27, 2004

	Number of enterprises (thousands)	Number of enterprises (% of total)	Value added in EUR million	Share of total value added in the sector (in %)	Number of persons employed (1000)	Share of total employment in the sector (%)
Business services	3 900.6	100.0	739 621	100.0	19 433	100.0
Computer services	500.6	12.8	154 257	20.9	2 570	13.2
Legal, accounting & management services	1 409.0	36.1	221 644	30.0	4 391	22.6
Architectural & engineering; technical testing	833.0	21.4	108 250	14.6	2 442	12.6
Advertising	193.6	5.0	33 852	4.6	845	4.3
Labor recruitment & provision of personnel	65.4	1.7	74 526	10.1	2 912	15.0
Other business services	899.0	23.0	147 092	19.9	6 274	32.3

Source: *A statistical Portrait*, 2008; EC, 2007a, p. 373.

An analysis of employment growth in computer services shows that the fastest growth took place in eastern and southern Europe. On the other hand, employment decreased in northern and central Europe. Analyzing trends in other business services, a high growth rate was identified in southern Europe, especially in Spain, Portugal, Romania, Hungary, and France. At the same time, the role of capital cities as places where other business services are located has diminished for a long time (EC, 2007b, p. 104).

A detailed analysis of business services in new member states[12] reveals the existence of similar regularities (Tables 7 and 8).

---

[12] Due to incomplete data, EU15 regions were not taken into account.

Table 7: Twenty EU10 regions with the largest share of those employed in Sections K 72 and K 74 NACE as a percentage of persons employed in non-financial sectors

Region	Share of persons employed in Section K72 – computer and related activities (%)	Region	Share of persons employed in Section K74 – other business services (%)
Közép-Magyarország	3.80%	Praha	18.96%
Praha	3.62%	Közép-Magyarország	16.54%
Bratislavský kraj	2.80%	Bucuresti	14.71%
Bucuresti	2.47%	Bratislavský kraj	12.10%
Mazowieckie	1.76%	Dolnośląskie	12.06%
Yugozapaden	1.48%	Mazowieckie	11.95%
Pomorskie	1.47%	Dél-Dunántúl	11.43%
Slovenia	1.45%	Yugozapaden	10.61%
Jihovýchod	1.26%	Közép-Dunántúl	10.21%
Malopolskie	1.21%	Dél-Alföld	9.69%
Jihozápad	1.20%	Jihovýchod	9.60%
Estonia	1.19%	Észak-Alföld	9.43%
Dolnośląskie	1.12%	Estonia	9.25%
Dél-Dunántúl	1.12%	Małopolskie	9.23%
Dél-Alföld	1.12%	Zachodniopomorskie	9.00%
Śląskie	1.06%	Észak-Magyarország	8.97%
Latvia	1.02%	Nyugat-Dunántúl	8.91%
Stredné Slovensko	1.00%	Střední Čechy	8.84%
Vest	1.00%	Slovenia	8.82%
Střední Morava	0.98%	Moravskoslezsko	8.64%
Max.	**3.80%**	**Max**	**18.96%**
Min.	**0.25%**	**Min.**	**3.06%**

Source: Own calculations based on Eurostat data.

Table 8: Share of persons employed in business services (NACE K 72 and K 74) in relation to non-financial business economy employment in EU10 regions, in 2005 (%)

Region	Percentage share
Severozapaden	3.31%
Severen tsentralen	3.59%
Yugoiztochen	4.18%
Sud	4.38%
Nord-Est	4.44%
Yuzhen tsentralen	4.46%
Sud-Vest	4.88%
Západné Slovensko	4.95%
Centru	5.20%
Nord-Vest	5.24%
Severoiztochen	5.31%
Sud-Est	5.66%
Stredné Slovensko	6.00%
Vest	6.00%
Lithuania	6.71%
Východné Slovensko	7.21%
Warmińsko-Mazurskie	7.36%
Świętokrzyskie	7.37%
Podkarpackie	7.51%
Latvia	7.79%
Střední Morava	7.94%
Severovýchod	8.00%
Wielkopolskie	8.80%
Severozápad	8.80%
Lubuskie	8.89%
Opolskie	9.07%
Kujawsko-Pomorskie	9.24%
Śląskie	9.34%
Jihozápad	9.41%

Region	Percentage share
Moravskoslezsko	9.58%
Střední Čechy	9.63%
Nyugat-Dunántúl	9.84%
Észak-Magyarország	9.85%
Zachodniopomorskie	9.97%
Pomorskie	10.03%
Slovenia	10.27%
Észak-Alföld	10.37%
Małopolskie	10.44%
Estonia	10.44%
Dél-Alföld	10.80%
Jihovýchod	10.87%
Közép-Dunántúl	11.15%
Yugozapaden	12.09%
Dél-Dunántúl	12.55%
Dolnośląskie	13.18%
Mazowieckie	13.71%
Bratislavský kraj	14.91%
Bucuresti	17.18%
Közép-Magyarország	20.34%
Praha	22.58%

Source: Own calculations based on Eurostat data.

The regions presented in Table 8 were classified into six groups. The regions whose participation values were lower than the median value of participation diminished by two quartile deviations were recognized as the first group, whereas the regions whose participation values were higher than the median value of participation plus two quartile deviations were recognized as group six.

Regions classified into the first group are regions of a very low share of persons employed. On the other hand, regions classified into the sixth group show a very high share. This classification is heartening because no Polish region was classified into the group with a low or very low share of persons employed in business services. Two Polish regions were classified into the last two groups with a high and very high share of persons employed in business services.

The number of regions in individual groups, the limit values of participation indicating the group of regions and their levels of participation are presented in Figure 1.

Figure 1: Number of EU10 regions in individual groups, values indicating the groups of regions and their levels of participation

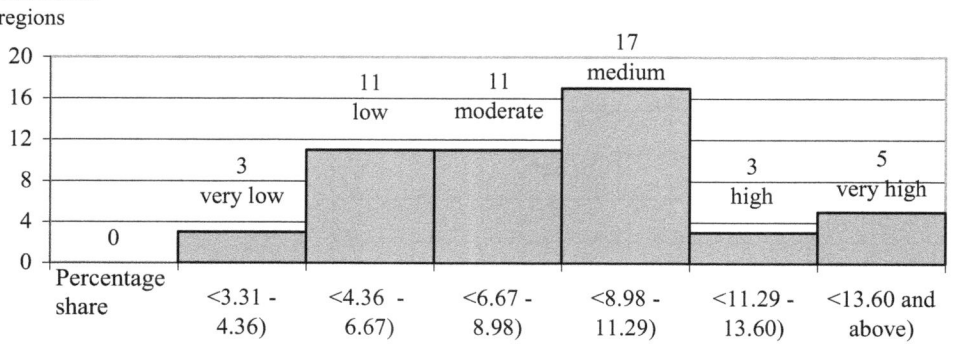

Explanatory note: Median value (Me=8.98); Quartile deviation Q=2.31.

Source: Own calculations based on data presented in Table 8.

In comparison with other EU27 countries, Poland's services sector is not innovative, as indicated by the service sector innovation index (SSII). Only Bulgaria, Latvia and Romania (in descending order) had worse indices (EC, 2008a, p. 5).[13]

Selected aspects of the innovation activity of service-sector enterprises in Polish provinces in 2004-2006

The analysis of the innovation activity of enterprises in 2004-2006 was based on a survey conducted by the Central Statistical Office (GUS, 2007) among enterprises from industry and the service sector. In 2004-2006, Polish industrial enterprises had a higher share of innovative enterprises (23.2%) than the service sector (21.2%). At the same time, considering the size of enterprises according to the number of employees, the most innovative are large enterprises (with more than 249 employees), regardless of the sector in which they have their core

---

[13] At the same time, Poland was classified as a "catching-up" country, together with the following economies: Malta, Lithuania, Hungary, Greece, Portugal, Slovakia, Bulgaria, Latvia and Romania (EC, 2008a, p. 6).

business. The share of innovative enterprises in industry was 65.5%, while in the service sector the figure was 53.5% in 2004-2006. A higher share of innovative enterprises in the service sector was only recorded for businesses with 10-49 employees, in comparison to industrial enterprises (Figure 2).

Figure 2: Share of innovative enterprises in the service sector and industry in 2004-2006 (according to the size of enterprise)

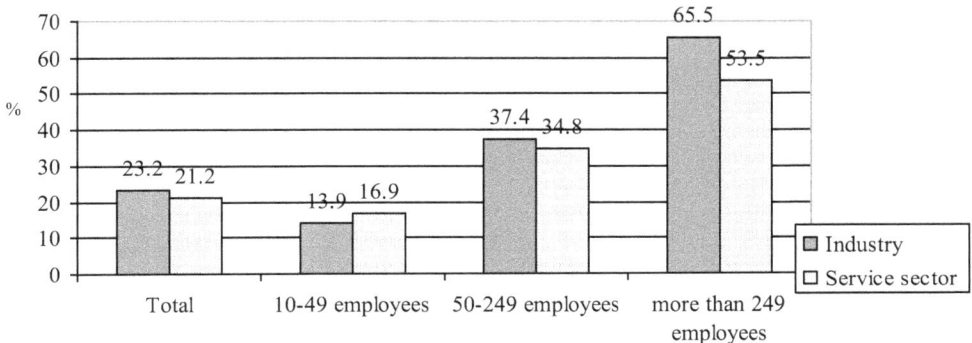

Source: GUS, 2007, p. 175.

In 2004-2006, enterprises from the service sector introduced mainly non-technological, i.e. organizational and marketing, innovations. The proportion of service-sector enterprises that introduced such innovations in 2004-2006 was 49.9%, up from 42.9% in 2001-2003[14] (Figure 3).

In Poland, the most innovative services are those involving research and development, insurance and pension funds, computer services, postal and telecommunication services, and financial intermediation (Gomułka, 2006, p. 186).

The innovation activity of service-sector enterprises is regionally diversified taking into account both the types of innovation introduced and the volume of expenditure incurred on innovation activity. A high proportion of innovative enterprises in the service sector in 2004-2006 was registered in the following prov-

---

[14] A representative sample of enterprises from the service sector was surveyed—according to primary activity conducted by businesses (according to the Polish Classification of Activities): branch 51 – wholesale and commission trade, excluding motor vehicles and motorcycles; section I – transport, warehouse management and communication; section J – financial intermediary; section 72 – computer and related activities; group 74.2 – architectural and engineering activities and related technical consultancy; group 74.3 - technical testing and analysis (see GUS, 2007, p. 132. Unless otherwise specified, the data concern businesses with more than 49 employees.

inces: Dolnośląskie, Podlaskie, Świętokrzyskie, Mazowieckie, Pomorskie and Śląskie, where this proportion was higher than for Poland as a whole (Table 9).

Figure 3: Share of innovative enterprises in the service sector in 2001-2003 and 2004-2006 (%)

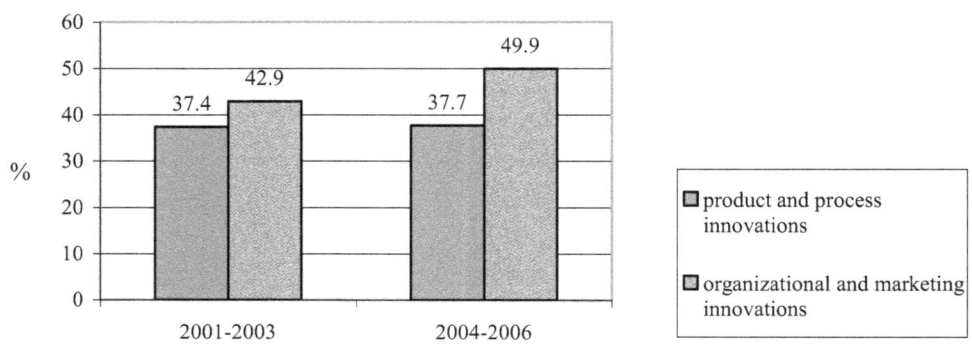

Source: GUS, 2008.

In 2004-2006, innovative enterprises accounted for 37.7% of the total number of enterprises (with more than 49 employees) in Poland's service sector. New or significantly improved products were introduced by 23.2% of service enterprises. The highest percentage was registered in Świętokrzyskie province, at 29.8%. A total of 31.6% of service enterprises introduced new or significantly improved processes in 2004-2006. The highest percentage of service enterprises that introduced new or significantly improved processes was registered in Świętokrzyskie province, at 40.5%, followed by Mazowieckie province, with 39.4%.

In 2006, machinery and equipment accounted for 48.5% of the total expenditure made by innovative service-sector enterprises, while "other expenditure" (including software) accounted for 19.2%. Expenditure on the marketing of new and significantly improved products accounted for 4.4%, and expenditure on buildings and land represented 11.5%. Expenditure on research and development constituted 11% of total expenditure by enterprises in the service sector, and expenditure on the purchase of technology in the form of documents and rights accounted for 4.1% of total expenditure. Companies' own funds represented 91.4% of total expenditure in 2006 (current prices); and bank loans accounted for 5.4% of total funds used to finance innovation activity. Other sources of financing included the state budget (0.9%), non-repayable funds from abroad (0.6%); and "other funds" (1.6%).

Table 9: Innovative service-sector enterprises with more than 49 employees by type of innovation in 2004-2006

Items	Innovative service enterprises as a percentage of the total number of enterprises			
	Total	New or significantly improved products	of which: new to the market	New or significantly improved processes
Poland	**37.7**	**23.2**	**11.8**	**31.6**
Dolnośląskie	37.9	18.7	11.7	31.3
Kujawsko-pomorskie	21.3	14.0	2.2	16.9
Lubelskie	29.9	20.5	5.1	20.5
Lubuskie	28.4	10.4	3.0	28.4
Łódzkie	27.2	14.8	10.5	22.8
Małopolskie	35.6	24.8	13.3	27.3
Mazowieckie	45.2	29.2	19.1	39.4
Opolskie	32.5	15.0	3.8	32.5
Podkarpackie	22.9	13.2	6.9	19.4
Podlaskie	46.3	20.0	3.8	31.3
Pomorskie	39.8	23.1	10.9	34.8
Śląskie	40.2	27.0	11.1	35.1
Świętokrzyskie	46.4	29.8	8.3	40.5
Warmińsko-mazurskie	37.5	25.0	5.6	30.6
Wielkopolskie	35.3	23.4	9.4	26.4
Zachodniopomorskie	29.1	12.6	7.8	26.2

Source: GUS, 2007, p. 147.

Enterprises active in sectors such as post and telecommunications, followed by those active in financial intermediation, incurred the greatest expenditures on innovation activity in the services sector (Figure 4).

Enterprises from the service sector work with other businesses in joint projects concerning research and development and other activities. Service-sector enterprises that in 2004-2006 actively worked with other enterprises (or institutions) in innovation activity (pursuing joint research and development projects, for example) constituted 23.6% of the total number, whereas in industry the figure was 23.9%.

Figure 4. Expenditure on innovation activity in service-sector enterprises by type of activity in 2006 (current prices)

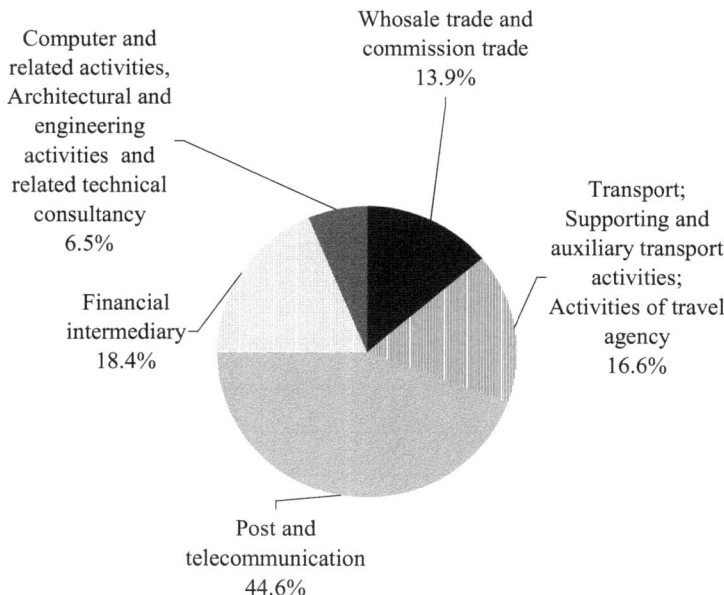

Source: GUS, 2008.

In terms of the type of activity conducted, 49.8% of all enterprises active in financial intermediation worked with other enterprises and institutions in joint innovative projects; in postal and telecommunications services, the figure was 47.2%.

In 2006, expenditure on innovation activity by enterprises in the service sector amounted to ZL 7,231.5 million (in current prices) and varied from one region to another. The highest expenditure was incurred in Mazowieckie province, accounting for 79.3% of total expenditure incurred by service-sector enterprises in Poland's provinces. The figure for Śląskie province was 4.2%. The lowest expenditures were incurred in Warmińsko-Mazurskie and Opolskie provinces.

The highest share of enterprises that incurred expenditure on innovation in 2006 was recorded in Podlaskie province, followed by Mazowieckie province. In terms of expenditure per innovative enterprise, Mazowieckie province topped the list, followed by Łódzkie and Pomorskie.

Table 10: Expenditure on innovation by enterprises from the services sector per enterprise and the percentage share of enterprises incurring expenditure on innovation, in 2006 (current prices)

Items	Percentage of enterprises that incurred expenditure on innovation	Average innovation expenditure per enterprise, in thousands of zlotys (current prices)
Poland	**33.9**	**6202.0**
Dolnośląskie	36.9	1725.2
Kujawsko-pomorskie	19.9	1789.9
Lubelskie	29.1	2303.4
Lubuskie	28.4	1440.3
Łódzkie	25.3	4048.9
Małopolskie	32.7	2304.8
Mazowieckie	40.8	14708.4
Opolskie	31.3	556.8
Podkarpackie	22.9	1872.8
Podlaskie	45.0	713.3
Pomorskie	35.3	3391.3
Śląskie	35.4	2165.7
Świętokrzyskie	38.1	833.8
Warmińsko-mazurskie	30.6	765.2
Wielkopolskie	28.3	948.6
Zachodniopomorskie	26.2	1049.2

Source: *Nauka i technika*, 2007, p. 151.

The lowest expenditure was recorded in Opolskie province. In Podlaskie province, the volume of expenditure incurred was among the lowest in 2006 (according to current prices) even though the region had the largest proportion of enterprises incurring expenditure on innovation. In Świętokrzyskie and Podlaskie provinces, the percentage of innovative enterprises is relatively high though their expenditure is low.

Summary and conclusions

1. The size of the service sector determines the modern structure of the economy and at the same time its competitiveness. In EU regions with a low level of economic development, there have been changes in the type of activities pursued. This also applies to Polish regions. However, the specialization of the regions also depends on factors specific for a given region.

2. The business services sector is developing dynamically in both Poland and all of Europe. This is shown by an increasing number of employees in this sector. In part, this trend is promoted by the outsourcing of these services, which results from the development of modern technology. Supporting the development of data communications technology in Poland will make it possible to provide these services via electronic channels. Today Poland is an attractive country as far as services are concerned, and, according to A.T. Kearney, it ranks 18th worldwide in terms of attractiveness for companies investing in business services (A.T. Kearney 2007, p. 2).

3. The analysis of the service sector's development shows that Poland's service enterprises are increasingly innovative. However, the level of innovation is still low in comparison with other EU countries. One barrier to innovation and further development in the sector is that enterprises do not have enough funds of their own. It is also important to take action to improve ICT usage by enterprises in the sector.

4. It is necessary to promote and support activities designed to enhance innovation in Poland's service sector by establishing foundations for the sector's long-term development. Supporting the process of introducing innovation, through measures such as financial support for the smallest enterprises, should facilitate the sector's development.

References

A Statistical Portrait of European Business. News release 7/2008 – 15 January 2008.

Alajääskö, P., (2006). "The Demand for Services; External But Local Provision". *Statistics in Focus*. No. 2006/26.

Alajääskö, P., (2007). "EU-27 Business Services: Thriving in the Wake of Outsourcing and Liberalization". *Statistics in Focus*. No. 76/2007.

Dołęgowski, T., (2002). *Konkurencyjność instytucjonalna i systemowa w warunkach gospodarki globalnej. Implikacja dla sektora usług*, Monografie i opracowania 505, Warsaw School of Economics, Warsaw.

EC, (1999). *Sixth Periodic Report on the Social and Economic Situation and Development of the Regions of the European Union*. Office for Official Publications of the European Communities. Luxembourg.

EC, (2004a). *Regions: Statistical Yearbook 2004*. Office for Official Publications of the European Communities. Luxembourg.

EC, (2004b). *Business Services—An Analysis of Structural Foreign Affiliates and Business Demography Statistics, Data 2001*, Office for Official Publication of the European Communities, Luxembourg.

EC, (2007a). *European Business: Facts and Figures – 2007 Edition* (2007), Office for Official Publications of the European Communities, Luxembourg http://epp.eurostat.ec.europa.eu/cache/ITY_OFFPUB/KS-BW-07-001/EN/KS-BW-07-001-EN.PDF.

EC, (2007b). *Eurostat Regional Yearbook 2007*. Office for Official Publications of the European Communities, Luxembourg.

EC, (2007c). *Rozwijające się regiony-rozwijająca się Europa. Czwarty raport na temat spójności gospodarczej i społecznej* (2007), Urząd Oficjalnych Wspólnot Europejskich, Luksemburg.
http://ec.europa.eu/regional_policy/sources/docoffic/official/reports/cohesion4/pdf/4cr_pl.pdf.

EC, (2008a). *European Innovation Scoreboard 2007. Comparative Analysis of Innovation Performance*.
www.proinnoeurope.eu/admin/uploaded_documents/European_Innovation_Scoreboard_2007.pdf.

EC, (2008b). *Science, Technology and Innovation in Europe*. Office for Official Publications of the European Communities. Luxembourg.

Flejterski, S., Panasiuk, A., Perenc, J., and Rosa, G., (2005). *Współczesna ekonomika usług*. PWN. Warsaw.

Gomułka, M., (2006). "Indeks innowacyjności dla branż usług i przemysłu". In: M.A. Weresa (ed.) *Polska. Raport o konkurencyjności 2006. Rola innowacji w kształtowaniu przewag konkurencyjnych*. World Economy Research Institute. Warsaw School of Economics. Warsaw.

GUS, (2007). *Nauka i technika w 2006 roku*. Informacje i opracowania statystyczne. Główny Urząd Statystyczny, Warsaw.

GUS, (2008). *Działalność innowacyjna przedsiębiorstw w latach 2004-2006, notatka informacyjna*. GUS, Warsaw.

Johansson, U., (2008). "Regional Specialisation in the EU's Business Economy", *Statistics in Focus* No. 34/2008.

Kuczewska, L., (2006). *Stan i tendencje rozwoju usług biznesowych w Polsce*. Instytut Rynku Wewnętrznego i Konsumpcji. Warsaw.

Kwiatkowska, W., Kwiatkowski, E., (2005). "Konkurencyjność gospodarki a struktura zatrudnienia – hipotezy teoretyczne i weryfikacja na przykładzie Polski i wybranych krajów". In: R. Piasecki (ed.) *Konkurencyjność gospodarki Polski*. Studia i Monografie No. 11. Kolegium Wydawnicze Społecznej Wyższej Szkoły Przedsiębiorczości i Zarządzania w Łodzi. Łódź.

Misala, J., (2007). "Międzynarodowa wymiana usług w świetle teorii". In: A. Szymaniak (ed.) *Globalizacja Usług: Outsourcing, Offshoring i Shared Services Centers*. Wydawnictwo Naukowe INPiD UAM. Poznań.

OECD, (2000). *The Service Economy*. http://www.oecd.org/dataoecd/10/33/2 090561.pdf.

OECD, (2005). *Growth in Services, Fostering Employment, Productivity and Innovation. Meeting of the OECD Council at Ministerial Level*. http://www.oecd.org/dataoecd/58/52/34749412.pdf.

Offshoring for Long-Term Advantage. The 2007 A.T. Kearney Global Services Location Index. http://www.atkearney.com/shared_res/pdf/GSLI_2007.pdf.

Rogoziński, K., (2000). *Usługi rynkowe*. Akademia Ekonomiczna w Poznaniu. Poznań.

Rylke, M., (1970). *Organizacja usług w gospodarce narodowej*. PWE. Warsaw.

Szukalski, S.M., (2007). "Wyzwania europejskie w perspektywie 2050 roku - skutki dla rozwoju usług". In: *Usługi w rozwoju społeczno-gospodarczym Unii Europejskiej*. Instytut Badań Rynku, Konsumpcji i Koniunktur, Ministerstwo Gospodarki. Warsaw.

UKIE, (2006). *Delokalizacja w rozszerzonej Unii Europejskiej - perspektywa wybranych państw UE. Wnioski dla Polski*. Urząd Komitetu Integracji Europejskiej, Departament Analiz i Strategii. Warsaw.

Chapter 7

Towards a Policy for Supporting Innovation in the Service Sector: The Rationale for Policy Action and Further Steps

Beata Lubos[1]

Abstract

At both the state and EU levels, there is a serious debate about the role of innovation in the services sector, the existence of market and system failure, and the expected role of national and European authorities in pursuing a policy aimed at supporting innovation in services. Experts agree that services greatly contribute to the creation of GDP. This fact has been proved especially in knowledge-intensive services (KIS). However, KIS differ from other services in innovation, especially with regard to the innovation model. Innovation in KIS is mainly driven by technology, while non-KIS enterprises usually implement non-technological innovation. This constitutes a challenge from the policy-making perspective. The crucial question is how to support the innovation activity of entrepreneurs operating in the service sector. The key issue for now is to map the existing instruments supporting innovation activity and check if they equally support innovation in manufacturing and services. This study attempts to determine if service investments in technology are more likely to obtain public support than investments based on the implementation of non-technological innovation.

This article covers the following issues: a theoretical approach to innovation in the service sector, statistics on innovation in the service sector, barriers to the development and support of innovation in services at the EU level, the rationale for policy action shaping Poland's innovation policy perspective towards supporting innovation in the service sector, and best learning cases from other countries.

Innovation in services – a theoretical approach

The concise definition of innovation states that it is based on successful production, assimilation and exploitation of novelty in the economic and social spheres, while the broad definition describes innovation as the renewal and enlargement of a range of products and services and the associated markets; the establishment

---
[1] PhD student, the Warsaw School of Economics, Poland, Beata.Lubos@mg.gov.pl.

of new methods of production, supply and distribution; the introduction of changes in management, work organization, and the working conditions and skills of the work force. According to the OECD publications, innovation is the implementation of a new or significantly improved product (good or service) or a process, a new marketing method, or a new organizational method in business practices, workplace organization or external relations (OECD, 2005).

Innovation has a great influence on the competitiveness of economies as well on individual branches, including manufacturing and services. The role of innovation in the service sector is huge, especially when we take into consideration the proven contribution of this sector to economic growth. The dynamic development of services and increased competition among service providers make innovation a crucial challenge and necessity.

Innovation in the service sector is classified by Howells and Tetcher (2001) into four groups: services dealing only with goods (for instance, transport, logistics), services concerning information (for example, call centers), services based on knowledge (for instance, consulting), services provided to people (for example, medical care) (OECD, 2005, p. 38).

Figure 1: Three dimensions of innovation in services

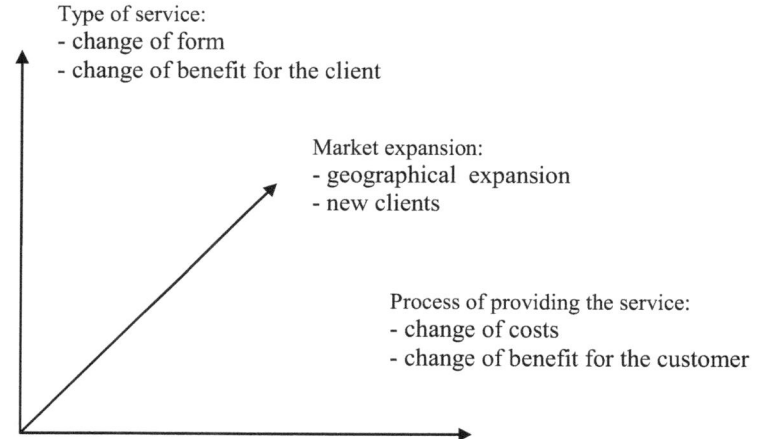

Source: Niedzielski, Szulkin, 2006, p. 53.

On the other hand, W. Rall highlights the three main dimensions of innovation in services. The service is innovative when its form or the client's advantages are changed. This does not have to mean the creation of a totally new service, but, for instance, a change in quality or a combination of previously separated services. The second dimension of innovation in services is the process of providing the service, which may change the advantages for the customer and decrease the costs for the service provider. This second dimension is closely linked to ICT and the potential of the people providing the service—especially their knowledge and creativity. The last dimension of innovation in services is the market expansion aimed at attracting new groups of clients and the geographical expansion of the company (Niedzielski and Szulkin, 2006, p. 52). Unlike innovation in manufacturing, innovation in the service sector is mainly based on four pillars: qualifications, creativity, entrepreneurship, access to various sources (not only financial, but also consulting and advisory services, for example). The whole process is influenced by technology, regulations, the stage of development of society, and the development of other sectors of the economy.

Figure 2: Four pillars of service innovation

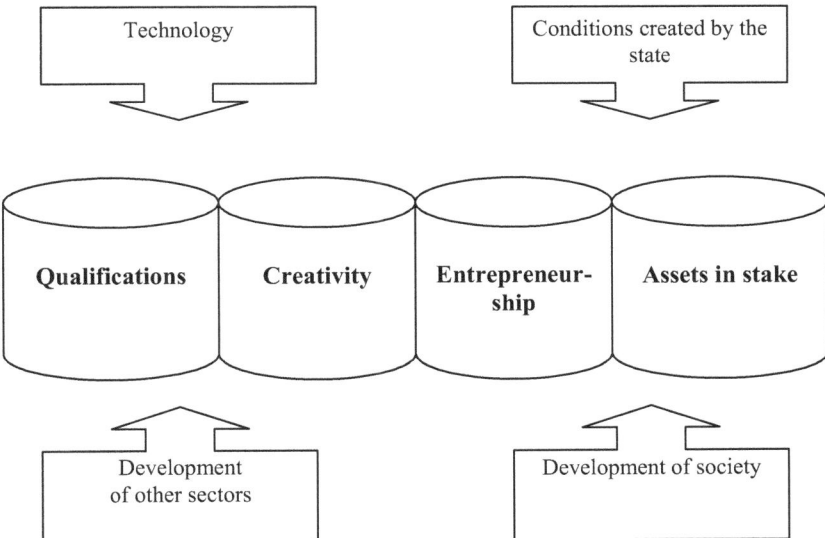

Source: Niedzielski and Szulkin, 2006, p. 53.

Innovation in the service sector—statistics

The European Union sees great potential in the development of innovation in the service sector. This explains why it has undertaken a number of activities aimed at increasing the innovativeness of service providers and services offered on the EU market. The first step for the European Commission was to undertake analytical work on measuring innovative activity in the service sector. A document entitled *2006 TrendChart Report: Can We Measure and Compare Innovation in*

Services was the first to present the methodology of measuring innovation in the service sector and the results of its innovativeness.

The Service Sector Innovation Index (see Figure 3) shows the average country performance for the 24 indicators which have been assigned to seven themes: 1) human resources; 2) innovation demand; 3) technological knowledge; 4) non-technological changes—such as organizational innovation; 5) sources of knowledge; 6) commercialization; and 7) intellectual property.

Figure 3: 2006 Service Sector Innovation Index (SSII) in EU-27

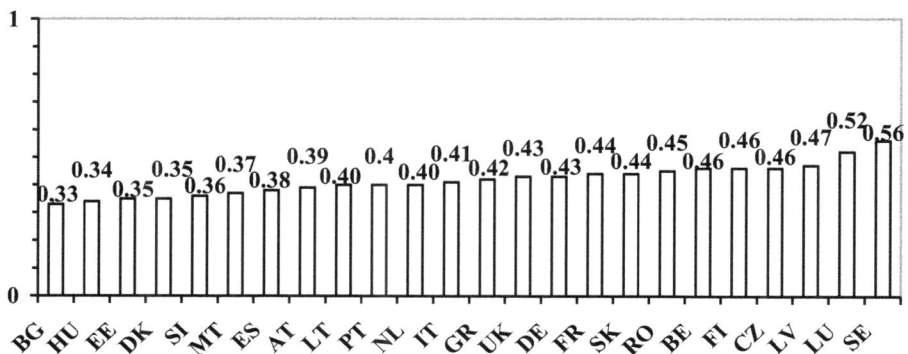

Note: data for Cyprus, Poland and Ireland were not available.

Source: Kanerva, Hollanders and Arundel, 2006, p. 34.

Sweden and Luxembourg perform best on this index, while Bulgaria and Hungary come last. As noted above, some of Europe's better performers on the EIS perform poorly on the SSII, including Denmark, Austria, and the Netherlands. Some of the new member states perform quite well, especially Latvia, the Czech Republic, and Romania, which outperforms many highly developed countries such as France, Germany and the UK. The indices for country performance in the four service subsectors show top rankings for Sweden, which leads in three of the subindices. The SSII indicator was not calculated for Poland, Ireland and Cyprus because of a lack of data (Kanerva, Hollanders and Arundel, 2006).

The SSII was calculated for both manufacturing and the services sector, with the use of an identical set of indicators. The results show that the manufacturing sector does only slightly better than services (see Figure 4). In fact, when looking at the seven themes separately, services outperform manufacturing in four of these: sources of knowledge, non-technological change, innovation demand, and human resources. Conversely, the manufacturing sector, not surprisingly, performs better on two themes that largely measure technical innovation: technological knowledge and intellectual property (Kanerva, Hollanders and Arundel, 2006).

Figure 4: Innovation performance - services versus manufacturing

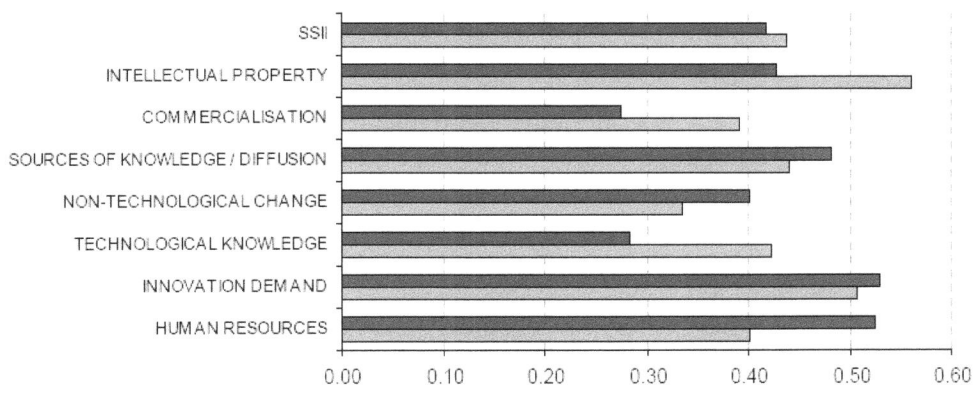

Source: Kanerva, Hollanders and Arundel, 2006, p. 5.

Figure 5 compares the innovation performance of member states in services, as measured by a selected number of service-related indicators, with an index for manufacturing constructed with an identical set of indicators.

Figure 5: 2007 Service Sector Innovation Index (SSII) in the EU27 compared with manufacturing performance across EU member states

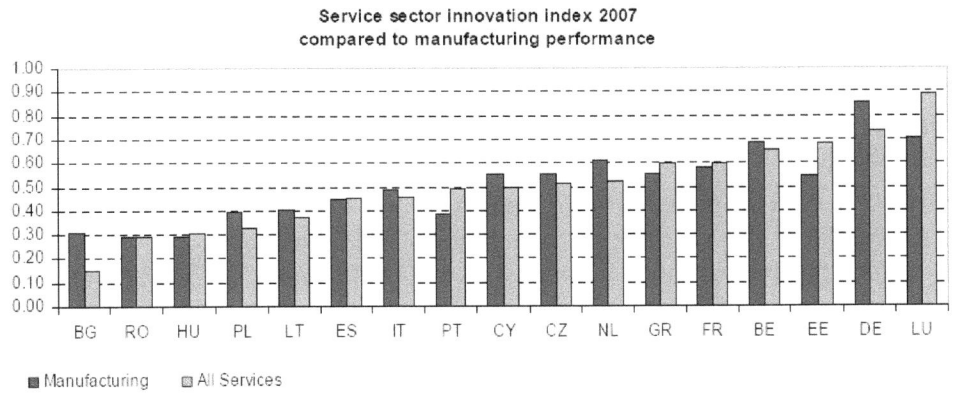

Source: CEC, 2007a, p. 12.

On average, the national difference in innovation performance between the two major sectors is highly correlated, although there are a few differences between performance in manufacturing and services. For example, Luxembourg and Estonia perform better on services than on manufacturing, which is explained by the fact that these economies heavily rely on services. On the other hand, Bulgaria, Germany, the Netherlands and Poland perform better in manufacturing CEC, 2007a, p. 12).

The Service Sector Innovation Index can be also calculated for selected service industries, such as (1) wholesale trade, (2) transport, storage & communication, (3) financial intermediation, and (4) computer and R&D and other business activities. However, many countries have been left out of the indices due to missing data (including Poland). As with the aggregated SSII, several countries that are generally considered to be poor innovation performers (based on technical innovation) perform much better on the sub-sector indices, while several countries that are good performers on technical innovation perform comparatively poorly in specific service sectors. The indicator scores in wholesale trade are highest for Sweden and Luxembourg. For the transport, storage and communication sector, composite indicator scores are highest for Latvia, Sweden, Slovakia, Finland, and the Czech Republic. For the financial intermediation sector, Portugal and Italy perform the best, while in the "computer, R&D and other business activities" sector, the best performance is in Sweden, Belgium, Luxembourg, and Portugal (Kanerva, Hollanders and Arundel, 2006, p. 36).

The European Commission asked the ESRC Center for Research on Innovation and Competition and the Institute of Innovation Research from the University of Manchester to produce a report on innovation in the service sector, which was finally published in 2004 under the title *Innovation in Services: Issues at Stake and Trends* (CEC, 2004). The report covers research on innovation in four service sectors: road transport and logistics; information processing; design and related activities; and care for the elderly. The research focused on the extent of change in enterprises, technology used, and human resources management, including the qualifications of the work force and the necessity to train staff.

Competition in ***road transport and logistics*** covers paying attention to the different aspects of the process of providing the services, especially its quality. This means that typical innovation activities do not occur too often, while "hidden innovation" is expected to play a more significant role. Implementation of new services in this sector has low priority; however, a lot of attention is paid to the qualifications of the work force. In the research carried out, new technology was not ranked high among indicators contributing the most to the company's success. This indicates that new technology is not easily adopted in road transport and logistics, which explains why this sector can be classified among "passive technology adopters." (CEC, 2004, p. 71). There is probably more space for organizational innovation.

Information processing companies put much emphasis on the quality of services provided. Due to the fact that services in this area are often heavily standardized, little effort is made to introduce innovation. This sector, as well as road transport and logistics, is a passive member of the innovation arena (CEC, 2004, p. 78).

With respect to the ***design and related activities*** sector, the human factor including the skills of the work force should once more be strongly stressed. The quality assurance process has a crucial role to play. Changes in the design sector do not rely on technology; the sector often introduces non-technological innovation (CEC, 2004, p. 85).

The ***elderly care*** sector stresses the role of human resources, adapting to the needs of customers, the quality of services provided and non-technological change in procedures and organization (CEC, 2004, p. 92).

The research yields the following conclusions:

- organizational and process innovation and all non-technological related forms of innovation play a crucial role;
- the quality of the services provided is of special importance;
- enterprises are reluctant to introduce new services;
- implementation of new technology is not seen as a success driving force;
- the key success factor is the high qualifications of staff and good training.

These conclusions exclusively apply to services that are not knowledge intensive. Knowledge-intensive services (KIS) tend to rely heavily on technological change.

Barriers to the development of service innovation

Before designing a policy aimed at providing support for innovative service companies, the crucial thing is to define the barriers which service companies face when they want to innovate. According to the *2006 TrendChart Report: Can We Measure and Compare Innovation in Services*, the main barriers in this field are:

- customers' unwillingness to pay for innovative and therefore more expensive services,
- high cost of innovative activity,
- high risk connected with the implementation of innovation,
- lack of a sufficiently skilled work force,
- useless and inadequate training programs (Kanerva, Hollanders and Arundel, 2006, p. 18).

Research on innovation among manufacturing and service enterprises has also been carried out by the European Commission as part of the Innobarometer project (Table 1). The main problems, in both manufacturing and services, included the need to access new innovative customers and markets and problems with mobilizing human resources. Manufacturing and services differed significantly in "finding or using new technologies," which confirms that service sector innovators usually implement non-technological innovation.

Table 1: Barriers to innovation in manufacturing and services (Innobarometer 2004).

	Manufacturing	Services	Significant difference
Accessing innovative customers/markets	33%	33%	no
Accessing/mobilizing human resources	32%	35%	no
Accessing/mobilizing financial resources	27%	25%	no
Finding or using new technologies	26%	18%	yes
Knowledge sharing or networking	20%	22%	no
Protecting company's knowledge	12%	13%	no

Source: EC, 2004, p. 109.

The European Commission's report *Innovation in Services: Issues at Stake and Trends* shows the barriers for implementing innovative ideas which were identified in four sectors: road transport and logistics; information processing; design and related activities; and care for the elderly (Table 2). For road transport, information processing and design, the results are the same—the most significant barrier is that customers do not accept new ideas, their costs and the risks involved. As far as the elderly care sector is concerned, the most important barriers are regulations and customers who do not accept innovation, its costs and risks.

It is worth taking a look at barriers hampering the innovative activities of Poland's service enterprises. The country's Central Statistical Office has carried out a survey (GUS, 2005, pp. 28-29) in which it asked enterprises if, in 2001-2003, at least one of their innovation projects was: seriously delayed, did not start at all, or encountered serious problems while it was in progress. A frequent reply from companies was that they had problems carrying out their projects (7.6%). Many enterprises said that the existing market situation ruled out innovation

(36.2%), or that they did not need to innovate because they had done so earlier; they also listed a number of reasons why they believed innovation was impossible. The same research shows that the high costs of innovative activities are still the most important barrier to innovation for more than 50% of service enterprises.

Table 2: Extent to which various factors impeded innovation (rank in brackets)

	Road Transport and Logistics	Information Processing	Design and Related Activities	Elderly Care
Customers are unwilling or unable to pay	85% (1)	78% (1)	82% (1)	71% (2)
Cost or risk of innovation is too high	81% (2)	77% (2)	82% (1)	69% (3)
Regulations hinder innovation	75% (3)	59% (5)	57% (7)	75% (1)
Customers are unresponsive to new services	70% (4)	60% (3)	73% (3)	40% (9)
Lack of key staff to affect change	63% (6)	56% (7)	60% (6)	60% (4)
Innovations are too easily copied	69% (5)	60% (3)	61% (5)	48% (6)
We are too busy to innovate	61% (8)	57% (6)	69% (4)	48% (6)
Innovation is not necessary	63% (6)	43% (10)	56% (8)	46% (8)
Organizational structure pampers innovation	61% (8)	47% (8)	40% (10)	52% (5)
Lack of key technologies to affect change	57% (10)	45% (9)	54% (9)	40% (9)

Source: CEC, 2004, p. 119.

Overall, the most important barriers hampering innovation in service enterprises are the high costs of innovative activities (just like in manufacturing) and a range of barriers connected with people, including a lack of openness to innovative services among customers and untrained staff.

Support for innovation in services at the EU level

As they develop their policies for supporting service innovation, EU decision makers are aware that the service sector plays an increasingly important role in the economy. The sector accounts for about two-thirds of employment and GDP and is the only sector of the European economy that has generated jobs over the past two decades. However, the share of service firms that innovate is still lower when compared with the level of innovation in the manufacturing sector, with the notable exception of ICT services, where R&D expenditures seem to be as important as in manufacturing. Moreover, the empirical evidence suggests that non-technological innovation plays an important role in the service sector.

Under Communication COM(2006)502 *Putting Knowledge into Practice: A Broad-Based Innovation Strategy for the EU*, the Council of the European Union obligated the Commission to prepare, by April 2007, an overall assessment of innovation in services and evaluate the related need for policy adjustments, while taking into account the various forms of non-technological innovation.

As a first step to follow this request, the Commission published in July 2007 a Staff Working Document *Towards a European Strategy in Support of Innovation in Services: Challenges and Key Issues for Future Actions*, which analyzes the specific patterns of service innovation and identifies the main challenges to the support of innovation in services with the view to fully exploiting their innovative potential and fostering the growth of the service economy in Europe.

The next step was to start public consultations on the Staff Working Document on innovation in services, which was held from October to the end of December 2007. The objective of the consultations was to get feedback from stakeholders on the challenges and key issues of a policy framework to support service innovation, as identified in the SWD. In general, the analysis presented by the Commission's SWD is strongly supported by a large majority of the respondents.

To make sure that the research and the findings of SWD are relevant for all member states, the European Commission organized a workshop entitled "Towards a European Strategy in Support of Innovation in Services", which was held in Brussels with academic and industrial stakeholders on Feb. 4, 2008. The workshop participants agreed with the main findings of SWD and offered further insights into existing market failures and the scope and motivation of member states to support innovation in services.

Taking into account the work that had already been done, the European Commission undertook to draft, by September 2008, a Communication setting out a European Strategy in support of service innovation.

In line with the recommendations drawn from the Communication *Putting Knowledge into Practice: A Broad-Based Innovation Strategy for the EU*, the Commission announced the establishment of a pan-European platform to better link universities, entrepreneurship and finance in order to foster innovative start-ups in the services sector. The European Innovation Platform for Knowledge-Intensive Services (KIS-IP) has been implemented under the Europe INNOVA initiative. The aim of KIS-IP is to accelerate the take-up of services innovations in Europe. The initiative focuses on innovative service solutions in technological and industrial fields by developing and testing new or better innovation support mechanisms for innovative small and medium-sized enterprises (SMEs). The objective of KIS-IP is to foster technological as well as non-technological innovation in services, by helping innovative SMEs better exploit research results and facilitate the search for investors and business partners. KIS-IP will develop new tools for innovation support, addressing particularly the needs of innovative service companies with the ambition to grow and internationalize fast.

The platform consists of three sector networks and one horizontal action. The three sector partnerships address the specific needs of innovative services companies in ICT services, renewable energy and satellite-based applications, and are expected to become the driving engines of KIS-IP. Each partnership is supposed to assess the specific research and skills needs of potential high-growth companies active in knowledge-intensive services and help them establish links with research, finance and business partners. The partnerships will design, test and validate improved support mechanisms to the benefit of KIS start-ups, with the aim of facilitating access to finance and networking with the below-described clusters.

The Achieve More cluster aims to address barriers and challenges to the development of KIS ventures in the ICT sector (software), by developing a new, integrated tool kit that will be delivered through a network of 50 business incubators, 15 ICT clusters and five finance organizations. Specific workshops for coaches and business support professionals will be organized with business support services, investors and cluster organizations to promote the use of the new tools.

The KIS PIMS cluster will support services that cover the whole life of new technologies for renewable energy (solar, wind, hydro, biomass, geothermal), including the planning of new systems, installation and commissioning, maintenance/repair and scraping of old systems. New support mechanisms will be tested through innovation vouchers issued by three national agencies through five clusters in Austria, Finland and France.

The KIS4SAT cluster will establish an innovation support platform needed to stimulate the launch and development of potentially high-growth knowledge-intensive services ventures in the field of satellite downstream applications, by stimulating cross-fertilization of expertise among 25 regional clusters in this field and encouraging networking and partnership between various research, finance, space industry and regional organizations. A voucher program will be developed and implemented in a practical manner in cooperation with 30 regional agencies (INNOVA, 2008).

A horizontal support action will facilitate coordination between the three sector partnerships and promote the dissemination of their results. Furthermore, a European repository on new organizational and business model innovation in services will be created and further promoted through a handbook on the facilitation of organizational innovation in services. As a new element, a "business club" of 100 young innovative service companies in Europe with high growth potential will be established, providing a platform for mutual learning and exchange of practical experience. Another key element is the organization of a prestigious annual European KIS Venture Contest leading to a European service innovation award (INNOVA, 2008).

Polish approach towards support for innovation in services

Innovation indicators for industry and services show that the service sector is less innovative than industry in Poland. According to data by the country's Central Statistical Office (GUS, 2007) innovative enterprises in the service sector accounted for 37.7% of the total number in 2004-2006, while in industry the figure was around 42.5%. The most innovative service sector was "insurance and pension funding, except compulsory social security," where 69.5 % of enterprises claimed to be innovative. A total of 23.3% of innovative enterprises in the service sector introduced new or significantly improved products in 2004-2006; 11.8% introduced new-to-the-market products; and 31.6% introduced new or significantly improved processes. The figures for industry were 29.3%, 14.3% and 35.9% respectively. In 2006, 33.9% of service enterprises reported expenditure on innovation activity (the corresponding percentage for industry was 37.3%), and average innovation expenditure per enterprise was ZL6,202,000 for services and ZL4,888,700 for manufacturing.

Table 3: Expenditure on innovation in Polish enterprises

Type of business	Expenditure on innovation in Polish enterprises in 2006 (in millions of zlotys)						
	R&D	Acquisition of disembodied technology and know-how	Buildings, structures and land	Instruments and equipment	Of which: import	Staff training for innovation activity	Marketing for new or improved products
Services	797.8	296.5	829.9	3505.1	276.3	92.7	320.3
Industry	1516.7	337.6	3781.5	9743.3	4175.0	41.6	471.6

Source: GUS, 2007.

Table 3 shows expenditure on innovation in both services and industry. From the point of view of innovation policy, the largest differences are in R&D, technology and know-how, and equipment and buildings, where industry spends far more than the service sector; and in staff training, where the service sector spends more than industry. This proves once more that industry is more knowledge-, R&D- and technology-intensive, and that human resources are still the crucial factor for services.

While in conventional services the need for technological innovation is relatively low, knowledge-intensive business services (KIBS) such as computer and R&D services are badly in need of such innovation. The latest available data from a Community Innovation Survey (CIS-4) show that 34% of all service sector firms are technical innovators, compared with 39.3% for manufacturing firms. The difference for product innovation is 22.1% versus 26.8 %, and the difference for process innovation is 25.7% versus 29.9%. The only exception are KIBS firms, which are more likely than manufacturing firms to introduce product and process innovation (51.5 %). On the other hand, service firms excluding KIBS are far less likely than manufacturing firms to introduce product and process innovation (30.2%). There is also a notable difference in the percentage of KIBS firms versus manufacturing firms that introduced product innovation (42.0% versus 26.8%) or process innovation (35.3% versus 29.9 %) (EC, 2007).

The dual character of services explains why designing a policy aimed at improving service sector innovativeness is quite a challenge. The crucial thing is to design support programs and map the existing instruments for supporting innovation, while trying to determine if they equally support innovation in manufacturing and services.

Analytical work on service sector innovation carried out by the Polish Ministry of Economy was inspired by the EU and the Commission Staff Working Document *Towards a European Strategy in Support of Innovation in Services* (EC, 2007). The ministry consulted several experts on the issue and checked the rationale for policy action. The Institute for Sustainable Technologies provided the ministry with the findings of a study showing a market failure in this field and the reasons for intervention. Recommendations included in the report are being carefully analyzed in order to draft a proposal for a support program.

Now that the innovation policy is perceived as a horizontal one, the government does not provide any set of instruments specially dedicated to service innovation. In addition to a range of instruments, service innovators can obtain support for the implementation of technological innovation, mainly in KIBS.

A law of July 29, 2005 "on some forms of support for innovation activity" introduced: (1) the possibility of supporting the implementation of new technologies in enterprises, via technological credit, which can partially be written off with the use of budgetary resources, and (2) tax breaks for the purchase of new technology, which allows companies to include an extra 50% of the value of purchased technology among business costs.

A wide variety of support programs is now available under the Innovative Economy Operational Program (IE OP), which is financed from EU structural funds. The main objective of IE OP is the development of the Polish economy on the basis of innovative enterprises. The program embraces the priorities of the National Strategic Reference Framework for the years 2007-2013. A total of 9.7 billion euros is available under the Innovative Economy Operational Program. The funds are intended not only for direct support for entrepreneurs, businesses and scientific institutions providing entrepreneurs with high-quality services, but also for comprehensive support to ensure the development of an institutional environment for innovative entrepreneurs. The IE OP supports technological (product and process) innovation as well as organizational innovation in manufacturing and services, which contributes directly or indirectly to the establishment and development of innovative enterprises. The program supports innovative activities that generate the highest value added for the economy and enterprises, and contributes significantly to strengthening the competitive ability of the Polish economy on the international market. IE OP instruments have been divided into eight priority areas:

1. R&D in new technology,

2. R&D in infrastructure,

3. Capital for innovation,

4. Investment in innovative undertakings,

5. Diffusion of innovation,

6. The Polish economy on the international market,

7. Information society—establishment of e-government,

8. Information society—increased innovativeness of the economy.

The fourth priority area, *Investment in innovative undertakings,* covers the co-financing of projects designed to apply R&D results in practice. Support is granted to projects undertaken by businesses and aimed at implementing their own or purchased technology. Funds for R&D work are also available under the first priority area.

In addition to support for R&D investment in enterprises, there is an advisory program and the co-financing of projects aimed at launching R&D, including the financing of preparations by enterprises applying for R&D center status.

Support intended for services is provided under IE OP submeasure 4.5.2. *Support for investments in modern services,* where strong preference is given to investment projects by enterprises operating in the service sector, especially those connected with launching R&D activities. Support is provided for two types of projects:

- new investment covering the purchase of fixed assets and tangible/intangible assets, as well as the creation of at least 200 new jobs, leading to the establishment or development of:

• centers for joint services (for example, finance, accountancy, human resources management, administration, banking and insurance, market research),

• IT centers (for example, software development, application tests, design and implementation of networks, product optimization, and database management),

- new investment concerning starting up new R&D activity, covering the purchase of fixed assets, tangible/intangible assets and an increase in employment—with at least 10 new jobs created for R&D specialists—leading to the establishment of R&D centers not eligible for financing under the law "on some forms of support for innovative activity."

Under the Innovative Economy Operational Program, innovation is defined as the implementation, in business practice, of new or significantly improved solutions involving products (goods or services), processes, marketing or organization.

It is usually difficult to introduce new or significantly improved solutions as a result of non-technological innovation. This probably explains why businesses find it extremely difficult to meet the main IE OP criteria while applying for funds for non-technological projects.

One conclusion is that, apart from KIBS, which is chiefly driven by technology, other service sectors may in fact obtain less government support under the 2007-2013 financial perspective. This may justify the need for policy intervention in order to support non-technological innovation in both industry and services—in order to maintain the horizontal approach to innovation policy.

An additional recommendation is to focus on building the crucial competencies and skills needed to handle the innovation process in enterprises. This is important for both manufacturing and services, but it seems that this feature has greater influence on the service sector, where the human factor is the essence of business and a main driver of change.

Best practices—policies for supporting service sector innovation in Ireland and Norway

Policies aimed at supporting innovation in the service sector are increasingly popular, in part due to the active role of the European Commission in promoting innovation in services. In line with the Commission Staff Working Document, most EU countries are developing or at least rethinking instruments aimed at promoting innovation in the service sector. Some countries, including Norway and Ireland, have made huge progress in this field, and can in fact be seen as pioneers in the development of innovation support programs for the service sector.

The Norwegian innovation policy is not designed to take care of specific sectors, but rather to increase the overall innovative activity in the economy.

Table 4 gives a brief overview of the relevance of policy measures specified for five service groups.

Table 4: Policy areas of importance to services

	Support for generation of ideas	Improve the market for vital inputs	Bring the innovator closer to the market	Simplify market coordination	Innovation-friendly regulations	Support the development of new markets for private services
Problem solvers	High relevance	High relevance	High relevance	Relevant	Relevant	Relevant
Assisting services	Low relevance	Low relevance	Low relevance	Low relevance	Low relevance	High relevance
Manual distributive	Low relevance	Low relevance	Relevant	High relevance	High relevance	Low relevance
Digital distributive	Relevant	Relevant	Relevant	High relevance	High relevance	Low relevance
Leisure	Relevant	Relevant	High relevance	High relevance	High relevance	Relevant

Source: Ministry of Industry and Trade of Norway, 2006.

The main Norwegian recommendations with respect to the development of innovation policy friendly to service innovation are:

• to support the generation of ideas, including investment in measures focused on stimulating the market for venture capital and R&D;

• to improve the market for vital inputs (invest in skilled labor in order to improve knowledge and competencies);

- to bring the innovator closer to the market (promote innovation driven by interaction between agents in the market;

- to make it simpler for market players to coordinate their activities (the government can play an important role in solving possible coordination failures);

- to provide innovation-friendly regulations (limit extensive regulations);

- to support the development of new markets for private services (allow a more pronounced presence of private service suppliers in public sectors such as cultural services, health services, and transport)(Ministry of Industry and Trade of Norway, 2006, pp. 22-24).

Ireland is another example of a country that quite early started to think about innovation in the service sector. Analytical work began in 2006 and was managed by a government think-tank institution called Forfas. A report entitled *Services Innovation in Ireland—Options for Innovation Policy* provided Irish policy makers with nine key recommendations that can significantly improve the innovativeness of Ireland's service sector.

The recommendations are the following (Forfas, 2006, pp. 67-72):

1. To provide a statement on Services Innovation Policy;
2. To create a supportive and flexible Regulatory Environment;
3. To build a services innovation culture;
4. To provide a new and distinct business support framework for services Innovation;
5. To enhance services-oriented support for telecoms and broadband investment and infrastructure;
6. To enhance competitiveness and convergence through networks, clusters and centers of excellence;
7. To provide innovation and creativity through education and skills development;
8. To create services innovation policy and an international economic image;
9. To build the typology of Services Innovation and the development of policy and support measures.

The implementation of the above recommendations should be based on a set of four kinds of support actions, which are described in detail in Table 5.

Table 5: Strands and actions to be undertaken under a policy aimed at supporting innovation in services in Ireland

Strand 1—Innovation through New Business Models	Strand 2—Innovation in Service Delivery and New Customer Interfaces
– Promote a culture shift to allow new thinking regarding services and the relationship between customer value and profit opportunities. – Improved futures, foresight and competitive intelligence capacity and capabilities. – Increased emphasis on strategic planning and evaluation of possible futures for businesses and organizations. – Increased capacity and capability for creativity at all levels, including schools, institutes of technology and locations where businesses can be trained and supported. – Flexibility in workforce conditions. – Specific encouragement for the adoption of new business models involving temporary companies; part-time collaborations; portable employment portfolios etc.	– Investment in new, speculative ICT applications at sector, company and research center level. – Support for acquisition and implementation of ICT (without employment criteria). – Improved ICT infrastructure conditions throughout Ireland.
Strand 3—Innovation through New Services	**Strand 4—An Innovative Services Innovation Policy**
– Futures, foresight and competitive intelligence capacity and capabilities. – Centers of excellence in convergent thinking. – Feasibility supports for new service launches.	– Services innovation awareness raising and showcasing. – "Ireland's services innovation offer" to FDI marketing campaign. – Supportive and flexible regulatory arrangements. – Services innovation web portal. – Services innovation diagnostic tools and benchmarking techniques. – "Intellectual Property Rights protection" events program and advice service.

Source: Forfas, 2006, pp. 73-74.

Such an approach to policy making and the efforts of both Norway and Ireland to provide their service innovators with better framework conditions and accurate support programs, can contribute to improving the competitive position of these countries and give them a leading position in providing and developing new services. It can also provide a solid inspiration for Polish policy makers as they try to come up with the right innovation policy and design support measures for service innovation.

References

Arundel, A., Kanerva, M., van Cruysen, A., Hollanders, H., (2007). *Innovations Statistic for the European Service Sector.* Inno Metrics. Brussels.

CEC, (2003). *Communication—Innovation Policy: Updating the Union's Approach in the Context of the Lisbon Strategy. COM (112)2003*, Commission of the European Communities. Brussels.

CEC, (2004). *Innovation in Services: Issues at Stake and Trends*, Commission of the European Communities. Brussels.

CEC, (2007a). *Commission Staff Working Document: Towards a European Strategy in Support of Innovation in Services: Challenges and Key Issues for Future Actions*. Commission of the European Communities. Brussels.

CEC, (2007b). *R&D in Services—Review and Case Studies*. Commission of the European Communities, DG Research. Brussels.

Cunningham, P., (2007). *Innovation in Services: Thematic Report*, Pro Inno Europe. Inno Policy TrendChart.

Forfas, (2006). *Services Innovation in Ireland—Options for Innovation Policy*, Dublin.

GUS, (2005). *Działalność innowacyjna przedsiębiorstw w sektorze usług w latach 2001-2003*. Główny Urząd Statystyczny. Warsaw.

GUS, (2007). *Nauka i Technika w 2006 r.*, Główny Urząd Statystyczny. Warsaw.

Howells, J.R.L, Tether B.S., (2001). *Innovation in Services: Issues at Stake and Trends—A Report for the European Commission*. INNO-Studies 2001. Lot 3. (ENTR-C/2001). Brussels.

Kanerva, M., Hollanders H. and Arundel A., (2006). "Can we Measure and Compare Innovation in Services", 2006 *TrendChart Report*. European Commission, Brussels.

Ministry of Industry and Trade of Norway, (2006). *Innovation in Services: Typology, Case Studies and Policy Implications*. ECON Analysis, Meon AS. Oslo.

Niedzielski, P., Szulkin, A., (2006). "Innowacje w sektorze usług – zarys problematyki". In: G. Gromada, M. Nowak, M. Matusiak (eds.) *SOOIPP Annual – 2006: Innowacje i przedsiębiorczość dla przyszłości*. SOOIPP, Łódź-Poznań-Wrocław-Warsaw.

OECD, (2005). *Promoting Innovation in Services*. OECD. Paris.

OECD-Eurostat (1995). *Oslo Manual – Guidelines for Collecting and Interpreting Innovation Data*. Paris 2005.

Salter, A., Tether, B.S, (2006). *Innovation in services – Through the Looking Glass of Innovation Studies*. London.

Van Cruysen A., Hollanders H., (2008). *Are Specific Policies Needed to Stimulate Innovation in Services?*, UNU-MERT. Inno Metrics. Brussels.

www.europe-innova.org.

www.stat.gov.pl.

www.ingramcontent.com/pod-product-compliance
Ingram Content Group UK Ltd.
Pitfield, Milton Keynes, MK11 3LW, UK
UKHW062306230426
12049UKWH00005B/122